BEHIND THE UNIFORM

BEHIND THE UNIFORM

Policing in Britain and America

Ian K. McKenzie
Hon. Research Fellow, University of Exeter

G. Patrick Gallagher
Director, Institute for Liability Management

HARVESTER WHEATSHEAF

ST. MARTIN'S PRESS

First published in 1989 by
Harvester Wheatsheaf
66 Wood Lane End, Hemel Hempstead,
Hertfordshire, HP2 4RG
A division of
Simon & Schuster International Group

and in the USA by
St. Martin's Press, Inc.
175 Fifth Avenue, New York, NY 10010

© Ian K. McKenzie and G. Patrick Gallagher 1989

All rights reserved. No part of this publication may be
reproduced, stored in a retrieval system, or transmitted,
in any form, or by any means, electronic, mechanical,
photocopying, recording or otherwise, without the prior
permission, in writing, from the publisher.

Printed and bound in Great Britain by
BPCC Wheatons Ltd, Exeter

British Library Cataloguing-in-Publication Data

McKenzie, Ian, 1941–
  Behind the uniform: policing in Britain and
  America.
  1. Great Britain. Police compared with
  American police, 1900–1988   2. United
  States. Police compared with British
  police, 1900–1988
  I. Title   II. Gallagher, G. Patrick
  362.2′0941

  ISBN 0–7450–0515–2

Library of Congress Cataloging-in-Publication Data

McKenzie, Ian K.
  Behind the uniform: policing in Britain and America
Ian K. McKenzie, G. Patrick Gallagher.
  p.   cm.
  Includes index.
  ISBN 0–312–03193–9
  1. Police–Great Britain.   2. Police–United States.
I. Gallagher, G. Patrick.   II. Title.
HV8195.A2M33   1989
863.2′0941–dc20   89–31745

---

1 2 3 4 5   93 92 91 90 89

1606 C74

For Tricia: More than yesterday, less than tomorrow. (I.K.M.)

To Mary, my wife, whose support has meant so much to me since we first walked in the sunshine of our love. (G.P.G.)

If the members of an English force were assigned to police an American city, they would all be kidnapped within twenty-four hours; and if American police were transferred to an English jurisdiction, they would promptly be placed under arrest for abuses of police authority.

(an unidentified English Chief Constable, quoted in Smith, B., 1960, p. 11)

perhaps, but today?

Contents

Preface

On both sides of the Atlantic there are major misunderstandings about the structure and function of the criminal justice systems, differences in the law, and about the organization, structure and role of the police, on the other side of 'the water'.

We have spent many long hours in discussion on the nature of policing in our respective societies and there has not been one occasion on which one, or more commonly both, of us has not said, 'I never knew that before!'

In our attempts to teach students of criminal justice something about the systems, structure and philosophies of our own countries we have repeatedly found that although there are a number of excellent texts which deal with each country in isolation, or which make reference to the other whilst trying to make a point about what Mathias et al. (1980) call the 'vertical' elements of comparative studies, there are rarely texts available which seek to examine areas of comparison and contrast side-by-side (what those authors call the 'lateral' elements).

Criminal justice systems are, by their very nature, complex and difficult to define. The understanding of them depends on some knowledge of both the psychological and sociological elements of a society before they even begin to make sense. Our common experience has been that students – as opposed to academics – have the greatest of difficulty in understanding that the British are not 'Americans who talk funny' (or vice versa); that the world of TV cops is rarely the world of real cops; and that 'behind the uniform' lies a complex, multifaceted subculture, easily, but inaccurately, defined by concentration on one superficial element – usually that of policing with or without guns.

The micro-system of policing in a democracy is entirely dependent upon the macro-system of the society, not only to feed and nourish it through the provision of powers, but also to punish and control it through societal mechanisms provided for that purpose. Consequently, the 'lateral' elements of comparative studies are legion. In a book of limited size it is only possible to deal with a few selected areas, and because this is a book aimed, in the main, at a student audience, we have chosen to provide a fairly substantial section regarding the history and development of policing. The 'professional' reader may wish to move straight to Section 2!

That aside, it is our hope that this book will move students and other interested readers a little along the path of comparing and contrasting the 'lateral' elements of our two societies without too much damage to the 'special relationship' said to exist between us.

As always, there are many who must be thanked for their, sometimes unwitting, help in the preparation of a manuscript. Our wives, who have been unremittingly patient and supportive, are among those without whom this book would not have been possible. Thanks are similarly due to the many hundreds of police officers of both nations whose philosophies and comments have helped to initiate some of the ideas in this book, and consequently to the many 'advisers' in the Criminal Justice Faculties at John Jay College of Criminal Justice, New York City, and the University of South Carolina, Columbia SC, who provided the intellectual pegs on which to hang those comments.

Above all, the practical help and advice of Robert Reiner, who provided cogent, and entirely valid, comment on an early draft of this book is acknowledged without reservation.

The two-handed authorship of any book is a perennial problem. Issues of style, content and accuracy are constantly problematic. These difficulties are compounded in an exponential manner when the co-authors live 3000 miles apart. It is thus the case that much must be done with little or no reference, one to the other. Any errors of fact, style and content are thus entirely the responsibility of the British author in this endeavour. We know our 'special relationship' can bear that strain.

I.K.M.

G.P.G.

SECTION 1

Background, History and Context

CHAPTER 1

Cross-cultural Comparisons and Contrasts in Policing

The police of America are aggressive, corrupt and trigger-happy. Beset with jurisdictional and functional problems compounded by political interference and fiscal difficulties, they struggle against a growing tidal wave of Supreme Court decisions, civil litigation and downright hostility. The police of England and Wales are benign, avuncular, polite, independent and unarmed. Jurisdictional problems are a thing of the past, political interference is at a minimum, and there is no real hostility towards their activity. Scotland Yard is as efficient as Hill Street is chaotic.

Although, as with all stereotypes, there is some basis in fact, they are also generalized, inaccurate and patronizing. The truth is far more complex, for the special relationship between the two apparently bipolar policing systems, echoing that of the popular and political dimension, is more interrelated than many might suspect.

For decades senior American police officers and politicians have made a pilgrimage to Britain to examine and discuss British policing philosophies and practices with the hope that they would enhance and professionalize the US system. Innovations, from fingerprinting to forensic techniques were transported, like the emigrants of former centuries, from the Old Country to the New World.

But rising crime rates, riots and general concern about 'value for money', has, in recent years, reversed the tide. The new innovations in British policing have travelled east from across the Atlantic. Psychological Profiling, Policing by Objectives, Neighbourhood Watch schemes and much more are the new coin of the old economy.

Why has this change of direction occurred? What is the special relationship between the police of these two nations? Is the transfer of philosophies between two cultures who notionally speak the same language a wise or even viable course?

Superficially all police departments are the same. They have identical (or at least remarkably similar) organizational philosophies; usually expressed in writing in the form of an aim to prevent crime and preserve public tranquility; they may have similar equipment. But to assume congruence because the objectives and equipment are similar or because two or more police departments may administer broadly similar laws is to deny the reality that policing styles and the *unwritten* philosophies which lie behind and within them can radically alter not only the public perception of the role of police but also the perception of the police themselves about their own activity. Only by placing policing in its proper context both within the broad spread of a criminal justice system and at the same time, within the broader spread of the culture, the historical development of ideas about the control of crime and criminal activity, the philosophies and the psychology of the people and the associated mores and norms of the society, can one have a more complete understanding of the relationship of police to their macro-society.

Superficial comparisons are far too frequently misleading and sometimes downright dangerous. Without an understanding of deeply ingrained, underlying features of the society, many superficial differences and similarities are, for many people, difficult to comprehend. Many American police officers are bemused by the continuing ability of the vast bulk of British policing to be conducted by unarmed officers, and many are jealous of the facility for transfer with retainment of rank available to officers at most, if not all, organizational levels in the UK. Conversely, most British officers are stunned by the complexity of, and potential inefficiency inherent in, the local–state–federal structure of American policing, the political infighting and intrigue of senior management appointments, and the seemingly intractable problem of political 'interference' in 'operational' matters. On the other hand, as David Bayley points out:

> If it is a mistake to assume that police institutions operate independently of their social environment, it is equally mistaken to assume that they are shaped entirely by forces outside them. To assert that police organisations are constrained by social setting does not imply that they possess no margin of initiative. Interactions between police and setting are reciprocal. Not only may police institutions effectively choose to do differently in some respects, their actions may help to change the context within which they operate and so facilitate reform for the future. (Bayley, 1977, p. 8)

THE PROBLEMS OF COMPARISON

The admirable desire to compare and contrast both the societal and organizational structures which influence policing is beset with numerous methodological problems. Even within the UK there are differences between Scotland on the one hand, and England and Wales on the other. The law is different, the methods of recording crime statistics are not directly comparable, the laws of evidence and the rules which govern police practices are different.

Comparisons between any two countries suffer from similar difficulties and these are severely compounded when the comparison involves the complexity inherent in a multifaceted federal republic with a constitution which not only allows each of its component parts to make, interpret and enforce its laws, but at one and the same time overlays those organizations with a federal structure dealing with the complexities of nationally enforceable legislation.

In handling statistical material it is possible to overcome some of these difficulties by reclassifying both sets of data in such a manner as to allow meaningful interpretation to occur.[1] But by and large, that is not possible when one seeks to examine the reciprocity occurring between the nature of policing and its setting, the nature of laws and the structure of enforcement organizations.

For that reason we have chosen to concentrate on a number of very specific comparative questions. What is the constitutional position of the police, and how is their role seen by the courts and the legislators? How do controls which seek to 'police the police' operate?

At a local level, what are the mechanisms which control financial expenditure, the selection of chiefs of police, the training and organizational form of police departments and the discipline, conditions of service and rates of pay for serving officers? What are the (often controversial) laws which allow the police to exercise a proactive crime prevention role but which if used may bring the police into conflict with sections of the community (viz. Stop and Search or Stop and Frisk powers) and how does the use of these powers conflict with or conform to issues of constitutionality and the *philosophy* of each nation's legal structure?

What are the mechanisms, organizational responses and practical considerations which shape the response to public disorder, both in the form of limited on-the-street misbehaviour and in the larger context of riot, rout or unlawful assembly? What is the relationship of police to the armed forces in such circumstances, and what are the general conditions and controls which are present to deal with the use of deadly force in these and other circumstances?

Clearly some of these areas are potentially beset with the problems of comparison outlined above. Where complexity engendered by a multiplicity of available models is an issue, as in the discussion of police organizations, we have chosen to examine specific rather than general areas. Thus, for example, despite the huge variations in rates of pay, etc., for police officers in the USA the comparison we have undertaken (using previously unpublished research) is that of two loosely demographically comparable cities of London and New York rather than to attempt to deal with the 'big picture'.[2]

But, despite the specificity of these areas, we seek to place these data in their proper cultural and historical context and see no better starting-point than to examine briefly an issue which, although resolved in the United Kingdom, is still a bone of contention in the United States, and to put forward the proposition that it is cultural rather than practical difficulties which delay and, in the long term, may even destroy attempts to rationalize the policing of that nation.

AN OVERVIEW

More than sixty years ago, the American police system was noted by Frosdick (1920) as being hampered and constrained in its development by considerable administrational and organizational problems. These were later summarized by Donald E. J. MacNamara as:

political interference, public apathy (and in fact sympathy with the criminal), judicial irresponsibility, too short tenure for police administrators, lack of proper selection criteria and inadequate training for recruits, corruption, unenforceable sumptuary laws, a high crime rate, the impact of the narcotics traffic, uncoordinated police operations, and a host of other problems ... (MacNamara, 1950, p. 20)

Ten years later little had changed. The difficulties experienced by those operating in the law enforcement field in the USA continued to rest on the fundamental problems identified by Bruce Smith (1960, p. 1), who emphasized the historical background to them:

The police problem in America is as old as our system of local government. Springing from the creation of the first police establishments on these shores, it has continued to grow in complexity with the passing years. It is still a prominent feature of the American scene largely because of errors of long standing in the organisation and management of police and in the methods employed to ensure popular control.

In essence the problems of jurisdiction, varying standards, the relationship of the police and the population they serve with state and national government all hinge on the abiding need of the population to ensure that there is minimal 'central' interference with 'local' matters.

Such a jealous guarding of 'personal freedoms' is a part of the heritage and culture of the USA and springs, in part, from the ancestors of the modern American who frequently chose to leave the country of their birth as a direct consequence of abuses of those powers by officialdom, not infrequently assisted by 'police' as an arm of the authorities.

It is this emphasis on 'popular control', concern with preventing, or at least controlling, 'central interference' and so on, which gives American policing its particular style.

By contrast, over the years there has been a slow but inexorable movement in the United Kingdom towards a rationalization and restructuring of the police system. Although once centred in villages, towns, boroughs, cities and counties, political manoeuvring and, to some extent, lack of public concern, have resulted in the reduction of police departments from many hundreds to the 43 forces of today.

As long ago as 1949 Bruce Smith was able to write:

Under unusually able and far seeing leadership within the Home Office, implemented by the investigations and appraisals conducted by His Majesty's Inspectors of Constabulary, there has been improvement in some of the weaker jurisdictions, and by the Police Act 1949, most of the smaller forces were consolidated with neighbouring police establishments. Only 133 forces are retained in the service of almost 500 cities, boroughs and countries. (Smith, 1960, p 305)

Smith continues:

One other highly important feature should be noted: Nowhere in England, Wales, nor for that matter in Scotland, is there the slightest duplication of police authority. The police

Table 1.1 State and local law enforcement agencies by level of government.

	State	Total	County	Municipal	Township	Other	Grand Totals
			Level of government				
Coroners, etc.	310	1,768	1,659	108	1	—	2,078
Police depts	670	16,934	3,340	11,595	1,810	198*	17,613
Totals	980	18,711	4,999	11,703	1,811	198	19,691
Total percent	5	95	23.4	59.4	9.2	1	100

Source: Adapted from US Department of Justice (1980).
*Housing Authority/Port Authority and Independent Schools police.

establishments of city, county, and borough governments do not overlap in any way. Their powers are identical and they exercise a territorial jurisdiction that is distinct and exclusive. (Ibid., pp. 305–6)

Although the structure of policing in the UK was to be rethought in the 1960s, particularly in relation to the extension of jurisdictional authority and the definition of geographical police areas, the comparatively rapid movement towards a rationalization of policing in the United Kingdom is to be contrasted with the entirely more circumspect movement towards 'consolidation' in the USA.

The complexity of the relationships between local, state and federal government in the USA has led to a multitude of solutions to jurisdictional difficulties, fiscal problems and the ever-present desire 'in rural areas where small, financially-pressed communities [to] continue to function independently of county government' (Koepsell and Girard, 1979 p. 2). In consequence consolidation has largely been confined to police departments with less than 25 personnel, whilst in the bigger arena, informal arrangements; sharing of equipment and facilities; pooling of resources; formal, binding contractual arrangements falling short of actual merger; and the creation of 'police special service districts' where special arrangements are made for the policing of unincorporated areas of a county[3] have tended to occur as an alternative to actual consolidation, merger or (as it has always been called in the UK) 'amalgamation'.

CONSOLIDATION IN THE USA

Estimates of the number of law enforcement agencies vary wildly between 20,000 and 40,000 (the US Dept of Justice (1980) lists 19,691); most are at 'local' level (see Table 1.1) and more than 80 per cent have less than 25 officers (See Table 1.2).

Table 1.2 Number of police agencies by number of sworn officers.

| | | Number of sworn officers | | | | | | | | |
	1	2–4	5–9	10–24	25–49	50–99	100–99	200–99	300+	n/a
No. of agencies										
Total										
State 670	22	53	113	227	99	50	30	21	46	9
County 3,340	157	735	859	843	349	211	105	25	45	11
Munic'p 11,595	1,360	3,321	2,784	2,432	954	467	195	62	108	12
Town 1,810	11	381	415	522	239	115	25	–	–	2
Special district, etc. 198	8	15	39	71	32	19	7	3	2	2
Grand Total 17,613										
Percentage	9.4	25	23.9	23.3	9.6	4.8	2.1	0.6	1.1	0.2
Cumulative %	9.4	34.4	58.3	81.6	91.2	96.0	98.1	98.1	99.8	100

Source: Adapted from US Department of Justice (1980).

Academics have long argued that some centralization of resources, perhaps at state level, is the only rational solution to the lack of system in the system and in particular the proliferation of agencies at local level. The United Kingdom and Sweden (Becker and Hjellemo, 1976) are often cited as models of the 'sort of thing that can be done'. But there has been only limited enthusiasm for the process of consolidation even in small agencies.

AMALGAMATIONS IN THE UK 1960–87

By contrast, at the time of the setting up, in January 1960, of a Royal Commission on the Police of England and Wales (The Willink Commission), the number of police forces in England and Wales had fallen to 125 from more than 200. The Commission later made strong recommendations to Parliament that further amalgamations should take place. Following these recommendations, the Police Act 1964 reduced the number of forces; a constable's powers were no longer confined to his own and adjoining areas but extended throughout the whole of England and Wales; increased the number of inspectors of constabulary (with powers to examine, on behalf of central government, the efficiency and effectiveness of policing outside London).[4]

By 1974 the number of police forces in the UK had been reduced, with some heart-searching and some resistance, but little practical difficulty, to 43. The creation of larger and, it was hoped, more efficient police forces was aimed at combating British organized crime – which at that time had little, if any, connection with that seen in the USA – and at providing a better career structure for police officers. Small forces with few men and little facility for interchange meant, in the main, little chance of betterment for the ambitious officer.

The direct and practical consequence of the Willink Commission was the enactment of the Police Act 1964. This Act was aimed at allowing a balance to be struck between local autonomy and central control, defining, for the first time, the role of the chief constable and the functions of police and also giving to the Home Secretary the responsibility for ensuring (and promoting) the efficiency of every police force.

Local 'supervision' of forces was to be achieved by the creation of police authorities and, with the exception of the London Metropolitan Police, for whom there are different arrangements, the police authorities were empowered to appoint – and if necessary remove – the Chief Constable and to be responsible for the equipping, housing and maintaining of their local force.

As will be discussed in Chapter 4, definitions of 'equipping', 'housing' and 'maintaining' have proved problematic, most recently as a consequence of the prolonged industrial action by members of the National Union of Mineworkers (NUM). The appointment and particularly the removal of Chief Constables have similarly become something of a stumbling block.

NATIONAL POLICE FORCE

For all that, there has been no stampede towards centralization, and policing still rests firmly on autonomous units of local government as their link to the population.

One of the members of the Royal Commission, Professor A. L. Goodhart of Oxford University, went on record as strongly supporting calls for a national police force for England, Wales and Scotland; centrally controlled and regionally administered.[5]

The force of Goodhart's argument was that the real danger to democracy was not the existence of a strong, centralized police but in a weak, local police organization. He pointed out that the rise to prominence of Hitler and Mussolini had not been with the connivance and assistance of a strong centralized police force but by the use of small, privately controlled gangs of their supporters.

The British government did not accept the minority report, the majority of the Commission believing that, whilst there was nothing constitutionally wrong or politically dangerous with such a notion, the necessary improvements could take place within the framework of the existing policing structure in the United Kingdom.

CONCLUSION

Koepsell and Girard (1979) cite the following four major reasons for the existence in the United States of opposition to small agency consolidation:

1. That there will be a loss of local law enforcement service.
2. That there will be a loss of control over the level and quality of service.
3. That consolidation has proved no more effective than extant systems.
4. That in any case, consolidation may cost as much or more than any current system.

Although many of these arguments are dismissed by the authors as having little or no support from empirical research they (somewhat grudgingly) concede that there is 'certain justification' for the first of those claims.

> In addition to the psychological loss among the recipient communities, which is claimed to accompany consolidation, opponents purport that local officers know a community and its problems better than those of a consolidated agency; mergers dilute the relationship between local citizens and members of the law enforcement agency that serves them; and, the enforcement of local codes and ordinances suffer as a result ... (Koepsell and Girard, 1979, p. 9)[6]

In Britain, however, each *increase* in the involvement of central government with the everyday lives of the population, particularly through the provision of a comprehensive social security system, has provided the key for consolidation of policing services and the reduction of overall force numbers. The effectiveness of each force was theoretically to be increased.

This may be contrasted with the tendency in the USA for new police bodies to be created (perhaps by areas seeking incorporation, for example) in order to improve the service provided but without any attempt to sweep away or modify the old.

Furthermore, in the UK, bit by bit, the provision of police services has come to be seen by the population as a function to be performed or at least supervised by central government. Local police authorities there are, but increasingly their right to advise, direct and, above all, to control the delivery of service in their area is slipping away.

Now, none of this means that the movement towards centralization in the United Kingdom is right and the reluctance for such moves in the States is wrong.

It is interesting to note that current concerns with issues of accountability in the United Kingdom, although formulated in different words, are essentially the same as the four contrary arguments in respect of US consolidation discussed above. Academics, politicians and concerned citizens are increasingly asking: 'How can we, the local population, get some measure of say in local policing when the force covering our area has its headquarters many miles away, policemen and women don't stay long enough to get to know the area, and although we pay taxes we have no say in how the money is spent or how police are deployed in our little town?'

Furthermore, the problems of controlling police behaviour do not seem to have been affected by this overall policy of reducing the number of individual police forces. As we shall discuss in Chapters 4 and 6, concern over issues of accountability have been historically addressed in two totally different ways: in the USA through Supreme Court decisions and civil litigation, in the UK through national internal disciplinary proceedings, and a comprehensive system for dealing with complaints against the police. But things in the UK are moving more towards the American model.

In January 1986 the Police and Criminal Evidence Act 1984 came into the force in the UK. This Act seeks among other things to provide, for the first time, legislative controls over the actual on-the-job performance of police duties. In a very real way the Act has provided something that increasingly, we shall argue, seems to be like a Bill of Rights, at least in respect of those who come into conflict with the criminal justice system. The Act came nearly twenty years after the vast bulk of amalgamations had been completed and was passed by Parliament – with some strong resistance, much political rhetoric and a good deal of hot air – amid an atmosphere greatly concerned with the failure of previous non-legal 'controls' (the Judges' Rules) to ensure that suspects were properly handled by the police.

The provisions of the Police and Criminal Evidence Act are remarkably similar to those key decisions made by the Supreme Court of the USA which, by and large in the 1960s and early 1970s, sought to control (or at least manipulate) police behaviour in such well-known cases as *Miranda*, *Mapp* and *Escobedo*, and deal with the provision of legal advice, the methods of interrogation and the nature of detention and supervision of police prisoners.

We shall argue that this new legislation is a major change to the unwritten constitution of the UK and that there are certain consequences for policing which must be accepted by them; in particular that a good deal more flexibility in dealing with parliamentary amendments to this legislation and its adjuncts (which can occur far more rapidly than changes in constitutional law in the USA).

Banton (1964) sought to explain differences in police behaviour in the UK and the USA in terms of the nature and texture of interpersonal exchanges – what he referred to as degrees of *social integration*; Wilson (1968) chose to concentrate on *political* features of the police environment; whilst Bayley (1976) sought to explain differences in Japanese and American police behaviour in terms of *cultural* determinants.

It will be our theme that the behaviour of police is shaped by all of those factors but that the most cogent factor is that of the legal constraints under which the police operate. Those legal constraints reflect not only the norms and mores of the society, but are also, in the way they are framed and in their interpretation by the courts, indicative of expectations about the manner and style of delivery of service by police.

Those expectations are indeed rooted in the cultural determinants which Bayley examined and are thus closely associated with historically-placed attitudes about the development of organized policing; the use of such coercive forces at time of trouble; and the type and manner of service (Banton's 'interpersonal exchanges') law enforcement is expected to provide. It is to those areas that we now turn.

The remainder of this section will be given over to an attempt to place the the policing of the two nations in their historical and cultural contexts and to locate them in their respective criminal justice systems.

Section 2 will examine the way in which that affects the organization, management and training of police, and Section 3 will examine some of the issues associated with the practicalities of policing; and the consequent differences of approach apparent in the police systems under study.

Throughout, we shall seek to indicate why the tide of innovation has moved from the East/West passage of yesteryear to the West/East route of today, and to demonstrate that the stereotypes of policing, based on film and television portrayals of police activity, are rooted in reality but fertilized by myth.

CHAPTER 2

The 'New Police' and the 'New World': Disorder and Dissent

By the year 1700, London had developed a full-scale, urban-criminal society. A society in which thieves, forgers, pickpockets and counterfeiters were able to operate largely without constraint. By this time London was a city of about half a million souls, 'in which a thief may harbour with as great security as wild beasts do in the deserts of Africa Arabia' (Fielding, 1751), but growing at an alarming rate. In many parts of the city the developers – as developers often do – saw fit to build in the gardens of larger houses, and then add second and third rows of houses. The resultant maze of narrow streets, courts and alleys, criss-crossing the main thoroughfares, created an environment supportive of opportunist criminal activity.

Roving gangs of street criminals, adulation of highwaymen and other 'elite' thieves, and severe problems with drunkenness, were sufficient justification for Henry Fielding, Chief Magistrate at Bow Street Court, to set about trying to establish an effective group of 'thief takers' whose task would be to make the streets safer to pass along.[1]

Fielding, with the assistance of a government grant, appointed six householders to serve as paid constables for an extended period (more than the usual year). The men were not uniformed and became known as 'Mr Fielding's men', and later, 'the Bow Street Runners'.

One of the major advantages of the 'extended' period of service was simply that the 'Runners' became both skilled and knowledgeable regarding methods of investigation and the behaviour, style and whereabouts of active criminals in the city.

The 'Runners' were however, first and foremost, a reactive body (to use the modern phrase). Nevertheless, as Stead (1977) points out, Henry Fielding and his brother John were greatly influential in establishing thinking about the *object* of policing which was echoed in the next century.

In 1819, the public were stunned by violence that had occurred when the authorities had sought to 'police' a crowd of some 80,000 in St Peter's Field, Manchester, with 200 special constables, six troops of the 15th Hussars, one troop of horse artillery with two guns, a large part of the 31st Regiment of Infantry, several companies of the 88th yeomanry, 400 men of the Cheshire Yeomanry, and 40 of the

Manchester Yeomanry. Despite such an impressive show of force but largely because of ineffective and inefficient leadership – the local chief constable with the assistance of the Manchester Yeomanry went into the middle of the crowd in an attempt to arrest the leaders of the mob and not surprisingly were stranded and consequently powerless – things got out of hand.

The Hussars were directed to charge the crowd with drawn sabres and in the ensuing confusion eleven people were killed and 400 injured, including 100 women. The incident became known as the 'Peterloo Massacre', as a sarcastic reference to the Battle of Waterloo, which had taken place four years previously. Many of the Hussars threatened to mutiny because of their revulsion at being directed to charge at an unarmed crowd and the inability of the army to respond effectively, since it could only alternate 'between no intervention and the most drastic procedures' (Silver, 1967). This led to a rapid consideration of appropriate methods of riot control including a 'professional police force'.

PEEL'S 'NEW POLICE': ORGANIZATION AND OPPOSITION

Parliamentary opposition

Following the débâcle of Peterloo the Prime Minister, the Duke of Wellington, instructed his Cabinet to set up an organized police force 'without delay'. Such an instruction proved more than a little problematic. In the past many parliamentary committees (i.e. 1770, 1793, 1812, 1818) had been established to investigate the growing problems of crime and disorder in the nation (particularly in relation to frequent riots) and without fail the committee members had baulked at the notion of establishing a 'police force'. Indeed, in the year before Peterloo, a parliamentary committee (1818) declared that a 'severe system of police' would be 'inconsistent with the liberties of the people' and of necessity would be 'odious and repulsive' (Price, 1983).

Robert Peel became Home Secretary in 1822[2] and his abiding achievement, against such a background of resistance, was in his political manipulation of both Houses of Parliament to the extent that, when a committee was convened in 1828, the members, carefully selected by Peel, concluded that: 'It is absolutely necessary to devise some means to give greater security to persons and property' (Parliamentary Reports Vol. 4, 1828).

With little delay Peel introduced the Metropolitan Police Bill to Parliament on 15 April 1829. It became law later the same year. The purely reactive nature of Fielding's runners had, in the hands of Sir Robert Peel, developed into a 'theory of policing', when at 6 p.m. on Tuesday, 29 September 1829, following much parliamentary and public debate, the first officers of the Metropolitan Police marched out on to the streets of London.

The objectives of Peel's 'New Police' were clearly stated by him in a letter to the Duke of Wellington, dated 5 November 1829:

I want to teach people that liberty does not consist in having your home robbed by organised gangs of thieves, and leaving the principal streets in the nightly possession of drunken women and vagabonds. (Wellington: Supplementary Despatches, Vol. VII, p.287)

Peel had argued that the function of an organized, disciplined and responsible police was to *prevent and detect* crime. Such a view was an echo of the earlier views of Patrick Colquhoun, Jeremy Bentham and others who had sought to reform elements of the criminal justice system. Colquhoun had, for example, written in 1795:

> Police in this country may be considered as a new Science; the properties of which consist not in the judicial powers which lead to *punishment*, and which belong to the magistrates alone; but in the PREVENTION and DETECTION OF CRIMES, and in those functions which relate to INTERNAL REGULATIONS for the well ordering and comfort of Civil Society. (Colquhoun, 1795)

But not only was the political background volatile but the increasing population of the cities, particularly London, was producing social conditions which were extremely primitive and unhealthy. As the century progressed and the cities continued to grow rapidly, outbreaks of cholera and typhoid became more frequent and health standards in towns were noticeably lower than in country districts.

Many of the laws the police were required to administer related to the 'Use and Condition of Streets' and were an attempt by Parliament to improve the living conditions of Londoners. The Metropolitan Police Act 1839 contained many sections dealing with everything from driving animals through the streets to the use of obscene language and the throwing into the streets of any 'dirt, litter, ashes, or any carrion, fish offal or rubbish'.[3]

The ending of the Napoleonic Wars with France a few years before had resulted in the Vagrancy Act 1824 which contained numerous provisions for controlling vagrants, beggars and 'loose, idle and disorderly persons', many of whom were, in fact, returning unemployed British soldiers who had flooded the streets of the city to seek alms (and steal where they were not provided) from the population. Although the development of a 'professional' police is seen by some revisionist writers (e.g. Storch, 1980; Silver, 1967; Spitzer and Scull, 1977) as being a deliberate attempt to suppress and control the 'dangerous classes' as opposed to the more common notion of the need to (almost literally) 'clean up the city', the reality may be that there were elements of suppression but that these were ancillary to a growing pragmatism in the face of social change.

Reformation

On his appointment to the Home Office in 1822, Robert Peel had set about repealing many of the harsh and confused laws which had hitherto existed. The creation of the Metropolitan Police was, in this context, the final step in a series of reforms he had started, with his colleagues, a few years before.

Revision of the existing legislation was badly needed. A man could be hanged for innumerable offences, including stealing five shillings from a shop, stealing on a navigable river, taking forty shillings from a dwelling house, and so on. Peel and his colleagues succeeded in abolishing the death penalty for more than 100 offences. Punishments for 'minor' offences were also reduced, and 130 statutes concerned with larceny were consolidated into one Act.

THE SOCIAL ROLE OF POLICE

Despite a concerted campaign by the press and others it was the very social conditions in London which provided the key to the success of the New Police. Nineteenth-century officers carried out tasks that had a far broader base than the simple notion of law enforcement *per se*: 'Some were formal duties such as inspecting weights and measures or inspecting bridges, others were informal such as knocking people up in the morning for work' (Reiner, 1985 p. 58).[4] Involvement in the social side of life, and a commitment to behave in a civilized manner which ultimately led to increasing acceptance, was reinforced at every turn by the early Commissioners: 'By the use of tact and good humour, the public may normally be induced to comply to directions. Thus the use of force, with its possible disapproval may be avoided' (Richard Mayne, 1829). Although occasional reminders seem to have been necessary:

> The Commissioners think it right again to caution every man in the police force, at a time when an attempt is made to create a strong prejudice against them that they should do their duty with every possible moderation and forbearance and that they should not furnish a just ground of complaint against themselves by any misconduct.[5]

It is the case that this level of assistance provided by the New Police and the exercise of the social role of policing were the significant factors which enabled the gradual acceptance of a British, as opposed to a European, style of policing to develop and thrive in London and subsequently the rest of England.

It may have been that this concentration on the social role of policing was a deliberate effort to overcome the strength of opposition to an organized police force, by methods of ingratiation, as a cover to more coercive purposes (cf. Donajgrodski, 1977; Brogden, 1982) but whatever the case, it does seem, as Reiner (1986) puts it, 'to have played a part'.

PEEL'S NEW POLICE: PUBLIC OPPOSITION

The 'construction' of the Metropolitan Police took place against a background of considerable public, as well as parliamentary, suspicion of the motivation underlying the initiative. As Stead (1977, p. 76) indicates:

> In most English minds, the idea of police had come to mean the surveillance and

documentation that had taken a new, and in many ways still unexpired, lease on life during the Revolutionary and Napoleonic eras.

Add to this that the French and English were hereditary enemies it is not to be wondered that the English were highly prejudiced against the 'police state' ... The continental examples were a tremendous problem in the path of the English police reformer.

Public resistance to the development of an organized police force was loud and strong. But even more powerful was the fear that they would be *effective* in a manner defined by government rather than the people, and would thus become a vehicle for controlling and subjugating the working class.

As a consequence, one of the special objects of concern of the first Commissioners was the 'attitude' to be taken by officers to the public they would meet on their beat. It was strongly felt that any demonstration of 'bias' in dealings with the public would be fuel to the fire of overt resistance. Thus, in a written order to the force, the Commissioners addressed this matter. The Police Order (Instruction) read:

> He will be civil and attentive to all persons, of every rank and class; insolence or incivility will not be passed over ... there is no qualification more indispensible to a Police Officer than a perfect command of temper.

Within six weeks of the passing of the Metropolitan Police Act, in April 1829, more than 1,000 recruits had offered their services, police stations had been acquired and a Central Office had been created. An organizational structure – the geographical splitting of London into divisions, sections and beats – had been formulated, whilst the manufacture of uniforms and equipment had been put in train. A pay structure had been agreed.

On the question of wages, Peel had been intractable. He was convinced that policing was work for 'artisans' and was opposed to the employment of 'gentlemen' on the grounds that the work would be beneath them and that they would not associate with 'the men' (and, by inference, might side with the gentry). In regard to wages Peel argued that 'a three shilling a day man is better than a five shilling a day man'. Perhaps in anticipation of the rigours that his men were to suffer in obtaining public acceptance, he wrote: 'No doubt three shillings a day will not give me all the virtues under heaven, but I do not want them.'

A great deal of the time of the early Commissioners was spent in hiring and firing. The Commissioners themselves – Colonel Sir Charles Rowan, a distinguished soldier, and Sir Richard Mayne, a lawyer – were the only exceptions to the 'no gentlemen' rule and were paid at the rate of £800 per annum. (The constables pay amounted to about £50 per annum.)

Peel's policy of paying low wages ensured first, that the recruits came from the working classes and, secondly, that the notion of 'policing of the people by the people' was ensured.[6]

During the first two years resignations exceeded recruitment. By 1833 there were only 562 men who had been recruits in 1829, in a force now numbering some 3,398 men. However, the rapid turnover of officers in the early days probably had more to do with police/public relations than pay and conditions, for Peel's apprehensions regarding overt hostility and conflict were far from overstatement.

Not surprisingly, following the often acrimonious parliamentary debates of the past and as a consequence of the generally held view than an organized and efficient police would be the ultimate destroyer of democracy, forceful public hostility to the New Police was almost immediate.

The hostility was fuelled and possibly orchestrated by a campaign in the press. *The Times* was strongly critical of a concept of central control – the police 'authority' for the Metropolitan Police was (and still is) vested in the Home Secretary and no other – because of the apparent increase in powers it gave to the government. Others were concerned at the removal of the right of the 'local parishes' to make their own arrangements. Furthermore, a sector of the 'upper classes', the landed gentry, owners of country estates and with 'large numbers of personal servants to guard their plate and their wives' (Hay, 1975), objected to paying for protection which they felt they already enjoyed. The popular, 'working-class', view was to reject *everything* about the police.

An American writer recently indicated that:

> What people in our own age think when they hear the words 'English Police' is an unarmed police force of constables who are ordinarily courteous to tourists, patient and restrained in confronting crowds. (Thurmond-Smith, 1985, p. 5)

The people of London in 1829 (and later other cities (see Storch, 1975)) had another view.

Some writers claim that the reasons for the development of a professional police force was not simply to control and prevent crime but was, more sinisterly, an attempt to impose on the population control over both their working and private lives, and an even tighter discipline in the interests of a growing capitalist organization (Reiner, 1985). The 'industrial revolution' had, it is claimed, brought about both the criminalization of former work practices, such as the 'right' of workers to be paid in kind rather than cash, and of former recreational practices such as kite flying,[7] knocking at doors without reasonable excuse[8], and hoop-rolling.[9] These attempts at forcing the 'brutish' working population towards respectability and decency (Reiner, 1985) were placed alongside what were genuine 'public health' attempts[10] to clean up disease-ridden streets and to limit 'public mischief'.[11]

Whether these regulations were really an attempt by the 'aristocracy' to subjugate the 'proletariat' or not, strong resistance to the New Police was a common occurrence. Popular nicknames reflected popular attitudes. These ranged from 'Mr Peel's Bloody Gang' through 'the Blue Lobster Gang' to 'the Crushers' (Reiner, 1986), and attacks and assaults on these early constables were commonplace. Many officers were the victims of the very crimes they sought to prevent.

On 29 June 1830 PC Grantham was thrown to the ground and killed by a fierce kick to the temple. He had intervened in a fistfight between two Irishmen. Some weeks later, on 16 August 1830, PC John Long was stabbed to death when he tried to arrest three men near Gray's Inn Road. On 13 May 1833, Constable Robert Culley was stabbed to death following 'disorder' at a meeting of the Chartist Movement at

Coldbath Fields, also in Gray's Inn Road. The government had declared the meeting illegal but a notice giving this information to the people had the words 'By order of the Secretary of State' at its foot but no signature. Indeed, requests by the Commissioner of Police of the Metropolis for the order to be signed met with a stolid refusal.

The confusion about the legality of the meeting, coupled with the still strongly-held views of the populace that 'the police were an arm of a repressive government', reached its almost foregone conclusion when an inquest into Culley's death returned a verdict of 'justifiable homicide'. Not only that, for the verdict, which symbolized the deep suspicion with which the New Metropolitan Police was regarded (Reiner, 1986), was accompanied by the presentation of an engraved cup to one of the coroner's jury, and medallions to the others. The engraving indicated, in part, that the mementos would serve as 'a Perpetual Memorial of their Glorious Verdict of Justifiable Homicide, on the Body of Robert Culley, a Policeman, who was slain while brutally attacking people while peaceably assembled ...'.

ACCEPTANCE AND LEGITIMATION

The conventional view is that the public, particularly the middle-class/respectable public, were so horrified by this turn of events that the death of PC Culley became a watershed in policing history, turning overt resistance to (at a minimum) covert support, and directly influencing a movement towards acceptance and legitimation of a body which had until that time been seen as tantamount to an army of occupation.

The less conventional view (cf. Reiner, 1986) is that the gradual but growing acceptance of the police hinged on seven *deliberate* and well-thought-out policies initiated by Peel, Rowan and Mayne, and designed, in the manner of the best public relations firms of today, to 'appeal' to the public. The 'appealing policies' were:

1. *The appeal of a corporate image.* The establishment of a full-time, disciplined, meritocratic body with an image of policemen as 'disciplined members of a bureaucratic organization of professionals'. As the police force came to be seen as a vehicle through which working men could achieve higher social status, 'respectability and a career' (Cohen, 1979), so acceptance of the body increased.

2. *The appeal of an organizational philosophy.* Adherence to the rule of law, which coupled with the creation by the Commissioners of an atmosphere of strict discipline, cogent sanctions and some delineation of the wide discretionary powers granted to all constables (Reiner, 1986), was an element of considerable significance in securing public acceptance of the force.

3. *The appeal of a practical philosophy.* The doctrine of the minimal use of force and the concentration on the values of civility and self-restraint, had a powerful

effect in legitimatizing the police, even if its practical application remains dubious.

4. *The appeal of non-partisanship.* The notion of 'constabulary independence' and freedom from political control, including the fact that police regulations (to this day) prohibit officers from participation in political activity and until 1887 disenfranchised serving officers, prevented them from overtly showing support for any political party.

5. *The appeal of an identified non-law enforcement responsibility* (the service role). The development of policing practices which are not directly related to law enforcement or order maintenance is seen as having a powerful legitimizing effect mainly because it showed the police to be more than solely concerned with enforcement of the law.

6. *The appeal of a proactive police function* (preventive policing). A strong emphasis on seeing as the primary objective of policing the 'prevention of crime' and only as a secondary objective 'the detection and punishment of offenders' led to a strongly-held feeling that the potentially repressive nature of a police was in practice a benevolent, almost avuncular, one.

7. *The appeal associated with success*[12] (police effectiveness). The early part of the nineteenth century did in fact see a fall in the overall levels of crime, violence and disorder. Thus 'policing' could be shown to work: for Rowan and Mayne's declared measure of success 'the preservation of public tranquillity and the absence of crime' could be demonstrated to have come to pass.

It is argued that the *deliberate* creation of policing policy which sought to legitimize the nature and conduct of British policing (if, in fact, it was deliberate rather than fortuitous) is far removed from the development of policing in the USA where an essentially *ad hoc* process has spawned a complex, multi-layered and multifaceted body of police whose function may differ markedly from that of policing in the UK.

THE POLICE OF AMERICA

With the creation of the Metropolitan Police in London and the application of the 'New Science of Preventive Policing', American policing sought to emulate the managerial and organizational trends which had spawned the 'British model'.

However, as early as 1624, with the colonization of the area, now known as Manhattan, by the Dutch, attempts had been made to impose a law enforcement system which, not unnaturally, reflected European experience: a council to make and interpret the laws and a *Schout-fiscal* to enforce them.

The first Schout-fiscal of New Amsterdam (as New York was then called) was one Johan Lampo who was given specific instructions by the Director General of the Dutch Colony to punish each lawbreaker 'as the circumstances of his crime require, in order that the Indians may see that in both civil and criminal cases we do justice without regard to persons'.[13]

The gradual development of Dutch, British, Scandinavian and European colonies on the eastern coastline of the USA led in its turn to the development of similar localized 'policing', sometimes referred to as 'folk-policing'. Frequently such developments took place on a piecemeal basis and provide the key to understanding the generally parochial nature of American policing, together with some of its more contentious areas – lack of reciprocity, differences in training standards, etc.

According to Beckman (1980), colonization of the East Coast of America, and in particular the British colonies of Virginia, resulted in the creation in 1634 of the first Sheriff's Office. Based on a traditional, but by then defunct, role of the 'shire-reeve' in England (see Beckman, p. 24), the sheriff had all the powers required for the performance of his duty. But the fear in the population of central authority, which remains a deeply ingrained part of American culture even today, plus the apprehension that if a person stayed in post too long he would amass too much power, led to the creation of an elective post, usually on an annual basis.

For similar reasons the post of constable in the New England states was also an elected one, but in both cases the principle backfired since no electee was ever in post long enough to gain sufficient knowledge to carry out his allotted task efficiently.

The year 1664 saw the 'transfer' of control over New Amsterdam from the Dutch to the British who promptly renamed it New York, in honour of the Duke of York. Such a change of control did little to alter the structure of early policing. There were already similarities between American and British law enforcement initiatives, particularly in the provision of a body known as the 'rattle-watch' which may be seen as similar to the 'watchmen' who patrolled London.

These early 'New York cops' were, however, true 'civilians'; not wearing uniforms and occasionally having been sentenced to serve on the watch for crimes they had committed (Beckman, 1980).

The first uniformed police officers to appear on the streets of New York took up patrol in 1693. They were provided with 'a coat of ye city livery with a badge of ye city arms, shoes and stockings', the whole to be charged to 'ye account of the city' (Green and Young, 1980).[14]

The nineteenth century and on – immigration and organized policing

The bulk of immigrants in the latter years of the nineteenth century (1840–1900) came to the USA from European, British and Irish stock. They came to avoid starvation and the threat of the noose or lengthy imprisonment; to escape tyranny and the perception of tyranny.

In Ireland, hunger, resulting from the failure of the potato crop through blight in the 1840s which had claimed almost a million lives in only five years was the spur, but in Europe the threat of death came from other sources. In 1848 political unrest, revolutions, arrests and executions took place across Europe. Declarations of war,[15] revolution and riot were the order of the day. The selection of Jews as scapegoats was a common occurrence.

The unannounced arrival of secret police, the 'stoniest sound in the world: the midnight knock at the door' (Cooke, 1973, p. 275), the fear of whip and rope used with impunity, and with the approval, tacit or otherwise, of the authorities, were the keys to the development, in the growing immigrant population, of an attitude to authority strongly averse to the notion of central government in everyday life.[16]

By 1800 New York had established the first paid daytime police force. The day force operated when the night force was 'a-bed'. Philadelphia in 1833 and Boston in 1838 established their own daytime forces.[17]

In 1833 a delegation was sent to London from New York to examine the structure and organization of Peel's New Police. They returned greatly impressed and a reorganization of New York City policing was undertaken.

The examination of a successful model for an organized policing agency was the final key in a process of pressure for change in the face of fears of social disintegration and the search for a preventive role for the police. Some years before Charles Christian, a magistrate, had argued strongly in favour of a policing system that would act as a deterrent to crime not just deal with it *ex post facto*. New York authorities found such a model in Peel's *prevent and detect* philosophy and were filled with enthusiasm for it.

In 1844 New York consolidated its day and night watches and its first chief of police, George W. Matsell, was appointed by the mayor. Matsell's appointment was only for one year, but was renewable at the mayor's discretion. It was thus a 'political' appointment and paved the way for the politicization of the job of chief of police in a way never envisaged by Robert Peel.

By contrast, although it was the case that Peel had actually appointed his first two commissioners, he made it clear in documents that henceforth promotions to the 'superior stations' would be from within the force. As Stead (1977, p. 81) points out, 'This gave great incentives to do well *in the work*: the channels of advancement would not be blocked by importing outsiders to fill the supervisory posts' (emphasis added).

In Britain there has never been a publicly elected 'chief of police' and, although it could be argued that some senior appointments are political in nature, being undertaken by the members of the police authority (formerly watch committee), they are *never* in the gift of *one* politician.

It was Tammany Hall, the headquarters of a powerful political machine with an Irish-Catholic base, which provided the real fly in the ointment in any attempt to remove policing from the political arena in the USA. The Tammany organization sought political control of the city through manipulation of elections, the collection of 'graft', and its key element – the control of the municipal police. Tammany manipulation ensured that many chiefs enjoyed relatively long periods of tenure. So complete was their hold that when, in an effort to break their control, the New York State legislature put the police department under the control of a single commissioner appointed to a five-year term by the mayor and removable by him or by the governor, the new commissioner appointed as his deputy William Devery, who some time before had been the subject of a corruption enquiry and had been fired from his post as a superintendent in the city police force.[18]

The so-called 'single commissioner plan' for the organization of New York policing was expected to produce strong controls: but it did not work out that way. No New York City police commissioner ever survived a change of political administration and, as Reppetto (1978) indicates, in the first 77 years of its operation in the twentieth century the New York City force saw 32 commissioners, an average of one every 2½ years. During one decade, 1965–74, there were six incumbents.

For comparison purposes suffice it to note that in the entire history of the London Metropolitan Police (1829–88), there have only been 21 Commissioners, including Peel's first two joint-appointees (1829–50), a second 'pair' of Commissioners, one of whom was Sir Richard Mayne (1850–55) and Mayne himself as the first 'single Commissioner' (1855–68); an average of nearly eight years per Commissioner. Mayne himself could claim 39 years.

Pioneers – law enforcement and order maintenance

As the American nation developed, the cry of 'Go West young man!' was increasingly heard and a movement from the original East Coast colonies began. No one, least of all the pioneers, had any inkling of the size of the country they were crossing. Even in the early nineteenth century Charles Dickens went to St Louis, only 900 miles inland from the coast, and was convinced he had seen the West – the frontier. He declared it to be a fraud!

Contemporaneously with the movement west in the USA a similar movement was to be seen in Canada. Hundreds, if not thousands, of men, women and children seeking to make a new life for themselves and to make a fortune at the same time if possible, moved ever westward. But here, a deliberate and well-considered policy by the Canadian government – to establish a police presence first and only *then* to open the country to pioneers – had a profound effect. As Sewell (1985, p. 31) puts it:

> In what has become a hallmark of Canadian culture it is generally assumed that the police were sent to establish order so that freedom and liberty could be enjoyed – in stark contrast to the American notion that freedom and liberty come first, with order following far behind.

It is here that one may see for the first time a key to the most fundamental difference between American and British policing – the difference between the law enforcement nature of American policing and the order maintenance model of British policing.

Creating the ethos for the existence and maintenance order in a relatively crime-free environment, in which laws are rarely broken because there is no one there to break them, is a different order of things from attempting to do the same thing in an environment which is already crime-ridden and lawless.

Both Canada and the USA have historical links to the 'rugged individualist' notion, but it is only in the USA that it has extended to the structure (and organization) of policing. This is not intended to suggest that all modern Americans

are 'rugged individualists' at heart, but rather that the people-first law-second
practice in the USA created an environment in which the law officer – the model
sheriff exemplified by Gary Cooper in *High Noon* – elected by his peers, became a
symbolic torch-bearer; both the source of law enforcement *and* the local upholder of
'rights', rights that the federal government had provided but were not to be allowed
to administer, both by the Constitution and the people. When such a man was found
to be wanting, when corruption and avarice were discovered, it was to the
Constitution and the Supreme Court that the people turned. But for all that, as
McClure (1984) indicates, 'rugged individualists' remain as a singular force both in
the American culture and in the American law enforcement system.

The service role of policing   HERE

To be sure, as was the case in England, the early police of the USA must have
tempered their responsibilities as law enforcement officers with the performance of
'social role' work, the provision of assistance to those in distress and the helping hand
where it might be needed. But this may have been more a matter of expediency than
a defined role – for the elected official to do otherwise would have been political
suicide. But in any case, the officer, oriented in his work to a 'law enforcement first'
and to 'public service second' philosophy, brings to his job a different set of values
from the officer who considers order maintenance first and service second.

Faced with pre-existing lawlessness and a population deeply suspicious of
government intervention, the American officer then as now, and despite the fact
that Wilson (1968) observed 'service role' policing in action, performed his task with
enforcement skills not social skills. But, as Reiner (1986, p. 51) puts it:

> In the US ... the more freewheeling and aggressive style of policing evolved not as a
> consequence of social divisions but the political integration of American Society as
> something approaching a property-owning democracy. Popular participation in
> government meant confidence that the police could be entrusted to the political process
> rather than a tight framework of legal rules and regulations.

It was a confidence that was, regrettably and too frequently, misplaced.

Against a volatile background of immigration, expansion and growing concern
for the 'democratic' process, the fear of centrally controlled, oppressive, secret
police organizations, and the 'political integration' of a shared value system focused
in this context on an apprehension about the advent of *large-scale* organized policing
the new Americans based their law enforcement aspirations in the hands of locally
selected, locally controlled and locally administered police. The ship of hope too
commonly foundered on the rocks of human avarice. The involvement of local
politicians in the hire-and-fire decisions, let alone the freely available graft to both
politicians *and* police, held back acceptance of 'policing' as a viable community-
control vehicle for some years. The framework of confusion over issues of

reciprocity, jurisdiction and the nature of control was firmly laid and is, to this day, echoed all around the country.

NATIONAL DEVELOPMENT IN POLICE ORGANIZATION – UNITED STATES OF AMERICA

Local conditions and frequently the ethnic or national background of early colonial groups dictated the nature of the developing police function in America. However, in America's early history the corrupt nature of many local government officials, disputes over the jurisdiction of law enforcement agencies and the lack of commitment or vote-catching tactics of many law enforcement officials led inevitably to the recognition that state police forces were needed.

After the revolutionary war the pride which the newly declared 'nation' had was firmly centred on residence in a particular state, which was, naturally, better than all others. Having declared themselves 'states' rather than colonies, the interminable argument as to whether they were a Confederation or a Union of States would only be resolved by the bloody Civil War some few years later. Nevertheless the principle of self-governing, autonomous states outlived the revolutionary war and resulted initially in the 'Articles of Confederation' (1781) and later in the 'Constitution' (1787). It is important to recognize that by the time the Constitution was agreed the states already 'had had together the experience of one hundred and fifty years of *separate governments*' (Cooke, 1973, p. 147) (emphasis added).

A second 'conflagration', the Civil War (1862–65), also had its effect on the nature of policing in the USA. Until that time the system of sheriffs and constables had proved sufficient for the rural areas, while the more affluent towns and cities were developing small, if inefficient, police departments of their own. The social changes generated by the war, particularly the improvement of roads and the development of a comprehensive railway system, led to increased mobility of the population, not least the criminal, the hobo, and the economically disadvantaged. Furthermore, the industrialization that had taken place as a consequence of the war continued, and with the establishment of industrial communities (mostly of immigrant workers) and the development of industrial problems, frequently leading to strikes and disorder, it became apparent that 'traditional' law enforcement could no longer cope.

Haunted by a spectre of 'revolution' following an ineffective, but none the less surprising, uprising of the working class in Paris in 1871, the 'upper classes' of the USA, and more particularly the nation's industrialists, became obsessed with what could happen if 'radicals' should lead the workers against them. Disturbances in West Virginia, Baltimore and other major industrial areas had demonstrated the futility of relying on local law enforcement and the unsuitability of relying on the 'militia'.[19] Later disturbances, particularly at the Carnegie steelworks in Pennsylvania, became synonymous with violence from both strikers and police, the use of firearms and the employment of 'private' detectives (known as Pinkerton men after their founder) who were roundly beaten. A 10,000-strong militia managed to restore order, but the manifest fear of Marxist revolution resulted in numbers of strikers being charged with treason, although juries steadfastly refused to convict them.

Although many of the more affluent cities had been developing a model of policing based on London's, the authorities had manifestly failed to encourage similar models in the rural and industrial areas. Thus the failure of the local law enforcement agencies, fed by the fear of revolution by the workers, generated, at least in Pennsylvania, a desire to develop a state policing agency which could respond to industrial disorder and quell disturbances with the rapidity of a fire brigade quenching flames.

The traditional view of the development of state police is that, as a consequence of the corrupt nature of many local government officials, disputes over the jurisdiction of law enforcement agencies and so on, the creation of such a police in many states became inevitable.

However, a more radical view is that the state police model was directly attributable to the desire of major industry to maintain the status quo and to do so under the patronage of state government. As Mathias et al. (1980, p. 217) put it:

> The Pennsylvania State Police Force was established by the governor when he determined that the sheriff–constable system had broken down. . . . The distinguishing characteristic of the Pennsylvania Force was that it was answerable directly to the governor.

It might be assumed that a force answerable to a state governor was analogous to the Metropolitan Police and their direct supervision by the Home Secretary, but there are two major reasons why this is not the case. First, the position of governor of a state is more closely analogous to the post of Prime Minister (not Governor of a British Commonwealth country, from which the US title emanates), the Home Secretary being but a member of the British Cabinet and thus exercising only delegated powers from that Cabinet. Secondly, the model for Pennsylvania state policing was not that of British policing, but a modified version of national policing based on the models of the Philippine Constabulary and the Royal Irish Constabulary.

Strongly militaristic, required to reside in barracks, to be unmarried, armed with pistols, carbines and riot batons, the Pennsylvania state police were above all partisan, not only because of the level of political affiliation and control but also because they were almost exclusively American-born. According to Katherine Mayo (1920), their motto was 'One American can lick a hundred foreigners' – the 'foreigners' being immigrant Irish, Italians, Slavs, blacks and, with little regard for ethnic background, 'labour agitators'.

Known as 'The Black Hussars' (reminiscent of Peterloo?) the history of this police establishment is beset with tales of violence, authoritarian behaviour and 'forceful' involvement in labour disputes of all kinds. Even a number of the constables and peace officers of the state were hostile to their continued presence.

As time passed, the original rationale for the existence of a state police gradually faded, but the model did not. It offered certain advantages over alternative systems of policing: a professional force in place of small town constables and rural sheriffs; and the image of a disciplined and relatively incorruptible police, which appealed to those who were distressed by the nature of big-city policing (Reppetto, 1978, p. 134).

Although some states resisted until after World War I, the arrival of the motor car, with its added mobility for the criminal and the need to provide ever better road and highway facilities, finally persuaded them.

Today all states have some sort of state police or state highway patrol, although their duties vary widely. As Beckman (1980, p. 35) describes it:

> In some states such as Michigan, the state police have general powers. In others such as California, they are Highway patrols and only have authority pertaining to motor vehicle codes.... The state police are not the only law enforcement personnel in the state government. Other agencies ... include liquor control boards and commissions, departments of motor vehicles, state bureaux of narcotics, state fire marshalls and state gaming commissions.

Federal agencies

Finally there are federal agencies with policing responsibilities: the FBI, Drug Enforcement Administration, US Marshalls Service, US Customs, Bureau of Alcohol, Tobacco and Firearms, the Secret Service, Desert Rangers, US Park Rangers, US Border Patrol, US Capitol Police (US Bureau of Justice, 1980).

The proliferation of federal agencies is typical of the development of all policing in the USA for there is, even here, considerable rivalry, conflict over jurisdiction and sometimes downright political manipulation which would do the Tammany organization proud.

Such a proliferation of policing agencies is seen at local level as well. For example, South Carolina has 245 county, city and municipal police departments and a further ten state-wide law enforcement agencies. Furthermore, given the anomaly of the District of Columbia not being a 'state' but none the less the seat of government, there are over 25 law enforcement agencies, having different types of jurisdiction, within its boundaries. Separate jurisdictional responsibilities include: the DC Metropolitan Police, the Metro Transit Police, the US Park Police, the FBI, the US Capitol Police (1300 personnel covering 240 acres), the Smithsonian Institution Police, the Executive Protection Agency, the Secret Service, the Federal Protection Agency and so on.

NATIONAL DEVELOPMENT IN POLICE ORGANIZATION – ENGLAND AND WALES

The success of Peel's 'New Police' in London led rapidly to the development of similar police forces in other parts of the country. By 1835 many boroughs and most cities had established their own police forces and, in 1839, the county areas followed suit. Despite a concentration of some writers on the Metropolitan Police as 'the first' it is nevertheless the case that some of them (e.g. Oldham) simply converted former paid watchmen to paid policemen (see Emsley, 1983). By 1856 the British Parliament had agreed that the provision of a police force should be a legal requirement for the county councils and, at the same time, sought to reduce the number of small independent police forces which had developed. It became the responsibility of the Home Secretary, the post Robert Peel had held, to offer advice and direction to forces through the machinery of the Home Office. Although the operational arrangements were left to chief constables, many facets of administrative and fiscal policy were to be the province of the local 'watch committees'.[20]

However, there is a level of national government involvement, perceived as unacceptable by many American commentators and, while the existence of a set of national 'representative bodies' – the Police Federation (established by law in 1919 following a police strike), the Superintendents Association and the Association of Chief Police Officers – does tend to provide *some* standardization of policy, there is potentially the facility for common manipulation for the political ends of any particular government.[21]

It is also the case that British police officers, particularly those of senior rank, are taking a more substantial role in defining the 'politics of policing'. Although far removed from the overt political skills that the average chief of police in the USA is obliged to demonstrate, political statements – on the whole non-partisan, but none the less political for that – regarding the nature of crime, the causes of criminality and disorder and so on, are more overtly political than one suspects Robert Peel would have approved.

There are no difficulties in England and Wales in relation to jurisdiction or reciprocity. The Police Act 1964 not only reduced the numbers of forces and removed the final boundary anomalies but also gave police officers the power to act as such through the whole of England and Wales, a stark comparison with the USA where, despite the proliferation of motor vehicles, most states confine the law enforcement powers of local officers to their own area or a few miles from its boundary. Frequently their extension is only applicable in the case of 'immediate pursuit' of a fleeing felon.

Provision lies in the Police Act for officers to set up joint crime squads or traffic squads with other forces, to serve periods of 'central service' in Home Office-controlled establishments such as the Inspectorate noted above, regional training centres, research and planning functions, forensic laboratories, and at the Police Staff College (a central training resource for senior police managers).

There is a facility for officers to transfer from one force to another, taking with them their pension rights and without having to be 're-certified' as is often the case in the USA. The standardization of police training, selection and promotion (with certain reservations) has been a fundamental step in creating an aura of policing as a career for those who want it to be so.

With the exception of those central service functions noted above, there is no 'governmental' policing in the sense of tht provided by the federal agencies of the USA.

Immigration, Customs, Inland Revenue and so on are not considered police functions and their staff are not police officers within the meaning of the Police Acts.

However, with a role analogous to a combination of some of the functions of the US Secret Service and the CIA, the Special Branch, which draws its members from all 43 of the police forces, has some central resource facilities at Scotland Yard. None the less, each chief constable still retains responsibility for Special Branch activities within his own force area.

CONCLUSION

There is, as Reiner (1985) punningly puts it, a 'cop-sided' view of police history. That view, of vigorous resistance to attempts to smother at birth the new child of effective, efficient but, above all, organized policing has, in view of recent research, to be tempered by the knowledge that an alternative view exists. The proposition that organization of policing was not the altruistic exercise it was presented as, but rather a formidable attempt to keep workers in their place is essentially reliant upon a particular political orientation, and may or may not be true. What is clear, however, is that such views about the police were current on both sides of the Atlantic at one time or another. The significant difference seems to be that in the UK those notions were abroad at the very birth of Peel's 'New Police', while in the USA they reached their zenith not at birth but at puberty.

There is little doubt that the historical development of policing on each side of the Atlantic contributes strongly to the stereotypes identified in Chapter 1. The slow spread of population westward towards the Pacific; the pioneering, but above all individualistic value systems of the 'new' Americans; and the apprehension of, and downright bloody-mindedness towards government – any government – contrast strongly with the development of a policing philosophy in a comparatively stable environment in England. Street disorders at Peterloo and Coldbath Fields were the voice of protest at government policy rather than at the existence of government itself.

But the perceived *purpose* of policing differed between the nations. In England fears of government spying on legitimate activity may be contrasted with the more ready acceptance of a role of 'enforcer of the law' in a growing democratic society. But it is the very definition of that democracy which points to the differences.

For *all* the new Americans, democracy meant freedom from repressive government, freedom from unreasonable controls, and a real voice in the day-to-day running of affairs. This definition of democracy was supported by a set of annotated 'rights', at first assumed, later enshrined in the Constitution. The existence of police under these conditions becomes a function of that democracy. The *ad hoc* existence of local policing was seen as legitimate, a service to the community, and aimed at the protection of the population they served. The police existed because the people wanted them.

For *a few* Britons, on the other hand, democracy meant the freedom to elect people to speak on your behalf on all matters, a freedom given to only a small proportion of the population. The exclusion of the masses from any investment in the development of a policing system led inevitably to the conclusion that such an innovation as *organized* policing was illegitimate, divisive and aimed at repression. The imposition of police on the population was, as we have seen, regarded with the utmost suspicion. They existed whether the population wanted them or not.

Miller (1977) draws a direct link between the gradual process of democratization of British society and the gradual acceptance of police legitimacy, against which may be seen the comparatively ready acceptance of policing in the USA. The London police were introduced in a period of social conflict and amid suggestions that they would be used for political ends. Despite that they achieved approval if not approbation. On the other hand, Miller notes that the political situation in the USA was different. In England the working classes were ranged *en masse* against the 'ruling classes'; in America the working classes were split and divided amongst themselves: the Old Americans against the New. The new were the recent immigrants who were seen as a legitimate target for conflict both by the 'respectable' New Yorker and by those who acted on their behalf – in a democratic manner – the police.

Miller categorizes American police authority as 'delegated vigilantism' with its consequent acceptance of violence as the legitimate means of controlling the deviants. On the other hand, the attitudes of the London officer had, of necessity, to be entirely more circumspect and the social role of police became all the more important.

For the British it was relatively easy to develop the 'cop-sided' view of history and to live with it in comparative complacency. But for the American, it was not until conflict started to occur as a consequence both of attempts to organize state policing and of concern over police abuses of authority and its corollary, attempts to control that enthusiasm by the Supreme Court, that a reappraisal of the police role occurred.

But things may have changed. The British police have been dealt two severe shocks. First the upsurge of public disorder that occurred in the early 1980s, and second, the entirely legitimate (but not entirely separate) attempt by Parliament to control police behaviour through legislation which mirrors to a marked degree the work of the Supreme Court in the 1960s. The two models of policing are, it will be argued, moving closer together.

For all that, there remain substantial differences. Resistance to the notion of state-organized policing, for reasons of fear of central government power remain powerful in the USA to this day. But in the UK, the level of involvement of central government in the everyday lives of people is such that responsibility for policing, regardless of the cries by some for increased local involvement, is seen more to rest at that level. There is little doubt that in the event that national policing really becomes an issue in the UK, most of the population would be swayed by the 'more efficient' arguments presented in favour of such a change than by any real desire to ensure that local officers are truly responsive to local needs and by responding to the contrary arguments.

But they probably would not be asked. A powerful enough central government, with a supportive majority of chief officers, could (theoretically) produce that effect almost overnight. The constitutional position of the police is one which is far from crystal-clear but the increasing authority of the Home Secretary in, for example, responding to police requests to provide equipment in the face of police authority disapproval[22] may be seen as further erosion of local supervision in favour of central direction.

On the other hand, such a level of central involvement is unlikely to occur in a proliferation of very small police departments if the people are more directly involved. What, therefore, is the answer to the perennial jurisdictional, fiscal and political problems of US policing? Maybe there is an optimum level of consolidation which will produce the solution? More realistically, perhaps it is the change of attitude, rooted in culture and history, that needs to occur. Alternatively, it may be that constitutional, philosophical and political determinants are so powerful that the questions themselves become void. It is entirely possible that these differences between the two nations continue to make the rationalization of policing in the USA in the direction of the British model a non-starter. It may be, as we shall see, that the moves are in the opposite direction.

We have examined the development of two policing systems and have discussed the processes by which the unacceptable face of the parliamentary democracy of the privileged, produced, in Britain, a form of organized policing which slowly overcame the suspicion and fear of the police, of excessive, partisan government abuse of power. Whether such legitimation occurred as a consequence of design or good fortune remains debatable. What is clear is that as British society moved slowly but surely towards a fully enfranchised democratic society, the New Police became accepted as a legitimate vehicle for keeping the peace. By contrast, as we have discussed, the more open acceptance of the legitimacy of policing in the USA, as an arm of the people rather than an arm of government, was apparent even from the earliest days.

But as we have noted, both systems have passed through the same trauma. The problems of early acceptance in the UK were echoed when allegations of partisan behaviour and political manipulation were levelled at policing in the USA, both in the manner of early dealings with immigrants and later in allegations of racism and abuse of civil rights in the 1960s and 1970s.

The experience of many major American police departments in coming to terms with these problems is a major cause of the search for knowledge by British police officers in the USA.

Furthermore, it is the growing recognition that some criminal activity, for example, organized crime, international terrorism and illicit drug importation and manufacture (and more contentiously the response to industrial disorder through the National Reporting Centre, see Chapter 9) can only be dealt with in a national context, that has led the UK to adopt a national response to such problems. Although concealed behind notions of 'constabulary independence' (see Chapter 4), the existence of coordinated drugs squads, anti-terrorist groups and Special Branches are precise echoes of similar federal bodies in the USA.

CHAPTER 3

Constitutions and Courts: Due Process and Crime Control

Both the United States and the United Kingdom share a common legal heritage as well as a cultural one. The early emigration of the Pilgrim Fathers to the shores of the New World and the later development of the East Coast colonies of Great Britain ensured that the *early* constitutions of those colonies rested on the same base – the Common Law of England. As Mathias et al. (1980, p. 158) put it:

> The growth of the law in America followed English ways in its early stages; however because of the remoteness of the Colonies, procedures in American courts varied from their English counterparts.... The United States Constitution (1787) soon ensured that the American system of law, though it belonged to the same Common-Law family, would vary considerably from that of England which has no single constitutional document. Together with the Bill of Rights (1791) the Constitution has influenced American criminal procedures to such an extent that today they are clearly distinguished from their English counterparts.

It was only the insistent pressure of Thomas Jefferson[1] which brought about the first ten amendments to the Constitution:[2] the Bill of Rights. The Supreme Court (the one really new institution in the governmental structure devised in 1791) was, through that Bill of Rights, really given something to get its teeth into.

THE WRITTEN CONSTITUTION

The whole of the Constitution of the United States has a bearing on the nature of policing in the USA, although it is sometimes said that only the fourth, the fifth and the (later added) fourteenth amendments of the 'Bill of Rights' are of significance to law enforcement. In the course of this book reference will be made to most if not all the amendments of the Bill of Rights and all are therefore laid out in Appendix I.

THE UNWRITTEN CONSTITUTION

The British constitution is said to be 'unwritten' because it is not contained in one document or a series of linked documents like that of the United States of America or France.

According to Redmond (1966), the British constitution consists of:

1. Several statutes, e.g. Magna Carta (1215), the Bill of Rights (1688), the Act of Settlement (1715);
2. A series of conventions.[3]

In combination, this hotch-potch of legal documents, gentlemen's agreements and democratically agreed statute law, provide for the British nation most if not all of the 'freedoms' contained in the American document. But they are 'implicit rights' rather than the 'explicit rights' of the American Constitutional document. One of the most fundamental differences in the two nations is the direct psychological consequence of that written/unwritten dichotomy; namely that, for the American, with a history of escape from repression, the 'freedom and liberty' clauses of the document are constantly at the forefront of his dealings with authority, and with certain limitations can be cited at the drop of a hat. For the Briton, hundreds of years of history and a diffuse (but no less real) set of rights is quietly assumed and rarely discussed.

THE CHARACTERISTICS OF CONSTITUTIONS

The positive characteristics of a written constitution are said to be that it:

1. Lays down and safeguards liberties, privileges and freedoms and is, in theory, a *guarantee* of such rights.
2. Details how certain national things will be done, e.g. elections, the law-making process.
3. Perpetuates itself through the existence of *entrenched* provisions, e.g. that certain things cannot be changed without necessary procedures, voting majorities, etc.

There are also negative characteristics.

The very things that make a constitution successful also are its inhibiting factors. The rigidity of electoral processes, law-making and constitutional dictates, do, of necessity, make rapid change and speedy resolution of problems difficult, and this is particularly true in the case of liberty or interpretation of the 'rights' of the people.

The inflexibility of a written constitution, requiring for example three-quarters of the states to ratify a constitutional change, leads inevitably to lengthy delays in achieving that change (unless the rules are broken). In a rapidly changing society this can prove problematic to say the least.[4]

In Britain, with an unwritten constitution based on a notion of 'the liberty of the subject', the freedoms are such that the rights of the British are sometimes referred to as 'negative', a concept which allows a person to do anything, go anywhere and say anything *which is not unlawful*. For example, the freedom of speech provision of the first amendment to the US Constitution is echoed in the unwritten freedom for any member of the population in the UK to hold public meetings provided that the law is not broken in respect of 'obstruction' of streets, highways and other people.

Second, the absence of a written constitution coupled with the principle of 'parliamentary supremacy' does mean that Parliament can legislate on any matter it wishes. Thus, by a majority vote, changes in the apparent freedoms of individuals can be brought about. For example, although a total restriction of the freedom of speech notion would not be tolerated, consideration was recently given to, and legislation passed, which sought to restrict marches and processions by requiring the organizers to seek police approval of routes, etc.[5] Thus at one and the same time, a change in legislation is both passed *and*, by the very act of passing it, declared to be constitutional.

Because of this important principle, the courts in the UK are obliged to accept any changes to the law 'as passed' and without question. The courts at any level in Britain *never* review the *constitutionality* of legislation.

But above all such a system's major advantage is the speed with which constitutional change can take place. In the event of a constitutional crisis or a sudden upsurge in a particular type of behaviour considered to be unacceptable to the population, change can be instituted virtually overnight.[6]

The final arbiters in constitutional matters in the USA are the nine members of the Supreme Court, and although there is the opportunity for a good deal of 'citizen involvement' in the law-*making* process, *final* decisions on the constitutionality of Acts are left to the Supreme Court.

Effectively, since the decisions of the Supreme Court are by majority decision, five judges decide the extent of the 'liberty of the individual'. At least it could be said that British parliamentary consideration of constitutional matters does mean that 635 members have the opportunity so to do.

THE STRUCTURE AND ORGANIZATION OF THE BRITISH JUDICIAL SYSTEM

Supreme Court decisions in both nations are the final step in the consideration of appeals against the action of courts or individuals lower in the criminal justice system. There are, however, fundamental differences in both the cause for, and the outcome of, appeals in each nation. Space precludes a full examination of the structure of the judicial systems of the UK and the USA. Superficially, the systems appear similar. Both are pyramidal and hierarchical in form. At the base of each system are the 'inferior' criminal courts; at the next level rest the trial courts; and finally come the Appeal Courts. At the apex of each system lies a Supreme Court responsible for decisions about cases dealt with within particular criteria, the existence of which makes each system 'clearly distinguished' one from the other.

Although the rules which govern the presentation of cases in the inferior courts are different in each system,[7] those differences are most easily identified in an examination of the appeal systems. It is here that disputes about cases, and the grounds on which they are made, and the available decisions by the courts most readily point up the overwhelming concentration on procedural matters in the USA and a very different legal philosophy in the UK.

The inferior courts in the United Kingdom

At the lowest level, less serious cases of all kinds are dealt with by magistrates courts which also act as a filter for cases to be dealt with in the trial court (the crown court), although the concentration in this case is on the weight of evidence rather than the examination of 'probable cause' for action as it is in the USA. Such 'committals' can be either because the law allows the accused to select trial by jury or, in more serious cases, because the law requires that such cases be heard before a jury. The vast bulk of such 'committals' are dealt with on paper. According to Lidstone (1984), less than 8 per cent of committals were conducted otherwise than on paper.

Crown courts are trial courts, involve the deliberations of a jury,[8] and generally have the facility for imposing higher sentences on those convicted.

The appeal courts in the United Kingdom

Although some categories of case may be heard on appeal in the Crown Court, more normally a trial court, the majority of important and serious cases are dealt with by the Criminal Division of the Court of Appeal.

The Court of Criminal Appeal (CCA)

Consisting of a quorum of three senior judges (including the Lord Chief Justice) the court will hear appeals against both conviction (on any point of law as of right), and sentence (but not appeals by the prosecution against acquittal) provided that the CCA accepts the case.

With the permission of both the trial judge and the CCA, CCA will hear appeals against conviction on the basis of any fact or mixed fact and law. Procedural rules allow that cases may be presented and argued by barristers, and for witnesses to be heard, in person, before the court.

Divisional Court of the Queen's bench division

In many cases, when appeal is only on a point of law, appeal lies to the Divisional Court of the Queen's Bench Division. The court hears appeals from both magistrates courts and the Crown Courts, by way of a 'case stated'.

The Divisional Court consists of any two or three judges from the Queen's Bench Division of the High Court which need not include the Lord Chief Justice. Appeals from Crown Courts are only dealt with by the Divisional Court where the lower court acted as an appellate court. Where the lower court was a court of first instance the appeal is to the CCA.

Procedure
The appellant requests the lower court to set out in writing the point of law to be decided by the Divisional Court. The court can respond in one of two ways:

1. order the lower court to continue hearing the case while directing how the law should be applied; or
2. allow or dismiss the appeal itself if all the facts of the case have been heard and decided by the lower court.

The House of Lords

The final court of appeal is the House of Lords.

The 'Law Lords', also known as the 'Lords of Appeal in Ordinary', in a quorum of three, will examine appeals from the CCA and the Divisional Court, submitted to the court with the permission of either the lower court or the House of Lords itself. Application may be either by the defence or the prosecution and must be *on a point of law of general public importance*.

Decisions of the House of Lords are binding on all other courts and, although it was the case until 1966 that such decisions were binding on themselves, this is no longer the case. In a *Practice Statement* the House effectively changed its own rules and the former practice that, as Redmond (1966) put it, the House 'would not change its mind once it had laid down a precedent' was reversed. However, in the intervening twenty years no reversal of this kind has occurred in criminal cases.

Save for the Law Lords themselves then, a rule of law, once laid down in a judgment, itself becomes a precedent and can only be changed or overruled by an Act of Parliament or a reversal by the Lords.

THE JUDICIAL SYSTEM OF THE USA

The United States has a dual court system. The federal courts which have jurisdiction over federal crimes defined by Act of Congress, and state courts which have jurisdiction over crimes defined by state legislatures. Because each state is a sovereign government, there are in effect fifty separate court systems relating to state law which run alongside federal courts in a non-overlapping mode.

The state court system

The state court structure and organization are not unlike the British judicial system in that they are in the form of a pyramid. At the base are the 'lower' or 'inferior' criminal courts (courts of limited jurisdiction) which may be seen as analogous to the magistrates courts in England and Wales. At the next level rest the trial courts (courts of general jurisdiction) occupying a similar position and role to the Crown Courts. This level is followed by the intermediate appellate courts which match the Criminal Division of the Court of Appeal and the Divisional Court of the Queen's Bench Division of the High Court of Justice in their role as appeal courts for various categories of case. Finally, at the apex, there is the State Supreme Court (Final Appellate Court).

State appellate courts

Each state has at least one appellate court; many more populous states have two. The highest appellate court in most states is called the State Supreme Court. Defendants have no constitutional right to appeal but many states have provided such a right in their State Constitution.

The State Supreme Court is a single judicial body composed of from three to nine judges. The judges are either elected or appointed for terms of from six to ten years in most states, but the length of their term can vary between two years to life.

Judges come together as a group (*en banc*), or as a panel of two or three, to deliberate on cases, and do not have the power to try or re-try cases. Their sole function is to decide if errors of law (contraventions of the Constitution) have taken place. The court will therefore be restricted to *reviewing procedural factors* in the sentencing and conviction of the accused.

Such 'legal mistakes' include:

1. That the accused was in some way deprived of his/her constitutional rights.
2. That the rules of evidence were contravened at the trial.
3. That a guilty plea was accepted that the accused did not make voluntarily.
4. The admission into evidence of an 'illegally' obtained confession.
5. Issues over the incorrect empanelling (e.g. racial imbalance) of or directions to a jury.
6. Passing an *unlawful* sentence.

It will be noted that the most significant difference between the appeal process in the USA and that in Britain is that there is in the USA complete and overriding concern with the legal conduct of the case, a feature of less importance in Britain. In British courts, reconsideration of facts and the opportunity to consider again the guilt or innocence of the accused are conducted at all appeals save those to the Divisional Court (which is only concerned with points of law). Although procedural elements may be considered they are rarely significant to the outcome of the deliberations. In the USA, due process considerations, seeking to guarantee the accused his rights of fundamental fairness and justice, are of the utmost importance to the US system (Robin, 1980, p. 174). For example, in the USA, appeals against sentence can only be undertaken where there is a violation of the fourteenth amendment's requirement for 'due process' and 'equal protection of the law'. In Britain such appeals can take place on such grounds as the sentence being excessive bearing in mind the facts of the case.

The US appellate court, unlike the British appeal courts, never changes a conviction to an acquittal or resentences the defendant.

The court may, however, order the lower court (trial court) to:

1. Resentence the accused without using certain inaccurate or unsupported information which may be contained in 'pre-sentence' reports used in the lower court.
2. Conduct a retrial which excludes certain illegally obtained evidence.
3. Dismiss charges against the defendant in cases involving severe abuses of the law.
4. Direct the court-supervised selection of a more radically balanced jury.

The direction for a retrial as at 2 above does not, however, guarantee that the result of the case will be any different from that originally announced.

Precedent – United States of America

The rules of precedent require that all state courts in similar cases are bound by the principles established by the State Appeal Court.

THE FEDERAL COURT SYSTEM

Some 85–95 per cent of criminal cases in the USA are processed by the state courts. Almost all violent crimes are state crimes although there is occasional overlapping of jurisdiction (the perennial law enforcement problem in the USA) as, for example, with the crime of robbing a bank – both a state and a federal crime (provided that the bank is federally or nationally insured).

Federal crimes include: theft of mail, theft from interstate commerce, counterfeiting, income tax offences, transporting a stolen car across a state line, violation of federal drug laws, etc.

The federal court system is a four-tier hierarchical structure consisting of (1) US magistrates, (2) federal district courts, (3) courts of appeal, and (4) the US Supreme Court.

According to the Constitution, the US Supreme Court was to be established and the power was given to Congress to establish any additional lower courts that would be required.

Federal Courts of Appeal

Following an overload crisis in 1891, the constitutionally created Supreme Court initiated the development of eleven Courts of Appeal. The district courts are arranged in eleven circuits, and each of these has an appeal court. At least three judges must hear an appeal case. Appeals are made on the grounds of a review of constitutional factors, as in the State Intermediate Courts of Appeals. Cases are dealt with by way of court transcripts and motions, not by way of trials.

The United States Supreme Court

The Supreme Court has two kinds of jurisdiction over cases:

1. Original jurisdiction: cases may be taken directly to the court for decision. These are usually disputes between states or issues of the constitutionality of state law or regulation.
2. Appellate jurisdiction: the court has authority to resolve 'substantial federal questions'. Almost without exception these are disputes about the constitutionality of state statutes or interpretation of the Constitution.

The major work of the Supreme Court is none the less discretionary in its nature. The Court may review, at its own discretion, appeals by defendants and prisoners who have been convicted. Almost two-thirds of the cases come from the lower federal courts and the remaining third from state courts. Cases from state courts will not even be considered by the Supreme Court unless and until all state remedies have been exhausted.

It may refuse to hear cases which turn on 'political questions' – issues which fall within the province of federal legislators or the executive branch, will not give 'advisory opinions' or consider 'moot' cases and will avoid interpretation of the Constitution if a case may be resolved in any other way.

The court *must* hear cases when:

1. The highest state court has ruled that a federal statute is unconstitutional.
2. The highest state court has upheld a state law or a provision in a state constitution whose federal constitutionality has been challenged.
3. The federal Court of Appeal has declared a state statute unconstitutional or contrary to federal law and the state appeals the decision.

Unlike the House of Lords in Britain, the Supreme Court never changes a conviction to an acquittal or re-sentences the defendant.

The court may, however, order:

1. A new trial before a different judge.
2. The exclusion of a defendant's confession from consideration by the jury in reaching a verdict.
3. A change of venue because of prejudicial pre-trial publicity or community hostility which prevented an impartial trial.
4. Direct the institutional authorities to remedy the unconstitutional conditions of imprisonment.

As with other courts, the direction for a re-trial as at 1 and 2 above does not however guarantee that the result of the case will be any different from that originally announced: most new trials result in reconviction and imprisonment.[9]

Retroactivity and precedent

Because the Supreme Court deals with matters of constitutionality it may make rulings which are 'retroactive' in their effect. Such a practice, particularly in criminal cases where people may be serving prison sentences for matters affected by the new ruling, may throw the criminal justice system into confusion. For that reason the court will only make such a ruling when there is a danger that not to do so will 'impede' the criminal justice process or will result in convictions of innocent defendants. Unlike the British House of Lords, the Supreme Court has never been bound by its own decisions although in the court hierarchy the principle of *stare decisis* binds all lower courts. Such a practice in the Supreme Court has always given it some leeway to adjust to current social conditions, but equally may be criticized for removing any degree of certainty from court decisions, the reason one suspects that the House of Lords has not taken advantage of their self-given facility to reverse themselves.

Magistrates, judges and a special issue

The courts of limited jurisdiction are distributed throughout each state and are similar in function to the magistrates courts in the UK. In the cities in most areas of the USA they are referred to as 'magistrates courts', 'municipal courts', 'district courts', etc., while in rural areas they are often called 'justice of the peace' courts.

In the UK the magistrates courts are supervised either by 'lay' magistrates, or by a stipendiary magistrate. Lay magistrates (justices of the peace) are locally selected and appointed by the Lord Chancellor, and act, on a part-time basis, with the advice of a court clerk, a legally qualified man or woman, usually a solicitor[10] or a barrister[11] of five years' standing. Stipendiary magistrates are full-time appointees, barristers of a minimum seven years' standing.

In the USA supervision of the court is carried out by a man or woman who has the title 'judge'. Such a title may be the cover for a multitude of differing experiences and skills. In most jurisdictions lower court judges are lawyers, but in some they are not. The Constitution of the United States does not require judges to be members of the bar or lawyers. Indeed a Federal Supreme Court decision in 1976 refused to require lower court judges to be lawyers or have a legal background.

The quality of justice in the justice of the peace courts is questionable. Commonly, JPs have no legal training and may not even have graduated from high school. Many will not have progressed beyond tenth grade (about age 16). In South Carolina, up to 85 per cent of the criminal defendants are tried by inferior courts (Robin, 1980, p. 170) by justices whose legal knowledge is sketchy at best and whose courtroom is their workplace or their home: being a judge is merely a sideline. Only a small percentage of South Carolina's JPs are lawyers; many will never have opened a law book, and have only sketchy knowledge of the 'legal niceties' (Robin, 1980, p. 171).

In 1967, a Commission set up by the President to study crime and the criminal justice system in the USA reported that of the thirty-five states that had JP courts, the judges' income depended on the volume of cases they dealt with, their outcome, or perhaps, a percentage of the fines imposed (President's Crime Commission, 1967). Although the situation is improving, progress is slow.

The US judiciary

In thirty-three of the fifty states, some or all the judges are elected. In fifteen of these states candidates for judicial office appear on 'party tickets', i.e. are directly associated not only with politics *per se* but also with politicians.[12] The major problems of the US judiciary are summed up by Robin (1980, p. 185):

> Until recently it was virtually impossible to do anything about judges who were incompetent, disabled, senile, corrupt, unethical, racist, abusive, who shirked their duties, or who conducted court room proceedings without decorum and the appearance of justice. State and federal law usually provided for the removal of judges only through impeachment – a cumbersome and ineffective device for responding to the range of problems associated with judicial shortcomings.

However, following a lead set by the state of California, by 1978 thirty-five states had established judicial discipline commissions.

Although by no means fully comprehensive, many professional and private groups have become 'judge watchers'. Judicial importance is a problem which many feel could be greatly improved by the introduction of a system which sought to appoint better qualified people to the bench.

The British judiciary

In Britain, judges are headed by the Lord Chancellor, who is appointed by the Crown on the advice of the Prime Minister and is a government minister. Sitting as a member of the House of Lords, he is responsible for the general running of the judicial system and 'supervises' the Lord Chief Justice, and the Lords of Appeal in the House of Lords, as well as numerous other judges. All judges must be barristers of long-standing and experience, usually of between ten and fifteen years.

All judges are appointed *quam diu bene geserint* (for so long as they are of good behaviour) (Bill of Rights, 1668). They can only be removed from office for misconduct, and are immune from liability for anything they say or do in court. They usually retire at about age 75.

Although most Americans look askance at the idea of the British judge *always* appointed for life (where's the democracy in that?) the process must be seen against the background of the academic and experiential aspects of the 'career' lawyer in the UK. Given the academic ability, the eminence and the skills of advocacy any ambitious lawyer can rise to a (junior) judge's bench[13] but only after three years of study as a 'junior' and *at least ten years* as a 'barrister'.

Even the lay magistrates in Britain are supervised through the Lord Chancellor's office and are required to attend regular sessions on new legislation, police procedures, and so on.

Nevertheless, there is still considerable difficulty in dispensing with the services of an 'incompetent, disabled, senile, corrupt, unethical, racist, abusive' judge in the UK, although, in practice, they are few and far between.

BAIL

A function of major importance in the lower courts in the USA (and to a lesser extent in the UK) is the consideration of bail for those accused of criminal activity. In the American legal system prior to the early 1960s the lower courts relied on the principle of cash bail (pay or stay), the amount of cash required being set by the court according to the seriousness of the charges and the defendant's prior record. Sometimes courts set the level of cash bail at a high level in order to ensure that the defendant remains in custody pending trial.

The beginnings of a bail reform movement occurred in the 1960s when more use was made of the provision to allow defendants to be released in their own recognizance. However, monetary bail continues to be required and has led to the development of the 'bondsperson'. Few impecunious defendants can afford the sums demanded in 'cash bail' cases and seek the help of commercial bondsagents, who, in exchange for a fee, will deposit with the court the cash required or a 'bail bond' in that amount.

It will be recalled that the eighth amendment to the US Constitution deals with excessive bail. The Supreme Court has been remarkably silent about a definition of this phrase.

In British courts, at all levels, the setting of bail does not require money to be paid directly to the court unless and until the defendant fails to appear at the trial or subsequent hearing. Bail conditions may be set, e.g. to live at a particular address, or not to go to a particular address or neighbourhood, and guarantees for appearance may be taken from friends and relatives of the accused (sureties) but only in the form of an agreement to pay if the accused does not appear. In the absence of need for sureties the accused is released (on his/her own recognizance), again on a signed agreement to pay a sum of money should he or she fail to appear. There is no 'professional bondsman' occupation and although in theory sums set for forfeit are unlimited, in practice they are generally restricted to the maximum fine applicable for the offence(s) charged.

Civil libertarians in both nations are concerned at the tendency of courts to place defendants in custody prior to the trial proper either because in the UK sureties cannot be obtained, or the court refuses (on grounds that are specified in legislation) to allow bail, or in the USA because either bail is refused or the setting of bail is at such a high level that the defendant cannot hope to meet the commitment. So-called 'preventive detention' thus becomes the case. In both nations this is considered as a breach of the notion that a person is innocent until proven guilty.

Figures released by the Home Office show that in the UK almost 20 per cent of the prison population are 'remand' prisoners (i.e. awaiting trial).[14] In the period 1979–85 the remand population in British prisons has grown by more than 50 per cent, the number of persons sentenced to prison increased by less than 1000 (less than 1 per cent) in the same period.[15]

In recent years there has been a movement in the United States for bail reform, and following the Federal Bail Reform Act 1966 many states have passed laws that limit the role of bondsmen. Some states have sought to control the practice by introducing legislation that, for example, defines the role of bondsmen. In Oregon, Wisconsin, Nebraska and Illinois commercial bail bonding has been eliminated, whilst in 1976 Kentucky extended a similar restriction to the outright banning of bondsmen and set up a state-wide system of pre-trial services and agencies.

The effect of these measures is that there appears to have been an increase in the number of people being released before trial. In 1976 a study showed that, in twenty cities, the release rate had risen to 67 per cent against a low in 1962 of only 48 per cent (Thomas, 1976). By 1981 Toberg (1981) was able to report 85 per cent of her eight-site sample were released before trial.

In many states there has been some shifting of the nature of bail in order that issues over community safety may be addressed. For example, in 1982, voters in five states approved constitutional amendments limiting the right to bail to assure community safety in pre-trial release (US Dept of Justice, 1983).

In the UK concerns have recently been expressed over the workings of the Bail Act 1976 which operates on the presumption that bail will be granted and in Section 2 of the Act states that bail may *only be refused* if the court feels that the defendant may:

Table 3.1 Bail practices in the United States

Exclusion of certain crimes from automatic bail eligibility	7
Definition of the purpose of bail to ensure appearance and safety of citizens	13
Inclusion of crime control factors in release decision	7
Inclusion of release conditions related to crime control	15
Limitations on the right to bail for those previously convicted	9
Revocation of pre-trial release when there is evidence that the accused has committed a new crime	11
Limitations on the right to bail for crimes alleged to have been committed while on release	9
Provisions for pre-trial detention to ensure safety	8

Note: Many states have two or more of the above. Some have none (e.g. Connecticut).
Source: Adapted from US Dept of Justice (1983).

1. Fail to surrender.
2. Commit an offence on bail.
3. Interfere with witnesses or otherwise obstruct the course of justice whether in relation to himself or any other person.

In practice this means that evidence on oath to that effect must be presented to the court. It may be that the introduction of a Crown Prosecution Service (CPS), loosely analogous to the Public Prosecutor in the USA, has, by virtue of the fact that all objections to bail were, prior to CPS, made by police officers, had an unexpected effect. The advent of the CPS will be examined more fully in Chapter 10 but with respect to the issue of bail, it may be that objections to bail put by CPS advocates currently carry less weight than those formerly put by a police officer. (See Marwood (1987) for a complete exposition of this point.)

The concern in Britain arose because, following the trial and conviction of a man for the murder of a police officer in a riot in North London, it was found that the accused person had been on bail for *another murder* at the time of the officer's death. Some Members of Parliament sought to get the Bail Act amended to allow for a blanket refusal of bail in cases of murder, and others added robbery, rape and sexual offences. The Home Secretary on behalf of the government rejected calls for change. It is interesting therefore to examine some of the provisions in various of the United States which are shown in Table 3.1.

GENERAL DISCUSSION

The single most important difference between the judicial systems of the countries under discussion is in the overwhelming concentration on the procedural/constitutional aspects of the prosecution (and appeal) process on one side of the Atlantic and the emphasis on the other, on the facts of the case and the nature and content of the legislation itself.

This difference is perhaps best indicated by an examination of a 'rule of law' of fundamental and practical significance to police officers – the exclusionary rule.

The exclusionary rule – United Kingdom

Historically, the rule at common law authorized the use of illegally obtained evidence so long as it was reliable and trustworthy. This view of the law was supported in the well-known case of Kuruma, Son of Kamu.[16]

This case occurred in the former British Commonwealth country of Kenya and related to the enforcement of emergency regulations which were in force at that time. The regulations contained a power which allowed an officer of or above the rank of assistant inspector to stop and search vehicles and people for unlawful firearms and ammunition.

In the case in question the defendant was stopped without a warrant by a constable and a sergeant, who searched and found a quantity of ammunition. After initial conviction, the appeal process was initiated and it was held in judgment that even though the search was, in fact, unlawful, the evidence of the found ammunition was admissable and that such would be the case provided that no trick, threat, bribe or misrepresentation had been used to obtain such evidence.

In broad terms, therefore, evidence obtained by an unlawful search is not *automatically excluded*, particularly if it can be shown to be the 'fruit of a crime, the instrument by which a crime was committed or material evidence to prove the commission of a crime' (*Ghani* v. *Jones*, 1970). There is however a good deal of complex and occasionally contradictory 'case law' relating to specific instances – search with and without warrants, etc. The Police and Criminal Evidence Act 1984 has stopped short of creating a total exclusionary rule, allowing evidence to be admitted if it can be shown to be 'fairly' obtained.[17]

The exclusionary rule – USA

As noted in Chapter 2 the fourth amendment to the US Constitution protects 'the right of the people to be secure in their persons, houses, papers and effects, against unreasonable searches and seizures'. Through a series of decisions in the Supreme Court which were declared as having, in part, the purpose of 'policing the police' (Frinley, 1971), the exclusionary rule, which provides that evidence obtained by unreasonable search and seizure is not admissible in evidence, was extended from the federal courts to the state courts.

The exclusion of evidence illegally obtained had been applicable to the federal courts following *Weeks* v. *US*[18] for many years, but when, in 1949, the Supreme Court declined to extend the rule to the states[19] the groundwork was laid for later judicial review of this contentious issue. '[The Court] said that individual states should be left to develop their own ways of discouraging police violation of constitutional standards' (Driscol, 1987, p. 554).

Some 'individual states' had, by 1960, developed their own exclusionary rules but since 'experience had shown that other methods of encouraging police compliance were fruitless' (Driscoll, 1987, p. 555),[20] the Supreme Court were drawn again to consider the matter in a landmark case during the period of court activity sometimes known as the 'due process revolution'.

Mapp v. Ohio

The final decision related to the 'unreasonable' (probably warrantless) search of a house occupied by Doloree Mapp. The officers believed that a bombing suspect was hiding there and that gambling equipment was concealed inside. Later at the house, Ms Mapp was arrested and subsequently obscene materials were found.

Charged with the possession of obscene materials, she was convicted and sentenced to prison. On a final appeal to the Supreme Court in 1961 (the incident having occurred four years before, in 1957) the court held that:

1. The defendant's right to privacy under the fourth amendment had been violated.
2. The exclusionary rule is an essential part of that right.
3. All evidence obtained by searches or seizures in violation of the Constitution is by that same authority inadmissible in a state court.

Some twenty-six states had, until that moment, refused to acknowledge the exclusionary rule and many police officers were (and remain) disillusioned by a decision which they saw as elevating the rights of the criminal above those of the public and the law enforcement organizations. But the Supreme Court made it clear that, in part, their decision was based on 'the need to maintain judicial integrity' sometimes requiring that 'a criminal go free rather than have the government become a partner in law violation' (*Mapp* v. *Ohio*, 367 US 643 (1961)). This was a case in which the Supreme Court did not make a 'retroactive ruling' for although it had a bearing on judicial *integrity*, it did not have a bearing on the judicial *process* – the due process requirement of the fourteenth amendment.

If emphasis were needed, the role of the Supreme Court in 'policing the police' is clearly seen in the application of the rule only to evidence illegally obtained by *government officials*. As Watson and McAninch (1984, pp. 53–4) put it, 'If A should enter B's house and obtain evidence which could convict B of a crime and turn the evidence over to the police, the evidence could be used to prosecute B. This is so even though A might be prosecuted for illegal entry.'[21]

There has in recent years been some softening of the effect of the exclusionary rule in the USA. For example, in 1984 the Supreme Court amended the decision to allow the admission of evidence 'if it would have been discovered by lawful means'.

Although there are many changes taking place in the UK, particularly in terms of control over the handling of arrested persons, confessions, and so on, the legislators have stopped short of creating a *total* exclusionary rule. However, Parliament saw fit in the Police and Criminal Evidence Act 1984 to allow the courts 'discretion' to exclude evidence if it would have an 'unduly adverse effect on the fairness of the proceeding'. As Zander (1985, p. 116) points out, it remains to be seen how the judges will use this discretion.

> It is conceivable that they will interpret the section narrowly and admit evidence obtained by thoroughly deplorable methods on the pretext that it does not effect the fairness of the *proceedings*. This would emasculate the discretion. The whole thrust of the policy behind the new section is to give the courts power to express their disapproval of objectionable police methods by excluding the fruits of such action.

There are clearly some interesting days ahead, for in the past, British courts have categorically stated that judges 'ought not to exclude evidence to punish police officers for breaches of the ... rules' (*R* v. *Elliott* (1977) Crim LR 551). Judicial dispute seems likely.

Due process versus crime control

Nevertheless, the established existence of such a powerful rule in the USA controlling and constraining the behaviour of police officers on the street, and its contrasting dependence on judicial decisions in *individual cases* in England and Wales, does emphasize the force with which the 'due process' model of law enforcement, which places legal guilt over factual guilt, is conducted in the USA.

The British model is, by contrast, one of 'crime control' which emphasizes factual over legal guilt and will thus examine each case on its merits, concerned with innocence or guilt not constitutional issues. Such a process, of necessity, demands speedy process with comparatively minimal concern with minor formalities.

In the USA the defendant is protected, particularly through the appeal process – which is mainly concerned with constitutional issues arising from the trial – from violation of written rights. In Britain the defendant, and the case against him or her, is judged on the basis of the credibility of the evidence, the circumstances of arrest and 'matters of fact'. Constitutional matters are rarely if ever addressed by the judges, for they are the province of Parliament not of the courts.

But the 'due process' philosophy has more than an effect simply on the manner in which the police perform their task in the gathering of evidence. Like a stone in a pond, the concentric circles of the exclusionary rule's waves spread from that epicentre to touch police policies, training and attitudes. The rule has a pervasive effect on all areas of policing responsibility, not least because of the psychological effect on the police.[22]

Supreme Court decisions comprehensively seeking to 'police the police' have, until now, been a source of little concern to the police in the UK – the crime control model has held sway; but, with the advent of the Police and Criminal Evidence Act 1984, and the creation of a series of 'due process rules' in the form of the annunciation of 'rights' for arrested persons, things may well change. What is certain is that the psychological effect on the police population in the UK has been stunning, and stunned.[23]

The sudden realization that Parliament was no longer prepared to tolerate police failure to provide legal advice to suspects, or was concerned about the manner of street interrogation of potential suspects and so on, led to a full-scale reassessment of police activity at all levels of British policing.

Issues which we have examined, such as the nature of constitutions, the appropriate provision of bail, the manner of trial, and the structure and function of the judiciary, while significant, are peripheral to the major concern of the constant search in a democracy for the appropriate balance between individual freedom and personal rights, and the battle against crime and criminals. One solution, as we have seen, has been the crime control model, the other the due process model.

Many American officers at all levels are frustrated and disillusioned by the regular release of persons arrested and charged with serious offences as a consequence of failure to abide by 'rules'. On the other hand, the British officer, uncertain whether matters will be excluded or not, has over the years tended to develop a 'let's give it a run' mentality, and consequent abuses of the system have occurred. Not surprisingly, many American officers are jealous of the freedoms provided by the British model. Many British officers are horrified to discover the constraints under which their American colleagues work. Those concerned with issues of civil rights in the USA were, until recent changes, bemused by the '*laissez-faire*' attitude of the British courts and the judiciary to the absence of laid-down, enforceable legal rights.

Both of the apparently bipolar police attitudes are strong indicators of the necessity for the existence of some, if not complete, concern over procedural aspects of the investigation, arrest and charge of suspects in crime.

As we have shown, the existence of a due process philosophy is due, in part, to the desire of the Supreme Court to control and limit the worst excesses of the comparatively unprofessional elements in American policing in the late nineteenth and early and mid-twentieth centuries. For the police officer in both societies it is a reality, although a rarely acknowledged one, that the principle of 'innocent until proved guilty' is rarely a viable proposition. After direct observation of criminal activity, or hours, weeks or months during which evidence is meticulously gathered, sifted and evaluated, following an allegation of crime, such a dispassionate position is at best difficult and at worst an impossibility. The police officer, by virtue of his special knowledge of the evidence, gives no credence to such an unrealistic position.

The strength of procedural elements in the American judicial system is a deliberate design created to exercise control over this aberration by ensuring that defendants are protected. As Robin (1988, p. 4) puts it: 'The idea behind due process is to guarantee citizens fair and proper treatment by government officials', and this is so even if the manifestly guilty go free.

But the comparative laxity of a crime control model has exactly the opposite effect. The concentration on evidence rather than procedures has the effect of allowing, on occasion, the innocent to be convicted, even though police officers may have exceeded their authority or abused their powers.

The focus of conflict between the two models is pointed to by Beckman (1980, p. 217) who writes:

There is a real tension in our society between those who advocate more effective police work to combat crime and those who point out this country's constitutional aversion to a police state. The tension cannot be avoided by calling for 'law and order' and more aggressive police tactics. A balance must be found between security and liberty.

It is this balance that both societies seek. The incorporation of due process considerations into police practice in England and Wales through the provisions of the Police and Criminal Evidence Act 1984 is matched by the so-called 'retreat' from the decisions (and stringent provisions) of Supreme Court decisions in the 1960s and 1970s which we examined earlier. The hardening on one side and the softening on the other bring the models slightly closer.

SECTION 2

Organization, Accountability and Professionalism

CHAPTER 4

The Buck Stops – Where? Issues of Accountability and Control

There is a real danger in any democracy that the constant need to adjust the fine balance between individual liberty and the control of ever-rising crime rates will lead to a blurring of the distinction between the two. Subsequently, this may lead, in its turn, to both the 'restriction' of freedom and the control of criminal activity by criminal or at least non-constitutional methods. One only has to examine the nature of policing in a nation beset by 'political' unrest (cf. Jakubs, 1977) to become aware that, in the absence of local control of the police, it is all too easy for the police function to be dictated (and controlled) by central government fear or paranoia, rather than by a definition of the needs of a given society to control crime, maintain order or provide support.

But the nature of democratic law-making is such that much of the definition and interpretation of both the law and the police function has to be left to the discretion of the police themselves. There is a potential danger that the limits of the law and the nature of crime are, at least until the courts have their day, decided by an unelected body – the police. The question therefore becomes one of examining and making decisions about the nature of the police function in a democratic society, and in particular, the methods by which the checks and balances to ensure popular local control are managed.

The aim of this chapter is to examine the nature of central and local government supervision of, and involvement in, policing in England and Wales, and in the United States of America; to draw some direct comparisons and contrasts between them and to discuss the nature and practice of 'accountability' and 'control' in law enforcement agencies in the two nations.

COORDINATION AND CONTROL OF POLICING IN ENGLAND AND WALES

The Municipal Corporations Act 1835 established the modern police force in the towns of England and Wales on the, by now, increasingly successful model of the

London Metropolitan Police. These forces were placed under the control of a local police authority. Later the County Police Act 1839 allowed the creation of county police forces, but many counties failed to create any policing structure. In 1856, therefore, Parliament passed an Act which made the creation of full-time county police forces compulsory and established a number of principles, many of which remain today.

The most practical of these principles was the creation of a supervisory body, the HMIs – 'Her (or His) Majesty's Inspectors of Constabulary'. The HMIs were, and are, required to inspect, on an annual basis, and report to the Home Secretary on all forces, except the London Metropolitan Police.[1] The Home Secretary is obliged to submit a report to Parliament.

The major aim of the legislation was however to get the recalcitrant counties into line and to 'encourage' them to accept their responsibilities for policing. To this end, central government agreed to pay 25 per cent of the pay and clothing costs of the police from central funds, provided the force could be shown to be efficient. The HMIs were thus required to include in their inspection details of efficiency, particularly regarding numbers of officers and the discipline of the force. The effect of such legislation was, despite the existence of police authorities (then known as Watch Committees), to give a measure of 'direction' over policing to the Home Office.

However, by 1860, there were over 226 forces in England and Wales – thirteen of them with only one officer. Thus in 1866 a second Parliamentary Act effected a reduction of the number of forces to 183 by 1889. This was mainly achieved through an extension of the mechanism of the earlier Act. The central government grant was raised to 50 per cent of the pay and clothing costs but only in exchange for an assessment by HMIs that the numbers of officers in a particular location was 'efficient'. Efficiency was assessed on the basis of the ratio between the number of officers and the size of the population. Thus, many small forces were obliged to allow themselves to be absorbed by the larger county areas. Only the bigger (or richer) city forces were able to survive.

One of the practical consequences of the legislation was to reduce the measure of control of the local police committees over their forces. At that time they had influence over all appointments, promotions, disciplinary hearings (including punishments) *and* the daily duties of officers. The chief constable was only able to post his men and was required to seek directions on all but the most trivial matters.

The 50 per cent grant by the central government was, in effect, to allow the chief officers (through the delegated responsibilities of the Home Office) to make more and more decisions. The Home Office could always hold out the threat of withdrawal of the grant to the local authority if a force was 'inefficient'; and efficiency was, in part, construed as having a bearing on the right of the chief officer to exercise proper managerial control over 'appointments, promotions, disciplinary hearings (including punishments awarded) *and* the daily duties of officers'.

The passing by Parliament of the Police Act 1919 formally gave the Home Secretary the power to make regulations governing the pay and conditions of service of all police forces in England and Wales and allowed for the creation and introduction of a standardized 'Discipline Code'.

Although the police authority was to be involved in the selection process, no chief constable could be appointed without previous police experience, unless he had 'exceptional qualities'. Prior to 1919 few 'regular' police officers reached the top and the majority of chief constables were ex-soldiers, with little understanding of the practicalities of policing. Not infrequently, disputes arose between those who saw themselves as professional police officers (the regulars) and the 'outsiders'.[2]

The legislation followed a police strike in 1919 and the Act set up *national* negotiating machinery in the form of a Police Council and a representative body for the police, the Police Federation.[3]

In Britain, in exchange for a further erosion of the local authority's control, the central government grant for policing was extended to cover 50 per cent of all policing costs, not just the pay and uniforms of the previous arrangements.

Finally the on-going process of amalgamations was concluded (for the time being) through the Police Act 1964 which reduced the number of forces to its current 43, allowed police officers to operate in the whole of England and Wales, and provided a formal and complete structure for dealing with complaints about individual officers, police practices, and so on.

THE HOME OFFICE FORCES

These 43 forces are known as 'Home Office Forces', but there are, in reality, fifteen other police forces not covered by the full 1964 Act, particularly in relation to the regulations regarding the investigation and recording of complaints against police officers. These forces include the British Transport Police (BTP), the Docks Police, the Royal Parks Police and the Atomic Energy Authority Police (AEA), Ministry of Defence Police (MOD),[4] etc. They have limited and specific jurisdiction confined to their responsibilities. For example, the BTP are confined to the railway stations, trains and sidings; AEA to atomic power stations and AEA property, MOD to British armed services property, and so on. In most cases, powers of arrest extend to a limit of six miles from the 'force's' property.

The modern role of the Home Office provides for a Police Staff College, for centralized training of senior managers, forensic science laboratories, wireless depots, regional training centres, central research facilities and a number of other support functions. In the main these provisions are confined to use by and for the Home Office police forces.

So how much *control* is exercised over British police?

The information contained in the preceding paragraphs would lead most casual observers to believe that there is a comprehensive element of central control with some limited local involvement through the police authority, and it is this view which no doubt provokes some ill-informed commentators to typify British policing as having 'strong central control'. The reality may, however, be somewhat different.

POLICE AUTHORITY

In 1930, in *Fisher* v. *Oldham Corporation*, the Court of Appeal stated that, 'although a constable may be an employee of a local authority, his office was "of the Crown" ', i.e. independent from the executive and other arms of government.

A Chief Constable is, of course, for all his high rank, still a constable and as such should, in theory, maintain such independence: and such a view was expressed in 1958 when it was stated in a debate in the House of Lords that:

> No Police Authority or anyone else has authority to interfere in relation to the enforcement of the law by police ... full responsibility for enforcement is a matter which is reserved entirely to the chief officer of police; in the exercise of this responsibility he is answerable to the law alone and not to any police authority; that is the position both in the counties and in the boroughs.[5]

This non-legal, parliamentary, view was confirmed by a case heard in 1968 again by the Court of Appeal.

In a case brought to try to force a chief officer to operate the laws on gambling (not enforced because they were, in practice, so uncertain) Lord Denning said of the Chief Officer:

> His constitutional status has never been defined either by statute or by the courts. But I have no hesitation in holding that, like every constable in the land, he should be and is, independent of the executive. I hold it to be the duty of the Commissioner of Police of the Metropolis, as it is of every Chief Constable, to enforce the law of the land. He must take steps so to post his men that crime may be detected; and that honest citizens may go about their affairs in peace. He must decide whether or not suspected persons are to be prosecuted; and if need be bring the prosecution, or see that it is brought; but in all these things he is not the servant of anyone save of the law itself. *No Minister of the Crown can tell him that he must or must not keep observation on this place or that; or he must, or must not, prosecute this man or that one. Nor can any police authority tell him so. The responsibility for law enforcement lies on him.* He is answerable to the law and to the law alone. [emphasis added][6]

Lord Denning also expressed in his decision that the Chief Constable is free to make decisions about whether enquiries should be pursued, whether prosecutions should be brought, and whether an arrest should be made. It must be for the Chief Officer to decide on the disposition of his force and the concentration of his resources on any particular crime or area. He continued:

> No court can give him directions on such a matter. He can also make policy decisions and give effect to them ... but there are some policy decisions with which, I think *the courts* can interfere. [emphasis added]

The emphasis on the use of the legal process (the application for an order of mandamus) has, in effect, weakened both the role of the police authority and the Home Secretary in their supervisory/controlling capacity. In practice it has led to the Home Office issuing 'advice' rather than 'directives' to chief officers, and to chief officers occasionally refusing to reverse policy decisions which have been challenged by police authorities, using in effect the 'so, sue me' argument (although never so baldly put).

The real problem, however, is one of party politics.

The police authorities are made up of elected local 'councillors' as two-thirds of the membership, and local justices of the peace as the remaining third. In most cases the demand from the left wing is for the exercise of full democratic *control* in all matters of policing by the police authority. The right-wing view is, however, that the police in England and Wales are among, if not the, most *accountable* in the world, and that in general no more supervisory powers are necessary.

It is probably time that we presented a definition of accountability and control which will separate them for discussion purposes.

Accountability may be defined as any system which provides mechanisms to allow individuals or groups to assess and comment on decisions, practices and policies; and requires those making or pursuing such decisions, practices and policies liable to allow such assessment and comment.

Control may be defined as any system which allows individuals or groups directly to influence the making of decisions, the defining of practices or the initiation and development of policies; and requires those seeking to make such decisions, or to develop such practices and policies to seek the approval of such individuals and groups.

Accountability

Chief constables (and the political 'right' generally) would point to a number of factors in support of their 'most accountable' argument.

1. Accountability through prosecution. Despite the *Fisher* v. *Oldham* decision, and the main content of the judicial decision in *Blackburn*, the final words of Lord Denning, 'He is answerable to the law and to the law alone', mean that any officer can be held *accountable* to a court of law and/or prosecuted for an offence, if appropriate.
2. Requirements to make reports. The provisions of section 12 of the Police Act 1964 allow a police authority to require a report on any specified matter, a provision intended to have the same effect as requiring the directors of a company to be answerable to their shareholders.
3. Control of finances. As the chief officers are dependent on the local authority's purse, they would be unlikely to pursue offending policies in the face of a refusal to meet subsequent claims for expenditure.
4. Investigation of complaints. That the provision of legislation regarding disciplinary offences are such that 'independent' assessment and evaluation of complaints by members of the public are thoroughly and impartially investigated.
5. Non-political presence in police authorities. That, in any case, the presence of

JPs on the police authority ensures that matters of accountability over legal and law enforcement matters are made without political bias.

The absence of such accountability and hence *any* level of potential controllability would, however, be identified by the 'left' by noting that, in relation to the items above:

1. Accountability through prosecution. The law on criminal offences committed by police officers requires that final decisions are made by the Director of Public Prosecutions. Such decisions apply a higher standard of evidence than is expected in non-police cases and thus many officers are not prosecuted. Even if they are the courts are statistically less likely to convict.

2. Requirements to make reports. In the event that a local police authority requires a report under section 12 of the Police Act, the chief constable can appeal to the Home Secretary if he feels that the making of such a report would not be in the interests of the public. The Home Secretary it is claimed will usually support him, particularly if he is of a different political party than the majority of the authority members.

3. Control of finances. In November 1985, in the wake of substantial street disorder throughout the country, a policy decision by the Greater Manchester Police to purchase and store 'baton rounds' (rubber bullets) was disapproved by the police authority. The chief constable was able to bypass the local authority and the Home Office agreed to purchase (and store) them for the force.[7]

   Furthermore, since the government is able to exert control over the expenditure of local authorities no police authority is likely to 'go the financial stake' (Morgan and Swift, 1987) over a dispute with a chief constable over such matters. Although it is the case that 50 per cent of policing costs are met by central government it is also true that that grant is itself increased by 50 per cent as a consequence of the normal rate support grant. In practice this means that only 25 per cent of policing costs are met from local financial sources. Ill-advised financial policies on the part of a police committee could result in the withholding of a part of the police grant-in-aid with a consequent rise in the proportion of local input to the police budget.

4. Investigation of complaints. Whilst there is an element of 'independent assessment', the complaints are investigated by police officers themselves and any subsequent discipline is administered by the deputy chief officer of the force – as such allegations of bias are constantly made.

5. Non-political presence in the police authorities. The presence (or absence) of JPs is of no relevance. Whether directly associated with the law or not they are, or will become, 'politically motivated'. Statistically many JPs will be supporters of the 'right'. The political power of 'right' politics can then act to support the status quo. (Currently two party manifestos indicated an intention remove JPs from police authorities.)

Control

Despite the fact that the chief constable is subject to some central governmental administrative controls (viz. decisions about the pay and conditions of his officers, decisions about amalgamations, the requirement to explain his actions and the threat of dismissal if he is inefficient), and that he may call upon certain central resources, his legal independence in operational decision making, etc. (as defined by Lord Denning in his important decision regarding the constitutional role of police officers) precludes the opportunity for any kind of 'control' as defined, either by 'the left' who want it or the Home Office, who think they have got it!

Liaison and consultation

Although 50 per cent of the funding for policing comes from central government, the other half comes from 'the rates'. The Metropolitan Police covering an area of over 700 square miles and with more than 26,000 officers has no police authority, save the Home Secretary himself. Londoners are deprived of any vehicle for achieving either accountability of their police or control over them.

For many years there was marked resistance by the force to the introduction of any form of 'consultation' with the community they policed. The argument against the setting up of a police authority on the model of that used in the counties was that of:

1. The size of the force, covering a huge area, with a mobile population and diverse policing problems from area to area.
2. That, although Scotland Yard is the headquarters of *only* the London force (a fact not appreciated by many British people let alone Americans), a good deal of its departmental and operational work has a national flavour.

Much of the resistance in the Metropolitan Force resulted from the antics of some London councillors, who sought to form unofficial 'police committees', described by Standen (1983):

> In London, and perhaps many other areas, some members of the consultative groups do not have the interests of the community at heart, but sit on the committees for their own personal or political reasons. It is because of the existence of such people that police officers are suspicious of the committees.

But when in 1981, against a background of growing racial tension, police in South London set up an operation (known as Swamp 81), things changed with dramatic speed.

The aim of the operation was to flood the Brixton area with large numbers of officers in an attempt to control rising street crime. Although there was a local and informal community 'consultative' committee they were not consulted or even informed of the nature and purpose of the planned operation. Neither of the commanders of the operation

> believed it was wise, or appreciated the need, to consult locally before deciding whether or not to mount an operation against street crime. They saw such consultation as a danger to the success of the operation, as well as an intrusion upon their independence of judgement as police officers. (Scarman, 1982, para. 4.75)

Lord Justice Scarman in his report recommended the *legal requirement* for consultation to take place between the police and the community on a formal basis. Many forces, including London, set up local liaison committees prior to the introduction of legislation (the Police and Criminal Evidence Act 1984) which compelled their creation and came into force on 1 January 1986.

Fundamentally, however, the same battle-lines remain drawn. In a circular, offering Guidelines to Chief Officers for the creation of Liaison Committees, it states clearly that no one, including the Home Office, can interfere in the enforcement of the criminal law: 'Therefore deployment of police, method and timing of police operations, *and the stage these may be discussed*, are matters for the chief officer and his officers' [emphasis added]. So where does that leave things? First, with a fair degree of 'accountability' bearing in mind the pros and cons noted above; secondly, with little 'control', nor it would seem the opportunity to create it; and thirdly, with some 'liaison/consultation' but with limited parameters.

The supervision of police in England and Wales is as problematic now as it ever was. Jerome Skolnick (1966) wrote of the policeman's 'craftsman-like' conception of himself. 'Police behaviour seems to be influenced more than anything else by an overwhelming concern to show themselves as competent craftsmen.'

One does not tell the cabinetmaker, the master builder or the stonemason what materials to obtain, what tools to use, and how to achieve any particular aim. All one does is to tell him what you want and to refuse to pay or to direct him to try again if he does not come up with the goods. And this is very much the philosophy of British police officers. With a marked tendency to see themselves as the (professional) 'thin blue line' standing firm against anarchy (see Reiner, 1978a) with little overt support, the police service generally are unwilling to concede that democracy demands that their activities are supervised and are subject to criticism.

In a real way these arguments about accountability and control in Britain are *ad hoc* events. That is to say, they have only really come to the fore when various abuses of police power and authority have come to notice. They seek (or so it seems to the police) to impose a system of supervision on a body which has, save for a comparatively brief period at its inception, been legitimized in the eyes of a vast proportion of the population. But the police are an unelected body and, in the USA, the issue of accountability in a democracy has tended to depend more on the democratic process than in the UK. Election of police chiefs, appointment of police by elected representatives, and democratic controls through specially elected bodies to supervise police activity are a far cry from central government resourcing, non-specialist supervision (as in police authorities) and an autonomous constitutional position for chief officers which leaves most chiefs in the USA bewildered and occasionally somewhat envious.

Coordination and control of policing in the USA

Policing in the USA is typified by its diversity and lack of centralization. There is no element of centralized control, and the USA, of all Western countries, is unique in having a Cabinet that does not include a Secretary for Criminal Justice, or some such title.

Police departments in the USA are different in their conditions of service, pay, uniforms, badges of rank, equipment, methods of control, and not surprisingly many, if not all, are singularly proud of their autonomy.

The system of local government, seeking to ensure popular control, has continued to grow in complexity with the passing years. Issues of police supervision have been handled in an entirely different manner from those in the UK. But, because they are different, it does not make them any more successful.

Election and appointment

The earliest process through which such accountability was to have been achieved was the use of the ballot box. In the majority of jurisdictions today there is some kind of reliance on the popular vote to obtain some element of community involvement.

There has, over the years, been no appreciable diminution of elections of sheriffs although there have been some county police departments established in which the sheriffs have responsibility for only civil process, custody of prisoners and court security. They have no regular law enforcement involvement (viz. Davidson County, Nashville, Tenn.).

Although there are fewer and fewer direct elections for chiefs of police, the bulk of PDs are headed by an officer selected and appointed by the local mayor, him/herself an elected official. In some cases, however, the chief officer may be selected or appointed by a city/county administrator/manager, who is in turn answerable to a city/county council and is appointed by them.

Occasionally, local ordinances and rules may allow no direct contact with the police chief unless through the administrator/manager.

Notionally such a process does have some advantages. As Smith (1960, p. 183) puts it:

> One device for controlling military power is to place its general regulation and control in the hands of a non-professional administrator who is displaced with sufficient frequency to prevent eventual domination by the technically skilled military caste.

But we have already noted one of the consequences of such a process in Chapter 2, for the major stumbling-block is that the practice of 'displacement with sufficient frequency' leads, inevitably, to a severe lack of inclination for long-term planning and policy-making (cf. Goldstein, 1977).

In pure managerial terms the organization which, in its management structure, lacks 'stability' will be unable to 'maintain a simple consistent underlying form' and will fail to develop 'broad yet flexibile underlying values' (Peters and Waterman, 1982).

The constant change and threat of change inherent in such a system will not provide the 'champions' on whom Peters and Waterman (1982) place such value: those who are prepared to argue for and actively support that which they believe to be right.

Although many officers, particularly sheriffs, still have to seek election, the majority of senior police ranks are filled by appointment.

The power of appointment frequently lies with the mayor of a town or city and occasionally with a standing committee of the city council (the legislative body). Whatever the period of tenure, appointments to police office, whether high or low, are frequently made in accordance with strict partisan interests. Standards of consistent performance are frequently forgotten or displaced in the higher interest of political ambition (or expediency). Not infrequently political 'brinkmanship' and sometimes downright political manipulation are the currency of police supervision under such a system.

In 1968, following the assassination of Dr Martin Luther King, the Chief of Police in Chicago issued instructions that his men should use discretion in dealing with subsequent hysteria and violence. These instructions were immediately revoked by the mayor who said that the police were to 'shoot to kill arsonists and looters', an instruction only later amended after severe public protest (Bunyard, 1973).

In 1978 in Montgomery Co., Maryland, the patrolman's association disagreed with the chief of police about certain matters. With an election for the county manager's post due shortly, the association approached the opposition party and agreed to provide action support for them if, in return, they agreed to remove the chief on attaining power. The electoral promise was kept.

Essentially, the practice of 'appointment' in the gift of an individual (or a partisan group) is a subordination of executive authority to legislative government; a practice bound to lead to dissension, collision of policy, protracted debate and compromise (but not somewhat surprisingly to issues of constitutionality). Such practices do not further the development of police operations and administration, and may be positively damaging to them.

Administrative boards

The logical development from policies of direct supervisory functions given to politically motivated individuals or groups was to seek to exercise such a role through 'administrative boards' drawn or appointed from outside the legislature.

Smith (1960, p. 185) writes of the historical development of these boards in the following terms:

> Judges, mayors and city councilmen were propelled into the technical direction of police affairs. Private citizens who were engrossed with their own personal concerns and had no experience of supervising public undertakings were given similar responsibilities. Almost invariably such service was of a part time character. Often it was not only inexpert, but meddlesome.

In this description there is remarkable similarity between the administrative boards and the police authority in the UK. Particularly when one considers Smith's (p. 185) concluding remarks:

> However it does not appear that any of them ... ever rose above party and partisanship. Their composition as lay, inexpert, and representative body went far to assure that result.

State control

The logical and reasonable response to some of the problems of local 'control' is to place that supervisory function in the hands of the state.

After all, the state is the sovereign power; it has legislative powers, and logically it has duties to the population to ensure that those laws are kept. But, with some limited exceptions such efforts proved to be doomed to failure.

The reasons for their failure lie, in the main, on a surprising reluctance to provide an equitable arrangement between the state and the local communities. For, although still beset with problems, the strength of the British system lies in the provision, by the Home Office, of centralized resources and advice (and 50 per cent of the costs) *for all forces*, in return for the opportunity for localized accountability through the police authority. No such equitable arrangement was established by state authorities.

In the main, the states concentrated on exercising 'control' over city police departments and excluded those in the more rural areas. The total responsibility for financial arrangements lay with the local population who, through their sales taxes to the state, with revenue sharing giving a certain percentage back to the cities, provide the cash to state government. (One of the effects of financial cutbacks *vide* the Gramm, Rudman, Hollins Bill is the restriction of revenue sharing, which at time of writing may have unexpected results on policing in the USA.)

Often, during attempts at state control of policing, the finances were appropriated by the state under threat of fine or imprisonment. The local communities got nothing in return, save a reinforcement of their view that direct central government involvement, state or federal, is unacceptable.

Above all, however, state officials' attempts uniformly to establish standards of private behaviour in the population across a state proved an impossible aim. Ongoing disputes and battles between the municipal authorities and those managing the police on behalf of the state became commonplace. Policing costs rose and rose with little opportunity for the local populations to do anything about it, the state officials having no responsibilities to the local taxpayers.

The most successful system of state control was that in Boston, Mass. State control of policing proved sufficiently effective that the system remained at the head of police organizations for many years but for reasons not unconnected with political expediency the department was 'given back' to the city in 1962.

A system of partial state control still exists in some places in the USA (e.g. Baltimore, Kansas City, St Louis – where chiefs are appointed by the state governor) but by and large, the system of full state control, which once had huge support, has disappeared.

Public safety commissions

With the enactment of commission government charters in many cities came an opportunity to provide local 'control' of policing through the Public Safety Commissioner(s).

The outstanding feature of commission government is a combination of both executive and legislative powers in a small democratically elected commission. Usually the commission, consisting of about five people, allows each individual to be designated as responsible for particular functions. For the purposes of police supervision the incumbent is usually designated as the Public Safety Commissioner and is frequently charged not only with the management of the police department, but also with supervision of the fire department, building regulations, and (very infrequently) public health and welfare.

There are a number of factors which promote the success of such a process, not the least of which is the facility which the system allows for the development of some expertise on the part of the Public Safety Commissioner. On the other hand, tenure problems and the prospect of political intervention are still problematic, as is the difficulty imposed by the spread of responsibilities noted above which exacerbate the problems of competing demands for resources from finite budgets.

Increased local involvement

Much in the sense that the Scarman inquiry in England resulted in recommendations, and later legislation, to set up liaison committees, so some police departments have established complex systems for ensuring that the views of the community are adequately taken into account. Fairfax County Police Department, VA, has established a system of local involvement through local police station advisory committees; a representative from each station area committee coming together to form the Fairfax County Police Department Citizens Advisory Council, directly accountable to the Fairfax County Board of Supervisors.

DISCUSSION

In the main the concern of those seeking a police supervisory function on both sides of the Atlantic is with the 'value for money' aspects of their responsibilities. Such matters quite rightly are of some considerable concern, particularly in the USA, where the total lack of a central government contribution frequently means that even events which could be typified as 'national' in nature – the presence of Convention Centres, the United Nations, and multiple immigration centres in New York, the Olympic Games in LA, or the space programme which continues to draw thousands of tourists to Florida every year, are the responsibility of the local community alone.

Even when the LEAA was administering a multi-million dollar grant programme, made available to the states through the State Planning Agencies (SPAs) the federal government was unable (or unwilling) to tie this funding to any type of restrictive language, application of standards or any other requirements except those of fulfilling bureaucratic administrative necessities.

Concern must also be felt because of the rising cost of providing *any kind* of satisfactory police response and redoubled as the police representative bodies become more powerful, often seeking to manipulate public opinion through raising the profile of crime and 'fear of crime' as support for pay awards, and the purchase of technological support.

In a sense, the local involvement of the population to control 'the unacceptable face of policing' in the form of graft, abuse of rights, etc. is a matter regularly and reasonably conducted through the Supreme Court's decisions effecting police behaviour. Indeed a Police Foundation (USA) study conducted to assess ways in which the police service and the American Bar Association (1974) could work together to improve both law enforcement and the criminal justice system as a whole, recognized this when they wrote:

> Control over police practice should insofar as possible, be positive creating inducements to perform properly rather than concentrating solely upon penalizing improper police conduct.

Among the means the participants saw of accomplishing such accountability are the following:

1. Education and training.
2. Inducements to officers in terms of status and promotion, etc., based on criteria that are related to police function and goals.
3. The elimination situations in which the public expect a police response but which is inadequately covered by legislation.
4. Systematic efforts by prosecutors and judges to encourage conforming police behaviour through (a) a more careful review of applications for warrants, and (b) formulation of new procedures to simplify and otherwise provide easy access for judicial review of applications for warrants, thereby encouraging maximum use of the formal warrant process.[8]

The study also noted that the following methods were already in use:

1. The exclusion of evidence obtained by unconstitutional means.
2. Criminal and tort liability for knowingly engaging in unlawful conduct.
3. Injunctive actions to terminate patterns of unlawful conduct.
4. Local procedures for handling complaints against police officers, procedures which usually operate administratively within police departments (American Bar Association, 1974).

CONCLUSION

Since the inception of any philosophy of organized policing the search for what Goldstein (1977, p. 4) refers to as 'the perfect police agency' has continued on both sides of the Atlantic. The amalgamations of police forces in England and Wales (and in Scotland to an even more marked degree) were a step in that search for perfection. In the USA the development of a 'professional' model of policing, based on the work of August Vollmer, Bruce Smith and O. W. Wilson, aimed for the same Utopia. The model, one of organization based on military lines which sought to avoid the influence of partisan politics, stresses: 'operational efficiency ... centralized control, clean cut lines of communication, fuller and more effective use of police personnel, greater mobility, improved training and increased use of equipment and technology' (Goldstein, 1977, p. 2) is, even today, save in the big cities, rarely encountered. Remarkably few of the plethora of police departments in USA (probably because of their multiplicity) can match the ideal espoused by those early innovators. There is, in both the USA and the UK, a strongly-held belief that advances in technology are the lifeblood of professionalism. But it is common to find, as in South Carolina, that ten or more PDs within a county are unable to communicate with each other by radio and have on occasion little real inclination to do so. Even the valuing of technology as a professional tool is dependent on finance and consequently the willingness of the local population, desirous of their own police force, to pay.

Professionalism in any body springs not from tangible things like computers, optical fingerprint readers and such, but from the values and attitudes displayed by those at the very top of the organization. Thus issues connected with the accountability of chiefs which we have examined become issues directly associated with the professionalism of the whole organization.

The exemplar of accountability, lack of political interference and professionalism pointed to by those early writers in the USA was commonly that of a European (usually a British) model. But the British model for all its appeal is not without its problems. The very independence from political interference which Volmer and the others espoused has, through the legally supported doctrine of constabulary independence, had the effect of insulating chief constables from the realities of day-to-day policing, both as they affect the population and as they affect the officers within their forces. There is little, save the development of management skills (often neglected in favour of 'leadership' attributes in selection processes and not the same thing), that can improve the latter. The former may, on the other hand, as we have indicated, be attacked by recognizing that the up-through-the-ranks notion of suitability for high command may actually be, in some cases, little better than election, partisan selection or direct political manipulation.

The search for processes which can, in a democratic society, allow the unelected to wield power, but can also, at the same time, impose *popular* controls on them and exercise appropriate sanctions against them, is a formidable task. In this context, the whole debate about accountability becomes a debate about appropriate methods of selecting chiefs, and in particular, how one can move towards ensuring that the appointees are conscious of public concerns and are able and willing to respond to them rather than to pursue a 'hidden agenda' of personal aggrandizement or a 'police know best' philosophy.

But, as we have shown, the processes of election, partisan selection, 'career' police chief, and 'outsider' police chief all have their problems. These problems are compounded by the often too ready facility with which some American systems can dispense with a chief's services or the contrasting inability for UK police authorities to exercise other than limited controls and sanctions over chief constables.

An alternative solution to the problem may lie in a variation of the notion of lateral entry to senior rank, which has been considered and occasionally implemented in both countries.

Lateral entry to the police of those who have been comprehensively trained in aspects of policing, the law and so on, is substantially different from those ill-conceived schemes that assume that a manager from industry of commerce can, simply because he has some managerial skills, manage a police department. Exercises of this kind 'tested' in the past have all foundered on the rocks of lack of understanding of the practicalities, difficulties and sub-culture of policing. To use another metaphor: to try to erect an extension to an existing building is foolish unless there are adequate foundations for the new and unless the old is capable of supporting the new.

The recommendation of the President's Crime Commission (1967) that 'lateral entry' to police departments should be encouraged in the USA has met with a limited response; less has been done to develop the framework on which such entry should occur in order to reap maximum benefit. In the UK an attempt at 'lateral entry' in the middle ranks (the Trenchard scheme) was adjudged a failure. The issue of lateral entry remains a contentious one on both sides of the Atlantic.

Becker and Hejellemo (1976) hint strongly at the viability of adopting the system employed in Sweden which, in summary, combines elements of both lateral entry and up-through-the-ranks selection of police chiefs, and does provide a useful clue as to what can be done. The combination of local involvement and personal and professional qualifications for chiefs is a powerful one (cf. Goldstein, 1977, pp. 235–40, for a full discussion of this area), for as Smith (1960, p. 191) put it more than twenty years ago:

the police administrator drawn directly from civil life is more closely in touch with public attitudes, more sensitive to public needs, and therefore better adapted to the purposes and requirements of popular control. He is more likely to have enjoyed the advantages of broad interests and wide experience than is the man risen from the ranks, who has been subjected throughout his career to the deadening and narrowing effects of official routine.

It may well be that the Swedish system would not prepare a candidate for a chief's position, particularly in answering the problem of 'political naivety' discussed above. Perhaps what is needed is a 'typically American' solution to the problem by seeking to combine the best of the management development programme of the British Police Staff College at Bramshill, the Swedish 'lateral entry' model and the existing programmes at the National Academy (FBI, Quantico) and the Southern Police Institute. In Britain, some freeing of the restrictive, incestuous, 'in service' selection process could prove similarly beneficial.

But as always, it is, in the long run, the interaction of public attitudes, police practices, concern about crime and criminality, and the infringement of personal rights which determine the nature, and the underlying philosophy of, external police supervision.

CHAPTER 5

Organization, Pay, Recruitment Standards and Training: A Tale of Two Cities and Some Others

The literature of policing is replete with generalized and occasionally specific outlines of the administrative organization of police departments the world over. Frosdick (1920), Banton (1964), Wilson (1986) and Becker (1979) all produce administrative charts of police organizations from Brighton to Berlin, Syracuse to Sweden.

Many of these assessments and descriptions have already become out of date. The last ten years have seen the potential of organizational change enhanced a thousand-fold by the development of microchip technology. The consequential changes of attitude in society and the effects of increased leisure-time (sometimes enforced through unemployment) have also had their effect on the nature of policing not least because those attitudes are brought to the police by their new recruits, altering the style of policing.

What police officers actually do, and the rules and regulations about how they should do it, will be discussed later. It is the purpose of this chapter to examine the infrastructure of policing in the two nations under study but even that, baldly stated, is problematic.

The common belief that the centralized resourcing of policing in England and Wales has produced a standardized administrative form is misplaced. The relative autonomy and independence of the chief constable enables him[1] to devise and supervise a unique organizational structure, which, although it may have similarities, is specifically geared to community (and force) needs. There is in effect no typical administrative structure for the British police.

Equally, there is no typical organizational structure in the USA. The unique local nature of most police departments leads to a diversity of organization unmatched anywhere in the world. Unfortunately, for the purposes of this study it is also the case that there are *no* constants. Titles, uniforms, badges of rank, rates of pay, conditions of service, representative bodies, methods of control and even numbers vary to a marked extent.

There are, therefore, aspects of police administration in England and Wales, those that are centrally agreed and accepted by chief police officers – which are surprisingly few – which can effectively be indicated. There are also those aspects which are unique to each force. This book cannot hope to cover all 43 Home Office forces or all (or even some) of the plethora of police departments in the USA. Thus we shall concentrate on only one on each side of the Atlantic, using research specially conducted for this volume, each a huge city force: the London Metropolitan Police, and, for comparison purposes, the New York City Police Department.

Some of the data cited below are, in practice, national in nature and where this is the case will be so indicated.

THE METROPOLITAN POLICE

The Metropolitan Police force covers an area of approximately 787 square miles and comprises the Greater London Area (excluding the City of London), parts of the counties of Essex, Hertfordshire and Surrey, and part of the River Thames.

The estimated population in 1968 was 8,250,000. By 1976 this had fallen to 7,028,000 and by 1983 was estimated as about 7,025,000. The 1983 strength of the force was 26,806 plus 16,942 civil staff. Apart from a period of poor recruiting during the 1970s, the number of officers has been rising steadily.

The Metropolitan Police District covers 32 London boroughs which are the unit of local government. A percentage of the rates from each of the local authorities (called the police precept) is paid towards the cost of policing. Issues relating to the lack of an elected police authority for London are dealt with elsewhere in the text.

Senior ranks for the force are:

- *Commissioner*: appointed by the Sovereign and acting under the authority of the Home Secretary and relevant statutory provisions, he controls the force.
- *Deputy Commissioner*: appointed by the Sovereign, he has general responsibility for the control and operation administration of the force. He is the 'discipline authority' of the force and in the absence of the Commissioner is 'Acting Commissioner'.
- *The Receiver for the Metropolitan Police*: appointed by the Sovereign, he is not a police officer. He is the accountant for the force and on behalf of the Commissioner supervises and controls finance, supply and property management. He is also responsible for the efficiency of the Metropolitan Police Civil Staff.
- *The Assistant Commissioners* (AC): appointed by the Sovereign. Under the direction of the the Commissioner they are responsible for territorial operations, specialist operations, personnel and training and management support.
- *Deputy Assistant Commissioners* (DAC): for administrative purposes London is divided into eight police areas each of which is under the command of a DAC. The eight areas are in turn divided into a total of 76 divisions. In addition to the

area role, DACs fill various support functions either as command heads of specialized branches and units (e.g. Director of Information, Training, Complaints Investigation, etc.) or as Deputies to Assistant Commissioners.

Policy committee

The Commissioner, Deputy Commissioner, the four Assistant Commissioners, the Receiver and the Director of Information, together form the *Policy Committee* who come together regularly to discuss and formulate policy matters for the force.

Territorial operations (TO)[2]
The Territorial Operations Department has responsibility for all policing functions (including detectives) which can be performed on a geographical basis by subdividing the Metropolitan Police District. This includes both crime, operations and traffic.

The AC 'TO' has direct line command of all Areas and Divisions.

Specialist operations (SO)[3]
The Specialist Operations Department has responsibility for all policing functions which cannot be effectively subdivided territorially; this may be because of:

1. A high degree of specialism, e.g. Royalty protection.
2. A lack of relevance of territorial boundaries, e.g. special equipment and surveillance units, specialized crime squads.
3. The scale of the operation, e.g. regional crime squads, anti-terrorist unit.
4. The national nature of functions, e.g. Special Branch (SB).[4]

Personnel and training (PT)[5]
The Assistant Commissioner Personnel and Training (AC 'PT') is responsible for the formulation and application of a police personnel programme designed to service the present and long-term needs of the organization. He is responsible for all aspects of training in the Metropolitan Police.

Management support department (MS)
The Management Support Department is responsible for providing the range of services required by senior management to develop and monitor the performance of the force as a whole. The department includes a Forward Planning Unit/Policy Analysis Unit, Management Services Department, Complaints Investigation Bureau (CIB) and the Office of the Director of Information.

In addition to the Departments under the command of Assistant Commissioners there are various operational and support units as follows:

'E' Department – Civil Staff Establishments and Secretariat
'F' Department – Finance

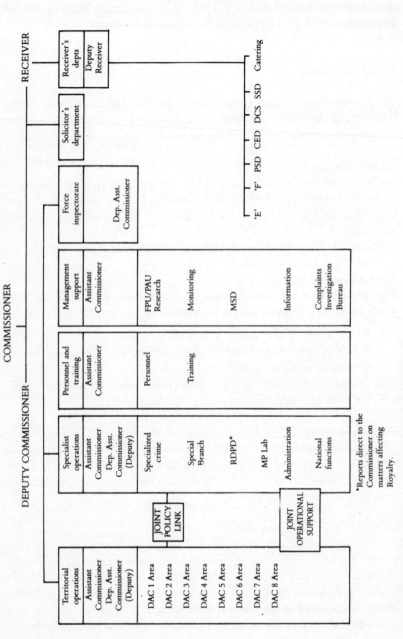

Figure 5.1 The organization of the London Metropolitan Police

HEADQUARTERS STRUCTURE

COMMISSIONER

DEPUTY COMMISSIONER

RECEIVER

Territorial operations	Specialist operations	Personnel and training	Management support	Force inspectorate	Solicitor's department	Receiver's depts
Assistant Commissioner Dep. Asst. Commissioner (Deputy)	Assistant Commissioner Dep. Asst. Commissioner (Deputy)	Assistant Commissioner	Assistant Commissioner	Dep. Asst. Commissioner		Deputy Receiver

DAC 1 Area
DAC 2 Area
DAC 3 Area
DAC 4 Area
DAC 5 Area
DAC 6 Area
DAC 7 Area
DAC 8 Area

JOINT POLICY LINK

JOINT OPERATIONAL SUPPORT

Specialized crime
Special Branch
RDPD*
MP Lab
Administration
National functions

Personnel
Training

FPU/PAU Research
Monitoring
MSD
Information
Complaints Investigation Bureau

'E' 'F' PSD CED DCS SSD Catering

*Reports direct to the Commissioner on matters affecting Royalty.

Property Services Department – (PSD)
Chief Engineers Department – (CED)
Department of Computer Services – (DCS)
Department of Supplies and Services – (SSD)

An organizational chart is shown at Fig. 5.1.

Organizational philosophy

Over some 155 years of existence the Metropolitan Police had become a huge
organization with considerable decision-making and administrative control centred
on Scotland Yard,[6] as the force headquarters.

On taking up his office in October 1982, the new Commissioner Sir Kenneth
Newman sought to consider a reorganization of the force with a view to a massive
decentralization of responsibilities. He saw four main causes of difficulty:

1. Because of ill-defined roles, large parts of the organization often worked
   towards their own ends rather than towards a shared purpose for the
   Metropolitan Police.
2. Too much energy and effort were wasted in keeping the organization going
   instead of serving the mainline job of policing.
3. The size and power of CO (Scotland Yard) was 'strangling the force', taking
   up valuable manpower and placing unnecessary demands on those left (at
   police stations).
4. There was a tendency for the organization to try to cope with problems by
   superficial changes in the bureaucratic system, rather than looking for real
   solutions.

The organizational structure indicated above was introduced during 1985 on a
phased basis in order to:

1. Reduce the size of HQ and make it offer more practical support at operational
   levels.
2. To shorten and clarify lines of communication.
3. To make the support functions at HQ more 'sensible and effective'.
4. To replace detailed instructions with broad policy guidelines and thus to
   encourage local decision-making.
5. To push decision-making downwards, thus enhancing the possibility of
   response to local needs. (Newman, 1984a)

The principal aim of devolution of responsibilities has been achieved by making the
police *division* 'the fundamental unit of policing' with 'maximum practical control
over the resources necessary to co-ordinate policing within its boundaries, and to
provide a comprehensive service response to community needs' (Metropolitan
Police, 1985a).

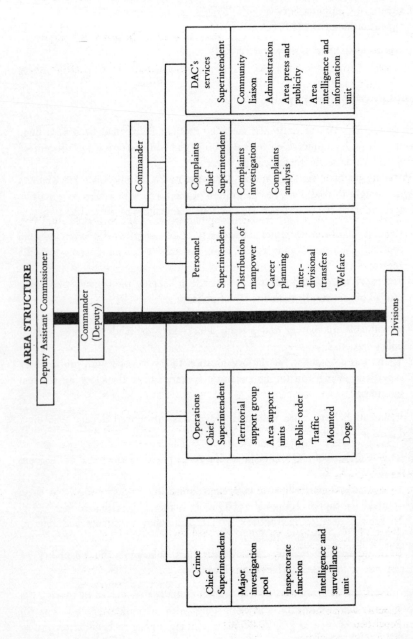

AREA STRUCTURE

Deputy Assistant Commissioner

Commander (Deputy)

Commander

Crime
Chief
Superintendent

- Major investigation pool
- Inspectorate function
- Intelligence and surveillance unit

Operations
Chief
Superintendent

- Territorial support group
- Area support units
- Public order
- Traffic
- Mounted
- Dogs

Personnel
Superintendent

- Distribution of manpower
- Career planning
- Inter-divisional transfers
- Welfare

Complaints
Chief
Superintendent

- Complaints investigation
- Complaints analysis

DAC's services
Superintendent

- Community liaison
- Administration
- Area press and publicity
- Area intelligence and information unit

Divisions

Figure 5.2 Organization of area structure: London Metropolitan Police

In order to produce a link between the policy-making and resource functions of Scotland Yard and the operational Divisions, an *Area Headquarters* level of command is provided to:

(a) Ensure coordination of divisional effort to achieve the goals and purpose of the force.
(b) Make known the views of Divisional (and Area) police staff to those formulating policy.
(c) Provide support and guidance to Divisions.

An organizational chart of Area functions is shown at Fig. 5.2.

NEW YORK CITY POLICE DEPARTMENT[7]

New York is a city with an estimated population of 7,071,338 people (in 1983), situated at the southern tip of New York state at the mouth of the Hudson River. The city is divided into five administrative boroughs: Manhattan, Brooklyn, the Bronx, Queens and Richmond. Only the Bronx is on the mainland of the USA, the other boroughs being designated as offshore islands. Unlike many cities in the USA the New York City Police Department is almost totally responsible for policing of the city. There is a small police department run by the Transit Authorities (Subway and Buses) and by the Housing Department, although the New York City Commissioner has administrative control over them. By comparison with many cities, jurisdictional problems, although they exist, are at a minimum.

The police area of the city amounts to some 320 square miles and the current strength of the department is some 23,033 officers and 5,792 civilians (Wait and Swindon, 1984). Over the years there has been enormous fluctuation of the numbers of sworn officers and a gradual increase in civilian employees. In 1975 there were 30,774 sworn officers and 2,627 civilians, but the fiscal crisis of that year and its continuing problems reduced the number of sworn officers to 25,031 by 1977, and to its current figure by 1983.

Comparisons between police strengths and population ratios are shown in Table 5.1.

Table 5.1 Police strengths and ratios: Metropolitan Police and New York Police Department.

	Metropolitan Police	New York Police Department
Regular/sworn officers	26,806	23,033
Population	7,025,000	7,071,338
Ratio police: population	1:262.06	1:307
Police area	787 sq. miles	320 sq miles
Ratio police: sq. mile	1:34.06	1:71.97

Senior ranks for the force are:

> *Commissioner*: appointed by the mayor of New York City. He is responsible for the overall policing strategy. He may either have a police or non-police background, although, with the exception of Commissioner Bob McGuire in the early 1980s who served for some five years and had no law enforcement background, in recent years the trend has been to appoint people who have served in the law enforcement area. The current Commissioner was previously the Commissioner of Corrections in New York and an officer in NYPD.
>
> *First Deputy Commissioner*: Appointed by the Commissioner, he serves as the Deputy to the former in his absence.
>
> *Deputy Commissioner(s)*: Public Information
> Community Affairs
> Trials
> Legal Matters

Policing operations are the responsibility of the *Chief of Operations*, the highest 'sworn officer' in the organization. Movement to Deputy Commissioner position is accompanied by a consequent return to civilian status.

The Chief of Operations is responsible for the following Bureaux and Divisions:

Patrol functions

The city is divided into seven 'patrol boroughs' (Manhattan and Brooklyn are, for patrol purposes, each divided in two). The patrol boroughs are subdivided into nineteen 'zones' (which were once called divisions), and the zones into 73 precincts.

Specialists

The other main functions of the Bureau are:

1. Special Operations Division
2. Street Crime Unit
3. Tactical Patrol Unit
4. Emergency Services Unit
5. Field Internal Affairs Unit
6. Harbour Unit
7. Mounted Unit
8. Traffic Division
9. Operational Detectives
10. Youth Services Unit
11. Internal Affairs
12. Task Force

Detective Bureau: comprising centrally organized specialist detective units, e.g. robbery and sex crimes.

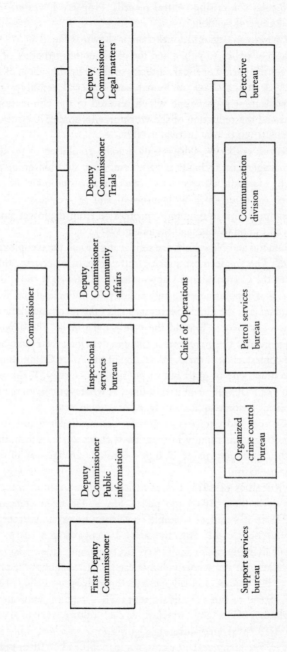

Figure 5.3 Organization chart, New York Police Department

Organized Crime Patrols Bureau: the bureau incorporates narcotics, public morals and the intelligence section.

Support Services Bureau: comprising central records, Property Division, Inspections, Management and Control Section.

Communications Division: an organizational chart is shown at Fig. 5.3.

The higher ratio of police to public and the parsimonious structure of the police department reflect the period of fiscal austerity suffered by the whole of New York City in 1975. A drastic cutback in human and material resources required a mammoth rationalization programme which resulted in the elimination of some operational units and the reduction of the workforce by some 5700[8] officers whilst the civilian support strength rose by over 1000.[9]

Promotion freezes, cutbacks, reorganization and a resolution of fiscal problems through 'crisis-management' techniques, have resulted in some on-going problems.

Career planning in middle management is inadequate; promotions and transfers of middle managers are often on a semi-informal and *ad hoc* basis; and there are substantial morale problems in relation to promotion from the lower ranks, ethnic minority hirings and so on (Waite and Swinden, 1984).

The cities of London and New York are similar in size and the complexity of their policing problem. The single most striking difference is, of course, the strongly political nature of the Commissioner's appointment. Although it could be claimed, and sometimes is, that appointments to high police rank in England and Wales are to some extent political (i.e. the Home Secretary makes the recommendation and he is not likely to choose someone 'beyond the pale'), once made, the appointment is unlikely to change even if the government changes, let alone the Home Secretary.

However, the consequence of the politicization of the Police Commissioner role is nowadays not so much one of graft but of political expediency. If the mayor says 'Clean up the Lower East Side' then it gets done, at whatever cost to the rest of the city. Policing policies become, quite simply, what catches votes.

Because of potential short tenure, each new Commissioner wants to make his mark quickly, putting ideas rapidly into action without paying much attention to any aspect of the 'management of change'; constant changes of direction and emphasis become the norm.

Despite the difficulties of 1975 it does make sense to attempt some financial comparisons between these two huge police forces. Financial comparisons are always difficult. Even if one does a simple conversion using the current exchange rate, the picture is no clearer. Any meaningful comparison needs to take into account the cost of living in each community. Cost-of-living indexes and so on take many months to work out and whole volumes can be written about the process. So, for the purposes of this volume, instead of converting dollars to sterling or sterling to dollars we have agreed to use a 'standard unit'. The 'standard unit' approach, in which an item which is of the same 'standard' in each culture is selected and its cost in each culture used to reduce different figures to a standard unit, is a well-established practice. For many years the cost of a loaf of bread or 1lb of potatoes was the standard unit. But more recently with the growth of huge international companies it is possible to select a more useful standard: *a Big Mac hamburger and small fries as produced to the same standard the world over in the MacDonald Corporation* (see Peters and Waterman, 1982). At 1983 prices the standard product cost $2.08 (NY) and £1.42 (London).

Wherever possible therefore, costings, rates of pay and so on, will be compared in 'standard units' (SU).

Budgets

The total annual budget for the New York City Police Department in 1983 was $865,023,000 (SU 415m), while that of the Metropolitan Police was £726,000,000 (SU 514m). Ninety-five per cent of the New York budget was disposed of on salaries ($819,350,000: SU 395m) whilst 63 per cent of the Metropolitan budget went towards wages and salaries including those of civil staff (£486,000,000: SU 345m). The overtime budget for each of the forces was:

New York City Police: $26,384,822 (SU 12.5m)

Metropolitan Police: £50,988,879 (SU 35m)

New York City Police officers perform a 42½-hour week; London officers perform a 40-hour week.

RANKS AND RATES OF PAY: SEPTEMBER 1987[10]

Although there is a less good match of responsibilities (functions) at middle-management level in each of the forces under study, the upper and lower functions match well. See Table 5.2 for details.

A conversion to the standard unit is shown in Table 5.3.

It will be noted that in general, even on this far from accurate measure, salaries in the New York City Police appear to be 35–50 per cent above those in London, even allowing for the fact that, in practice, the basic rates of pay for London officers can be enhanced by a further sum. All officers, of whatever rank, with the exception of the Commissioner, are entitled to either free accommodation (provided by the force) or a non-taxable 'rent allowance' in lieu.

Rent allowance

All police officers in England and Wales are entitled to free accommodation or 'rent allowance'. However, the maximum rates vary from force to force in accordance with a nationally agreed standard. Rent allowance is worked out according to a formula and varies according to rank. In the Metropolitan Police, the maximum rate

Table 5.2 Ranks, responsibilities and rates of pay (October 1987)

New York City Police Department			Metropolitan Police London		
Function	Rank	Pay $	Pay £	Rank	Function
Headquarters					
Management	Commissioner	94,500	65,000	Commissioner[5]	Management
Deputy	1st Deputy	92,500	49,983	Dep. Commr.[4]	Deputy
Operations	Chief of Dept	91,786	44,097	Asst Commr.[3]	Operations, etc.
Territorial					
Bureau/Boro' command	Chief	86,002	35,277	DAC[2]	Area command
Deputy	Deputy Chief	74,167	30,960	Commander[1]	Deputy
Zone command	Inspector	70,425	28,032	Chief Superintendent	Divisional command
Deputy	Deputy Insp.	66,882	25,650	Superintendent	Deputy
Admin.	Captain	63,548	20,142	Chief Inspector	Admin.
Patrol					
Shift Commander	Lieutenant	48,839	18,195	Inspector	Shift Commander
Shift supervision	Sergeant	42,595	15,294	Sergeant	Shift supervision
	Police Officer			Police Constable	
General patrol (Shift)	over 15 years	33,173	13,938	over 15 years	General patrol (Shift)
	over 10 years	33,073	12,597	over 10 years	
	over 5 years	32,937	11,499	over 5 years	
	on recruitment	25,977	8,352	on recruitment	

Note: All rates of pay are the maximum applicable at any level. Rates for Assistant Chief through Commissioner (NYPD) are fixed as are those for Commander through Commissioner for the Met.

All rates for NYPD are not representative of the rates in any other Police Department in the USA and may be enhanced at all levels by a 10 per cent night-duty differential and/or a higher rate for 'special' assignment duties. All rates in London are enhanced by a 'London allowance' of £1,011 (per annum) and a London weighting allowance of £948 (per annum) above the rates payable to officers serving elsewhere in England and Wales.

1, 2, 3, 4, 5. These ranks differ from those in county forces. Badges of rank coincide as follows: 1 = Assistant Chief Constable. 2 = Deputy Chief Constable. 3 = Chief Constable. 4 and 5 have no equivalent. Rate of pay for an Assistant Chief Constable is identical with that of a Commander in the Metropolitan Force. Rates for Deputy Chief Constable and Chief Constable are dependent upon the population of the area of responsibility.

for Constable–Chief Inspector is £3,722 p.a., for Superintendent and Chief Superintendent £4,318 p.a., and for Commander and DAC £5,009 (rates for 1986/87).

Specialist pay

Some specialist officers in both forces receive special pay, e.g. training instructors, dog handlers, etc., in the Metropolitan police; helicopter pilots in the New York City Police.

Table 5.3 Ranks and rates of pay standardized*(1987)

New York City Police Department			Metropolitan Police London		
Rank	Pay $	St. Unit	St. Unit	Pay £	Rank
Headquarters					
Commissioner	94,500	29,716	35,714	65,000	Commissioner
1st Deputy	92,500	29,088	27,463	49,983	Dep. Commr.
Chief of Dept	91,768	28,857	24,229	44,097	Asst Commr.
Territorial					
Chief	86,002	27,044	19,383	35,277	DAC
Deputy Chief	74,167	23,323	17,010	30,960	Commander
Inspector	70,425	22,146	15,402	28,032	Ch. Supt.
Deputy Insp.	66,882	21,032	14,093	25,650	Superintendent
Captain	63,548	19,983	11,067	20,142	Chief Inspector
Patrol					
Lieutenant	48,489	15,248	9,997	18,195	Inspector
Sergeant	42,495	13,363	8,403	15,294	Sergeant
Police officer					Police constable
over 15 years	33,173	10,432	7,658	13,938	over 15 years
over 10 years	33,073	10,400	6,921	12,597	over 10 years
over 5 years	32,937	10,056	6,318	11,499	over 5 years
on recruitment	25,977	8,169	4,598	8,352	on recruitment

*Divisor for Met. Police London, 1.82: divisor for NYPD 3.18.
Note: All Metropolitan rates with the exception of Commissioner may also include a 'rent allowance'
(see text).

Detectives

Detectives in England and Wales are paid at the same rate as their uniform colleagues plus a plain clothes allowance, according to rank. Transfer to the detective side is considered to be transfer to a specialism and *not a promotion*. In general there is a minimum of two years' service (the probationary period) required before officers in England and Wales can seek such a move.

Maximum rates of pay for detectives in the New York City Police are as follows:

Chief of Detectives	$72,000[11]
Commander of detectives (lieutenant)	$53,700
Sgt of detectives and det. 1st grade	$48,393
Detective 2nd grade	$42,595
Detective 3rd grade	$37,932

GENERAL ADMINISTRATIVE FEATURES

Recruitment – England and Wales

Regulation 14 of the Police Regulations 1979 sets down certain *minimum* criteria for applicants for the police, but Section 7(2) of the Police Act 1964 places the responsibility for such selection on chief constables. There is, therefore, a limited variation of the selection criteria from force to force. The minimum criteria are as follows:

1. Applicants for forces in England and Wales must be over 18½ years at the time of joining and generally under 30. Recruits will be accepted up to the age of 40 with previous experience in the armed services.
2. Physical requirements vary from force to force in England and Wales but, in general, applicants must be over 5 ft 8 ins in height for males and 5 ft 4 in for females.[12] Some chief officers may accept candidates who do not meet the height requirement if they appear to possess other 'compensating qualities'.
3. Applicants must be physically fit, with good eyesight and colour vision. The wearing of spectacles is permitted if they can correct defective vision to 20/20.
4. Applicants must be British citizens or a citizen of the Irish Republic (Eire).
5. There is an educational requirement in the form of a standardized written test (the Police Initial Recruiting Test (PIR)) but certain academic qualifications in the education system exempt some applicants from this test. Acceptable scores on the test vary from force to force. Currently a 50 per cent pass mark is the norm.

Background enquiries

Before interview substantial background enquiries are undertaken, usually involving a visit to the applicant's home, checks of two or more references and a check in the national Criminal Records Offices. Applications will not be accepted from those with other than the most trivial criminal records (and sometimes not even then).[13] Offences which involve 'some grave neglect to obey the law' involve driving whilst unfit through drink or cases which involve a number of minor offences which show a disregard for the law will usually result in a candidate being rejected at 'paper sift' stage.

If acceptable on other dimensions candidates may be interviewed if they have:

1. Been cautioned for an offence committed under the age of 14.
2. Been convicted or cautioned for using a vehicle without insurance.
3. Been convicted or cautioned for a 'regulatory' offence.[14]
4. Have been convicted on one occasion of drunkenness.

5. Been convicted or cautioned for a breach of peace.
6. Been convicted or cautioned of conduct likely to provoke a breach of the peace.
7. One caution or conviction for a criminal offence incurred prior to age 18 if there are extenuating circumstances concerning an otherwise excellent candidate.

Interview

Some forces have initiated a comprehensive two- or three-day assessment programme[15] but all will have some form of medical examination followed by an interview with senior officers of the force. In the event that the candidate has been accepted for interview despite caution or conviction as above the onus is clearly on the interview board to establish the circumstances of the offence and to be satisfied that repetition of the offence is unlikely.

Psychological tests

No psychological testing or lie detector tests are undertaken for any applicant to any Home Office force in England and Wales.

By way of contrast, in the USA, in the case of *Hild* v. *Brunner*[16] the New Jersey Supreme Court left standing a verdict against a municipality based on a failure to give psychological tests to prospective police officers. Similarly, in *Bonsignore* v. *City of New York*,[17] the district court upheld a jury verdict against the municipal defendant for negligence in failing to identify policemen psychologically unfit to carry guns[18] (Avery and Rudofsky, 1985).

UNITED STATES OF AMERICA

Residency

According to Beckman (1980), most police departments have a state residency requirement before a person may even apply.

But, in *Nehering* v. *Arioshi* a federal court in Honolulu declared as unconstitutional a Hawaii law which required police applicants to live in the islands for one year prior to employment.[19]

Furthermore, in *Uniformed Fire Fighters* v. *City of New York*, the New York Supreme Court overturned the City of New York's local residency law as a condition of initial or continued employment for police officers[20] (Eisenberg, 1981).

Other requirements

A typical list of other requirement is:

Age: between 21 and 30.
Height and weight: At least 5ft 9in (without shoes): height and weight in proportion.
Physical: Must be in good physical condition and pass a medical.
Vision: 20/40 in each eye without correction, corrected to 20/20 before appointment.
Education: Must be high school graduate or have completed a general education development test (GED).
Arrest record: Any conviction for a criminal offence may result in disqualification.
Written test: Many police departments demand the completion of a written academic test and many also require some form of psychological testing using standard psychometric tests.

It must be strongly emphasized that these requirements may differ markedly from one police department to another even among neighbouring agencies, and the reader is advised to consult Beckman (1980) for a comprehensive discussion of the value or otherwise of such criteria, with particular reference to the difficult area of recruiting from minority groups, etc. Some small PDs may have no standard requirements at all for recruiting purposes.

MINORITY RECRUITING

The Home Affairs Committee of the House of Commons (1981) recommended that 'police forces should take vigorous steps to recruit ethnic minority officers', a view endorsed by Scarman (1981) who stated: 'the Home Office should, in consultation with chief officers of police and the ethnic minority communities, conduct an urgent study of ways of improving ethnic minority recruitment into the regular police'.

On 31 December 1971 there were 47 black and Asian officers in the police service in the whole of England and Wales. On 30 June 1982 there were 386, including 160 in London (Home Office, 1982). By autumn 1985 there were 279 minority officers in London and 751 in the whole of England and Wales (Home Office, December 1985), and by spring 1987 the national figure had risen to 948 from a total of 121,500 serving officers in the country.[21]

In his report on the Brixton disorders Lord Scarman (1981) wrote:

> There is a widespread agreement that the composition of the police service must reflect the make-up of the society they serve. In one important respect, at least, it does not do so; in the police as in other important areas of society, the ethnic minorities are very significantly under represented. (para. 5.6)

In 1984, only 0.55 per cent of the police strength in England and Wales was recruited from an ethnic minority (and about 1.03 per cent of the London force), whereas people from minority groups account for 4.6 per cent of the national population, and about 10 per cent of the population in London (1981 Census estimate). The 1987 figures, whilst an improvement, still show that minority ethnic membership of the 43 British police forces still amounted to only about 0.8 per cent.

The issue of 'quotas' in minority recruiting

It is universally accepted in both policing and race/community relations circles in England and Wales that quotas are a singularly unsatisfactory method of increasing minority numbers. There is very real concern that standards should not be lowered to encourage recruiting and, although many confuse *affirmative action* with *positive discrimination*, the overall movement is towards attempting to alter the attitudes of minority communities towards those of their own group who seek to join the police.

Following a unique piece of research in which black officers themselves were asked the most appropriate strategies to adopt, Wilson et al. (1984) concluded:

> Our research indicates that there is no long-term solution to the problem of under-representation. The officers we interviewed have a clear view on this point – regard them and other potential recruits as people whose status is exactly the same as any other applicant. As far as they are concerned any other understanding may damage their status within the police service and, indeed, frustrate future recruitment. Public pressure from whatever source, which presses the police to remedy their recruitment problem in a short period of time, by some measure of positive discrimination or an overt advertising campaign, will not find the support of serving officers recruited from the ethnic groups they seek to influence. This does not mean that *some discrimination* in favour of ethnic minorities cannot be practised, neither does it prohibit the police from taking a public stance on their commitment to racial equality within their organization.

It is the notion that 'some discrimination' may be practised that leads us to the view expressed earlier that affirmative action – selecting the minority candidate rather than the majority candidate *when all other selection criteria are equal* – is preferable to positive discrimination in which the minority candidate is selected *whether or not the criteria are equal*.

Furthermore there are two underlying assumptions about minority recruiting which may be erroneous. First, that some of the 'black culture' and therefore some measure of tolerance will rub off on white officers, and second, that minority officers will be able to police minority areas more effectively.

Evidence from a number of studies reinforces the sociological view that there is no such thing as a *particular* minority culture common to all social classes of a minority group. Furthermore, in the USA, most of the black and minority officers come from middle-class backgrounds while police/minority friction stems, in the main, from the working-class (often ghetto) population and particularly from teenagers. At least one study in the USA showed that black officers were more aggressive towards black criminals whom they viewed as getting all blacks a bad name (Friedrich, 1977). The Wilson et al. study also confirmed that there is evidence that black police officers are 'de-racinated' by the black public who call them 'Uncle Toms', 'traitors' and 'coconuts' (i.e. black on the outside but white inside).[22]

The effect of quotas – New York Police Department

The resistance in British police circles to the quota system is largely based on observation of its effect in some US institutions.

Quotas, which aim to suggest that because a proportion of a large group is of a particular racial or ethnic origin, all sub-groups must be divided to represent the *exact proportions* of main group, are a double-edged sword. The appeal is that, in overall representation terms, quotas and even the lowering of standards to achieve them will provide the balance in a sub-group which is reflective of the large group. The disadvantage is what may happen later when the representation does not extend to sub-sub groups.

In 1983 11,534 officers of the New York City Police sat their promotion examination.

The Department operates a quota system at recruitment which is based on the observation that about 50 per cent of the city population is caucasian whilst the remaining 50 per cent is made up of minority groups.

When the examination results were published 968 white officers had been successful compared to 23 black and 44 hispanic officers.

Two official bodies representing the black and the hispanic officers in the police department alleged, in the New York courts, that the examination had been unfair because a disproportionate number of blacks and hispanics had failed. (The argument being that 50/50 population = 50/50 recruiting, should = 50/50 promotion.)

Typically of the American police system, the problem was complicated by the open opposition by the Mayor, Ed Koch, to quotas and the support of such a system by Federal Judge Robert L. Carter who was presiding over the law suits.

Faced with opposition from the Patrolman's Benevolent Association to the idea that non-white officers who had failed to achieve the required standard in the examination should nevertheless be promoted to fill 500 of the 1000 vacancies, the Commissioner decided to do just that – the agreement of the two associations to withdraw their law suits being a reciprocal arrangement (*Police Review*, 13 December 1985).

Importantly, particularly in the context of this book, there is no marked advocacy of 'anti-racist' policies, attitudes or behaviours amongst the general population in Britain. Evidence of racism in all aspects of public life grows (PSI, 1984) against a background of public apathy. Changes made in some US police departments came after decades of discussion and argument and then only as a consequence of support from federal legislation, directives and funds. In the end, however, the vital factor appears to have been a political one – the very political factor that gives American policing its unique flavour – strong political support for the police chief from 'City Hall'.

The police in Britain are dependent on the support of the public. As Sir Kenneth Newman, former Commissioner of the Metropolitan Police, has pointed out, there is great difficulty in assessing and responding to social change. The police cannot operate too far ahead of public opinion (Newman, 1984).

An Equal Opportunities Policy statement was made by the London Metropolitan Police in December 1986 (see Appendix II). It remains to be seen how this will affect operational policing, recruiting, and attitudes within the force.

PROMOTIONAL POLICY

The process of promotion to the lower ranks in England and Wales is as follows. For promotion from constable to sergeant and from sergeant to inspector, success in a written examination is the deciding factor. The process is different in the Metropolitan Police from the remaining 42 forces.

Constable to sergeant and sergeant to inspector

Metropolitan Police
In the Metropolitan Police any officer with more than two years' service may sit the sergeant's examination which is set and marked by the Metropolitan Police Examination Unit. The Inspector's Examination may be attempted by those officers who have served as sergeants for a minimum of four years. In both cases, the most successful examinees, who fill the top x places are promoted in order of success during the following year (x being the estimated number of vacancies for the following year). Those who do not do well enough in the examination to achieve one of these competitive places but who have nevertheless attained 60 per cent or more of the available marks are considered to be 'qualified' for promotion in the future (see below).

Currently no formal assessment of operational performance or managerial skill is undertaken, but the force is examining the introduction of 'assessment centre' technology in an effort to improve this aspect of consideration for suitability for promotion.[23]

Provincial forces
In the forces beyond the Metropolitan Police the two-year service criteria for the sergeant's Examination still applies but the examination is marked by the Home Office Examination Unit, and is standard throughout England and Wales.

The examination is qualifying in nature, that is to say, that the officer who reaches the required standard is considered 'qualified' to attend a subsequent promotion selection board, comprised of senior officers from his own force. Once qualified an officer remains so throughout his service. Any officer who has 'qualified' in the sergeant's Examination may take the inspector's Examination.

Table 5.4 Promotion process

New York City Police Department				Metropolitan Police London		
Promotion to rank	Service requirement	Process 1 2 3		Process 1 2 3	Service requirement	Promotion to rank
Captain	1 year for apt 1 day for exam	x x		x	3 years as Insp.	Chief Inspector
Lieutenant	1 year for apt 1 day for exam	x x		x	4 years as Sgt	Inspector
Sergeant	1 year for apt 1 day for exam	x x x		x	5 years for apt 2 years for exam	Sergeant

1 = Written examination
2 = Performance evaluation
3 = Other (role play)
apt = appointment

Since appearance before a selection board is at the discretion of the Chief Constable, many officers even though 'qualified' through the examination never achieve promotion. It is one of the anomalies of this system that many forces have large numbers of qualified officers who are never likely to be promoted (one force has over 40 per cent of its constable strength so qualified). In many cases officers are qualified through examination to the rank of inspector but remain constables despite expressed ambition, at the whim of senior officers. Not surprisingly this results in some substantial morale problems.

The strength of the Metropolitan system is that the ambitious officer, determined to achieve promotion, may do so purely on the basis of diligent study and the achievement of a 'competitive' vacancy. Officers who are not successful in the 'competitive' sphere but have 'qualified' may, at the discretion of the commissioner, be interviewed for a small number of vacancies as in the provincial forces. However, since the total number of vacancies for such cases in the Metropolitan Police is confined (by agreement with the Police Federation) to about 10 per cent of the total number of vacancies for the year, the real incentive is for the officer to retake the examination in the hope of achieving a competitive place. No such pressure is felt by the provincial officer.

Promotion to ranks above inspector

In all police forces in England and Wales, promotion to all ranks above inspector is through interview-type selection boards. No examinations are required. Again consideration is being undertaken of the suitability of the introduction of 'assessment centres', but to date little has been done.

Importantly, because of the level of standardization, there is little difficulty in an officer of any rank seeking appointment in another force and retaining his rank, or alternatively seeking such a transfer in order to gain promotion. The lack of standardization in American policing makes such moves rare, except at the very lowest (patrolman) and the very highest (chief of police) level. The patrolman who seeks to move from one state to another will find, almost without exception, that some kind of 're-certification' is required, usually by attendance at a police academy.

PROMOTION IN NEW YORK CITY POLICE DEPARTMENT

Some detail of the promotion system for the New York City Force is shown in Table 5.4. There is, however, no likelihood that similar systems exist anywhere else in the 20,000 police departments in the USA.

Training

Both the New York City Police Department and the Metropolitan Police have similar training programmes although both differ markedly from other programmes undertaken in each of the countries under examination. Training in London amounts to 20 weeks of formal training followed by a structured 'on the job' continuation training period of 'street duty' interspersed with 'in classroom' sessions. The initial 20-week course is held at the Hendon Police Training School[24] and consists of a mixture of formal teaching of law and police procedure and physical fitness but with an added dimension of 'policing skills training'. It is policing skills training which separates the training for Metropolitan Police recruits from courses held elsewhere in the country.

Again, London stands alone, and at the forefront of police training in England and Wales.

All other forces in England and Wales are, as noted previously, responsible for their own recruiting practices; in addition their recruits attend one of six regional training centres run by the Home Office. Each regional training centre may be responsible for training recruits from between three to six forces. The centres are serviced by a Central Planning Unit (CPU), a Home Office central resource body, which coordinates and plans training, trains instructors, provides support material and researches training and education innovations and aspects of the law and police procedure.

Recruit courses at regional training centres are 14 weeks in length and do not have the concentration on policing skills aspect, which will be discussed below.

One of the problems with the regional centres is that, since they service a number of forces, agreement on change and innovation must be sought from all the chief officers whose recruits may attend a centre. In practice CPU has the role of seeking the approval of 42 chief officers before such changes can be made.

Working for one force, and without the potential constraints of a police authority to challenge the decisions of a chief officer regarding training initiatives, no such problems occur in the Metropolitan Police Training School.

Training in New York City Police Department

New York City Police currently run a 22-week initial training course at the Police Academy in Manhattan. The syllabus encompasses the academic disciplines of social science, police science and law. These subjects, together with some physical activity, amount to over 400 hours of classroom attendance.

The most striking difference between the two training processes is the strongly classroom nature of training in New York and the strongly practical nature of training at Hendon (and in the regional training centres). At Hendon there is an area laid out in streets, with traffic signs, automatic traffic signals (traffic lights), road markings, and so on. There are rooms laid out as apartments, clubs, shops, and other premises. Instructors and recruits are encouraged to involve themselves in role-play whenever and wherever possible.

The opportunities for such markedly high levels of role-play are limited in New York and, although some takes place, it is usually of a rudimentary kind in the car park under the eight-storey building.

Above all, the two institutions (and in this they both reflect aspects of their country's culture) differ in the manner in which they present social science teaching. Both institutions allow about 25 per cent of their syllabus to this area and the differences in teaching practice are clearly stated by Bull and Horncastle (1983, p. 54).

> The most obvious of these differences lies in the title of the module: until recently Hendon used the term 'Human Awareness Training', and this has been replaced by 'Policing Skills'. New York uses the term 'social science' which is emblasoned across every sheet of the recruits' syllabus.... The practical outcome of this difference lies in the divergent strategies which the two institutions employ to teach social science/awareness training. Whilst NYC makes no attempt to disguise the fact that recruits are being taught social science, Hendon prefers to adopt a 'softly, softly' approach in providing the input.... The NYC approach is characterised by their free use of terms such as 'psychology', 'psychologists', 'sociology', 'behavioural science', 'psychological theories' and 'all police officers are psychologists'.... Hendon's approach is characterised by the trainers' efforts to integrate the ... input to the extent where it does not appear to the recruits to exist as a separate entity ...

The rationale for this approach typifies one theme of this book. The American population (if we may be allowed a stereotype) are far more accepting of psychology than are Britons. Social science and social scientists are seen by British police officers as on a par with social workers – do-gooders with their heads in the clouds.

There is clearly, however, a commitment to the principle of 'the police officer as a psychologist' and as such, the Hendon school is constantly improving the inputs. It remains true however that the British police officer is inherently sceptical of any material which they do not see as having immediate practical value.

Training generally in the United States

Given the diversity of policing in the USA, it is not surprising that there is little that can be said about training police officers that can be generalized across the country. The nation's capital, Washington DC, has a total of 28 police agencies operating within its boundaries, each with special jurisdiction, each with its own policies and procedures, basic training, uniforms and executives. The 'US Capitol Police', a 1400-person agency, has jurisdiction over a mere 240 acres including the Capitol building itself, the House of Representatives and the Senate and their office buildings, and the *outside* of the Supreme Court building (the interior of the Court has its own police force!). The Capitol police trains its officers at the Federal Law Enforcement Training Center (FLETC) in Glynco, Georgia.

But federal law enforcement agencies set their own standards and develop their own training and these may differ from the training and standards of those agencies with which they overlap or in the case of the Capitol police, with which they are coterminus.

Police Officer Standards and Training Commissions

Within each state there are minimum pre-employment standards and training requirements for police but it is only in the last five or six years that the last state passed legislation setting such minimum standards. All states now have an agency usually called a Police Officer Standards and Training Commission (POST) but these may have different names in some states (e.g. in Florida, the Criminal Justice Standards and Training Commission; in Arizona, the Law Enforcement Officers Advisory Council).

Under the required statutory authority the commissions or councils set a minimum number of hours of training and selection criteria.

Selection
Minimum selection criteria may be requirements regarding, for example, US citizenship, age, the possession of a high school diploma or equivalent, background investigations, fingerprint checking (through the National Crime Information Center (NCIC)), the absence of felony convictions, medical examinations.

Training
Some authorities have become more demanding in increasing the number of training hours to close to 400, setting on-going in-service requirements, certifying one- and

two-week courses for all levels, and developing specialized courses, and even developing a staff college programme as in California and an Executive Institute in Florida.

State variation

In some states where POST agencies set the minimum requirements, the larger departments might require their officers to go through twice the number of training hours than the smaller. In other states the POST agency only sets the requirement for the smaller departments. For example, in New York State the regulations apply to all agencies *except* NYPD and the New York State Police.

National Association of State Directors of Law Enforcement

All the POST agencies belong to the National Association of State Directors of Law Enforcement, which has attempted over the past few years since its founding in the early 1970s to provide a forum for the membership to keep apprised of the latest developments and to gradually increase each state's requirements. For example, there have always been outcries from the public when police cars have chased an offender and that car has crashed into an innocent third party. But because of searing criticism and the level of public attention being paid to the problem associated with police driving, especially in what are called 'hot' or high-speed pursuits, in the past few years concern has raised the level of awareness to unprecedented heights. A recent survey on driver training indicated that state requirements varied from forty hours of driver and pursuit training to no stated requirement at all. The Association has, therefore, recently started work on establishing a task force which will set up model instructor qualification and certification procedures and model curricula for driver training. Of course, there is no guarantee that any state will adopt the package but by involving the personnel from the various POSTs and instructors from the more progressive and innovative training academies, progress will be made. There will probably never be any degree of uniformity.

Regional training

To the British mind it might seem reasonable to consider that groups of states in the same geographical area might band together to produce uniformity in *regional* training packages. Unfortunately, it is not likely that such a regional grouping will occur. States will not band together, neither will they adopt the same basic training package, the same instructors' guide or even use the same job-task analysis to initiate the process of curriculum development. The sovereign status of each state means that the use of inter-state agreements of this kind will potentially be unconstitutional and courts have already indicated that to develop legally defensible curricula, states and possibly even agencies, would have to conduct *their own* job-task analysis.

In any case, to end up with any more universal acceptance of the training developed in another state, the POST council (composed usually of small city and county, and large city and county executives) must vote favourably for the measure. However, the local constituency represented by these council or commission members would have to be consulted and they might readily reject stricter requirements or wholesale adoption of another state's training package on both constitutional and parochial grounds.

The nature of POST requirements

To make the matter even more difficult, when the requirements are set by the state POST they usually are not sufficiently prescriptive even to have a good degree of uniformity throughout the state at the different training centres. In the 43 certified training courses in Florida there are currently no capabilities in place to guarantee that training on a specific topic such as driving is conducted or assessed in the same way. In this smaller states have an advantage. A number of them, like Montana, Idaho, or Wyoming, have only one training academy and all potential officers attend that academy. Then, but only then, the chances of uniformity are certainly higher.

The future in the USA

There is much to be improved in police training in the US. Some states still allow a police officer to be hired by a municipality and start work without having been certified (i.e. checked out by the state and having completed training). In some cases these men and women can function as a police officer for up to two years – carrying and possibly using a gun, enforcing the law, and doing all the things that an officer would do, but without having gone through any form of basic training. This is so because state requirements allow initial training to take place *within* a year or two of appointment. Most chiefs, particularly of smaller agencies, in need of immediate staff, use the intervening period as one of 'assessment of suitability' and will pursue that 'policy' until the last minute that the law allows. It is only at that point that they must then be sent to the academy to be assessed and certified as fit to do their job.

In South Carolina about 5–8 per cent of officers attending the Criminal Justice Academy are rejected – after they have been serving for up to a year – because they 'can't read or write' (McKenzie, 1986b).

Almost every promotion is made without pre-promotional training and very few supervisors receive post-promotional training. Firearms training, driver training, defensive tactics and legal training are particularly weak. Some officers are issued weapons such as shotguns by their agencies for which they have received no training.

The National Association of State Directors of Law Enforcement Training with strong leadership could come into its own and could become a force that will provide the guidance and direction to the police training community in the country. But the forces unleashed by the liability crisis and the wave of million-dollar judgments against police agencies have provided an impetus that is forcing greater attention to be paid to, and resources to be provided for, the training function. More of the gaps and inadequacies have been recognized and much more is being done to address them.

THE FUTURE IN THE UK

But police training in the UK, at least at recruit level, is not without its critics. A major study of police recruit and probationer training (probationers are officers in their first two years of service) undertaken by the University of East Anglia (MacDonald et al., 1986) is critical of much of current training particularly that of the regional centres. It points to:

- the 'authoritarian and militaristic' culture at training centres;
- is critical of 'parrot-fashion learning' of law and procedures at the expense of the social skills of policing. 'The art of policing, the deft handling of people and situations, remains largely untouched by initial training, except in a nominal sense';
- and calls for local police authorities to be given powers to oversee training in a manner not currently catered for.

In a comment which might be true of training centres on both sides of the Atlantic, Professor MacDonald was quoted[25] as indicating that 'This type of training depersonalises recruits. . . . It certainly does not produce the kind of police officer everyone says they want.' The sort of police officer the populations of the two nations want is problematic but it does appear that, particularly within the police, there is a strongly-held belief that policing is largely a matter of common sense. In a modern multi-culture, multi-ethnic, multi-layered society that is a dubious contention.

SPECIALIZED TRAINING

Racism awareness training

It is an unfortunate fact of life, but a true one, that as Panzarella (1984) observed: 'Books which do not have the word Police in their title rarely find their way into police . . . training programmes.' The same is true of the training programmes themselves.

The Police and Criminal Evidence Act 1984, following the urging of Lord

Scarman in the House of Lords, contains a section[26] which creates a specific disciplinary offence of behaving in a racially discriminatory manner. Although the inclusion of the section was resisted by the Police Federation as 'unfair' and 'unnecessary' (on the grounds that existing disciplinary offences adequately covered such behaviour), the Police Training Council Working Party on 'Community and Race Relations Training for Police' (set up following the Scarman (1981) inquiry) recommended that a team of researchers be set up at a prestigious university to develop research and training expertise, and concluded their report with a recommendation that 'racism awareness training should be introduced without delay and a pilot study be made of its impact'.[27]

They based their assessment on a volume of evidence including that of a number of controversial studies (PSI, 1983; Butler, 1979; Cochrane and Butler, 1980) showing overt and covert racism to be a problem in police community relations.

The 'pilot courses' were set up and run – with totally predictable results.

The Home Office Research and Planning Unit were tasked to evaluate the courses and Southgate (1984) highlighted many of the singular problems of 'grafting on' non-police-oriented training programmes, to those specifically designed for police. The former consequently suffering from a 'poor' response from police participants.

The racism awareness training model – frequently that of Katz (1976) – has been used to encourage social workers, probation officers and others in similar fields, on both sides of the Atlantic, to examine their own attitudes and to seek to change and control any discriminatory tendencies through such awareness. And herein lie two of the major problems which Southgate highlights:

1. In most (if not all) the organizations in which such training has been undertaken discussive, facilitated, student-oriented teaching/learning methods have been the rule.
2. Such 'courses' have generally been for 'volunteers only'.

With the exception of those recruits trained in the Metropolitan Police Training School at Hendon since 19 April 1982, under the 'policing skills' methodology discussed earlier, most police officers, particularly those of intermediate rank, are far more used to the didactic 'talk and chalk' methods of traditional policing training.[28]

Furthermore, many British officers actively avoid any attempts to encourage them to examine themselves. For police officers, relevance is of paramount importance. The nature of their work and the requirements of the courts and the judicial system, produce a pragmatic approach to life that, in general, rejects the need to understand emotions, feelings and perceptions.

As Southgate (1984, p. 6) says:

> Most courses they attend present them with facts rather than ideas, so that they are less than ready to acknowledge emotions, feelings and perceptions as facts. Policemen expect training to be clear and directly relevant to the operational task.

The officers who attended the 'pilot courses' were not only not volunteers but viewed their involvement with considerable scepticism. Some felt that they had been selected because they had been judged to be racist and others were uncertain of the role they were supposed to play. Above all, the officers had considerable difficulty in 'affording credibility to the trainers who they perceived as anti-police, politically radical, revolutionary or idealistic' (Southgate, 1984). Herein lies the major political hot potato.

For years, on both sides of the Atlantic, there has been a continuing debate about the use of non-police trainers in police training programmes. Frequently, these arguments have been over the level of expertise, teaching skills, ability to use audio-visual aids, and so on. If police officers as trainers are nothing else, they are in general exemplars of instructional technique and thus provide a high quality model against which others are measured.

Too frequently such 'outside' speakers have taken the opportunity offered to grind personal and political axes and to be openly critical of police behaviour – often in relation to individual and specific incidents – with little opportunity for considered and informed response.

Often the force of the 'more outside involvement' argument is that police should be more aware of the specific problems, perceptions and attitudes of minority (ethnic) groups in society and that such view can only be adequately expressed by minority group members, but that is a simplistic view of a complex problem.

The question of 'outside' speakers is really yet to be resolved.

Command training

Although estimates vary, there are 600–800 colleges and universities in the USA offering 'criminal justice' courses of one kind and another. Such courses in practice fill a number of needs, including:

1. To provide those intending to follow careers in law enforcement to obtain academic understanding and qualifications which will better fit the student for the task;
2. To provide, for interested parties, information and understanding about the nature of crime, criminality and the law enforcement response to such problems;
3. Through the nature of such education, to prepare and develop police officers and other law enforcement agents for advancement and career development.

No such system of criminal justice colleges or even courses exists in England and Wales.[29]

Professional police training in the USA is fragmented and, as usual, non-standard. However, the National Police Academy (run by the FBI at Quantico, VA), and the Southern Police Institute, seek to provide some managerial training for chiefs and others, although this is currently somewhat limited in scope.

The Police Staff College, Bramshill

Although no criminal justice colleges exist in the UK, the one unique feature of the policing scene in England and Wales is the Police Staff College.

Originally established in 1948, the Staff College (then known as the Police College) is the centre for advanced training for the police service in England and Wales. (Scotland has one of its own.) The Staff College is housed in an ancient country house in Hampshire and is known throughout the British police service by the name of that house, Bramshill.

The charter of the college reads, in part, that the aim of the establishment is 'to broaden the outlook, improve the professional knowledge, and stimulate the energies of men who have reached or are reaching the middle and higher ranks of the service'.

From the very beginning the college has sought a combination of professional studies and education. On the one hand, it seeks to study the techniques of policing and the society in which such policing takes place; and on the other, to develop men and women of 'middle rank' through an encouragement to study non-police matters – economics, politics, sociology, etc.

The directing staff of the College are a combination of well-qualified police officers and academics, the latter drawn from universities and polytechnics around the country. Those police officers attending the college as directing staff are seconded from their forces, usually for a period of about two years. The period is one of 'central service' in a Home Office establishment.

About 10 per cent of the available places for students are set aside for officers from overseas, once almost entirely police officers from British Commonwealth countries, but now worldwide in nature. Officers from the FBI and the Security Services of the USA have attended courses there.

Although a huge number of 'carousel' courses are run for short periods of about two weeks on specialized subjects – accounting, interpersonal skills, community relations, etc., the bulk of the College's time is spent in running the four, longer, main courses: the Junior Command Course, the Intermediate Command Course, the Senior Command Course and the Special Course.

The Junior Command Course

Open to chief inspectors and some inspectors, the Junior Command Course consists of 'general studies' to broaden the outlook and develop powers of expression in students and specific 'police studies', designed to increase professional knowledge and skill. The syllabus, spread over four months, includes studies of management, law operational planning, administration, etc.

Candidates for the course are nominated by their chief officer and those nominated are, in effect, the officers most likely on their present showing to be suitable for higher command rank.

There are about 140 students on each course.

The Intermediate Command Course
This course is open to officers who have attained the rank of chief inspector, and are likely to be suitable for higher rank, or those who are recently promoted to the rank of superintendent. The work is organized on a project-based system. Areas of study include social problems, leadership, management techniques, administration and organization, public relations, and a range of police subjects. The course lasts four months.

Senior Command Course
A comprehensive and professionally conducted selection procedure, run under Home Office control by the Civil Service Commission (another government office) in an 'assessment centre' format, seeks to reduce a large number of applicants from forces all over the country, to about 24. Known as the extended interview, the process examines the applicants, who are superintendents or chief superintendents, and are destined for the highest ranks, over a three-day period. The assessors are a combination of senior police officers who have been specially trained, psychologists and, uniquely in the British police service, a non-service member – usually a person drawn from industry, commerce or the academic world.

The course lasts six months and is organized in a series of study/project modules; each of which involves lectures, the preparation and presentation of papers by the students (either singly or in groups). Some projects involve visits to other establishments both inside and outside the police service, including industry and commerce. At least one opportunity is provided for officers to visit and study the police of another nation.

Themes of the course projects are concerned with higher police management at chief officer level and include such issues as accountability, public order and the control of disorder, personnel management, aspects of crime and traffic, proposals for legislation and any other important developments in the police sphere. Sociological and cultural issues are also addressed.

As a general rule, no officer will be promoted to any rank above commander in the Met. or assistant chief constable in the provinces unless he/she has successfully completed the Senior Command Course.

The Special Course
Although, as will be noted from the earlier discussion (see Table 5.4), the normal length of service for an officer to achieve promotion to the rank of sergeant is five years, it is possible, through two separate but linked processes, to accelerate the process.

Each year up to sixty people are selected to attend the Special Course at Bramshill which lasts for one year (most recently in 'sandwich' form with a period of operational police duty sandwiched between two academic slices). Selection for the course is undertaken from a large number of applicants and uses the Extended Interview format noted above used for selection for the Senior Command Course.[30]

Applicants are in two categories:

1. Serving officers who have passed the constable to sergeant promotion examination and as a consequence of high performance standards during the two-year 'probationary' period are considered by their chief constable to be of high potential.
2. Persons seeking to enter the police service under the Graduate Entry Scheme. This scheme was introduced in 1968 in an effort to encourage university graduates to join the police service by offering the accelerated promotion prospects of the Special Course.

Those successful as graduate applicants (category 2 above) will be required to serve the two-year probationary period and to pass the promotion examination but will then be automatically entitled to a place on the Special Course.

Serving officers (category 1) will, if successful in the Extended Interview, attend the next available Special Course.

All students attending the Special Course will be promoted to the temporary rank of sergeant whilst on the course; on successful completion will become substantive in that rank; and will, after satisfactory performance in the rank for one year, be automatically promoted to the rank of inspector.

The course consists of a combination of academic and practical modules, is regularly examined both in written and observational terms, and is subject of close scrutiny to assess whether the officers possess the qualities which will carry them high in the police service.

It will be noted, however, that for the successful candidate, a total period of about four years will have elapsed from joining to achieving the inspector rank (compare Table 5.4.).

CONCLUSION

Some of the other comparisons and contrasts will be left to the following chapters for more complete discussion. Suffice it to say here that three major areas of contrast exist among many areas of comparison.

First, despite a similarity of organizational structure (natural in militaristic models of organizations) a substantial difference in rates of pay is apparent. This differential is not accounted for by the differences in cost of living, etc., and is perhaps symptomatic of the status quo set by Robert Peel in his search for the 'three shillings a day' man, way back in 1829.

Indeed, in 1910 such a contrast still existed, for according to Richardson (1970), compared with that of the London police officers, the New York cop's job was definitely desirable. The wages were higher than those paid to many skilled mechanics, and although they worked long hours (sixteen hours at a stretch), discipline was lax and graft commonly available.

Although one would wish to make no suggestion that graft enters into the modern scene it is clear that such differentials have always existed.[31]

Nevertheless, back in Peel's time the constable who had the 'necessary education' could rise to the rank of inspector in *only* fifteen years, at which stage he would be earning 'roughly as much as a highly skilled craftsman or clerk. A Superintendent's pay ... was comfortable but no more and about as much as a senior insurance clerk might earn' (Price, 1983 p. 10). The balance of rates of pay in New York against those of England and Wales must, however, be seen in comparison with the levels of remuneration available to law enforcement officers outside the 'big city' areas.

In research specially conducted in 1986 by the Office of Agency Research and Services (OARS) of the University of South Carolina's Criminal Justice College, it was found that starting rates of pay in 196 of the 256 police agencies in the state ranged from about $4600 to about $17,600 (mean $11,737: median $13,162). These rates are fairly typical of those available to officers outside the urban areas and are, in part, responsible for the failure of law enforcement as an on-going career, to hold any thrill for the rural patrol officer in the USA.

Seen against the fact that the rural officer in a provincial force in England and Wales gets the same remuneration as his colleague in a town or city in his area, British rates of pay do not seem too bad.

Second, the absence of centralized standards and criteria for selection in the USA, even allowing for some minor differences in England and Wales, does mean that the public are never certain of the quality, training and potential skills of any officer they approach; to say nothing of the difficulties encountered by an officer seeking to move from one department to another which we discussed earlier.

As noted before, some efforts are being made to encourage 'accreditation' as a vehicle for both standardizing and raising the levels of such criteria but there is still a long way to go. The impact of the Standards of Accreditation Commissions can only be guessed, but the numbers of accredited police departments and those seeking accreditation is rising. Perhaps within the Accreditation Commissions lie the embryo of an 'Inspectorate' seeking, probably on a voluntary basis (typically American), both to raise and *maintain* the standards of the 'best' in US policing.

Finally, the existence of the Police Staff College as a centralized resource for ensuring the standards of senior police officers is a powerful vehicle for achieving that very goal.

But, however, it does little to enhance or improve the professional knowledge and understanding of officers of the lower ranks who are unable (as a consequence of their rank or through failure to be selected) to attend the College. The provision of Criminal Justice Colleges and the like, in the USA, is an effective means of encouraging the sort of understanding that is required for the 'street officer' to cope successfully with today's policing problems.

Where the facilities exist (e.g. the Houston Police Department) departments in the USA often take advantage of that fact by tying an officer's level of educational achievement to enhanced rates of pay (and even promotion).

Perversely, the Police Federation in England and Wales has been resistant to the notion of the provision of anything other than the most rudimentary educational programmes for police officers. There is a fear of academics and academia within the British police service, that at its worst denies the value of any and all 'book learning' and at best allows grudging acceptance of education and its value 'as long as it doesn't count for promotion'.

But it is our view that policing today, on both sides of the Atlantic, is too important to leave to three shillings a day men.

CHAPTER 6

Internal Regulations and Discipline: Professionalizing the Police

Despite the fact that the chief constable in the UK is subject to some central governmental administrative controls,[1] is subject to the threat of dismissal if he is inefficient, and may call on certain central resources not otherwise available, his legal independence and discretion in operational decision-making is absolute, at least in an *ante hoc* way.

But Wilson (1968, p. 7) has pointed out that in policing, discretion increases as one moves down the hierarchy; and right at the bottom line is the street cop.

Policing is unremittingly political (Reiner, 1985; Lustgarten, 1986) – not political in any overt partisan[2] sense but in the sense that it is a function which seeks to control and direct sections of the community on behalf of a population of citizens who are either unable or unwilling to do it for themselves.

Street cops pursue political activity simply because they are permitted and encouraged to exercise discretion. They define legislation, decide whom or whom not to arrest and when or whether to use a given piece of legislation. They also have the freedom to break the rules if they so desire. The individual nature of on-the-street policing means that supervision is a perennial problem. Furthermore, in the UK the constitutional position of constables is complex for, as Jefferson and Grimshaw (1984, p. 60), point out:

> there is no simple master/servant, employer/employee relationship between chief constables and constables. [They are] legally entitled to take independent action as well as to obey all lawful instructions of their senior officers.

In 1930, a case[3] in the Court of Appeal specifically stated that, 'although a constable may be an employee of a local authority, his office was "of the Crown"', i.e. independent of the executive and other arms of government. Both the *Blackburn* cases, and the *Fisher* v. *Oldham*[4] case clearly establish *in law* that the facility for the exercise of discretion provided to chief officers is equally applicable to constables, sergeants and other 'street' police officers.

Although there are some writers who take the stance (cf. Jefferson and Grimshaw, 1981, in a report commissioned by the Home Office) that the problems of subordinate control are wrongly analysed by others who misunderstand the nature of legal powers, many (Manning, 1979; Kinsey and Young, 1982; Baldwin and Kinsey, 1982) would support the view of Holdaway (1979) that 'the lower ranks of the service control their own work situation' (p. 12).

THE LEGAL POSITION

Although in part such autonomy springs from the need, on the simple grounds of expediency, to exercise discretion in the conduct of their duties, there is legal precedent as well.

In a recent case[5] it was held that a constable cannot be ordered by a chief constable to make an arrest unless the constable is satisfied that the facts warrant it. A constable cannot, on the other hand, be ordered *not* to arrest.[6]

It is clear, however, that a constable may take action himself in the face of inaction by his senior officers. In 1974, *The Times Law Reports* recorded a case in which a constable (PC Joy) took personal, private proceedings against a Member of Parliament for a driving offence *after a senior officer had declined to prosecute* (*The Times*, 6 July 1974: see also Gilbert and Kahn, 1975; Lustgarten, 1986).

Thus it is the case that, not surprisingly, a constable has a degree of independence analogous to Denning's view of the chief constable that, at a minimum, entitles him to make decisions as to 'whether prosecutions should be brought, and whether an arrest should be made' and, even in the face of the new Crown Prosecution Service, that independence might also legally include whether prosecutions should *not* be brought, and whether an arrest should *not* be made.

There is, therefore, a legal basis for the exercise of 'on-the-street' discretion but in the final analysis it is the ability of the police service itself to monitor and control constables and sergeants which determines the nature of those decisions.

SUPERVISION IN THE POLICE SERVICE

Control of the actual exercise of police discretion on the streets, particularly in the context of whether or not to make an arrest, is best summarized by a lengthy quote from the most comprehensive study of the workings of the police yet undertaken:

> The best way of putting this is to say that the constraints imposed by law on police officers in this field operate in a very indirect manner. The officer has to bear in mind that if he is seen to have exceeded his powers of arrest he will spoil his chances of getting a conviction. The force at a senior level may see successful actions for unlawful arrest as seriously damaging to its reputation and therefore its ability to achieve objectives to do with law enforcement; to that extent the management of the force may see it as being in their own interest to *discourage* officers from exceeding their powers. All the same, the chance that an individual officer will get into difficulty through exceeding his powers of arrest in a particular case is probably low ...

What this shows is that the law on its own cannot be an adequate or sufficient control. The constraints imposed by the law have tangible consequences – administer an actual kick to the police – in a few cases only. In order to achieve a consistent pattern of policing behaviour . . . it is necessary the police officers should genuinely accept the norms inherent in the law and for this we are dependent on the way the force is supervised, managed and organised. (Smith and Grey, 1983, p. 193)

There is no reason to believe that the situation in the USA is any different from that in Britain and given the fractured, conflict-laden, overtly political nature of American policing, it may be more severe.

Note that it is the view of Smith and Grey that senior officers will *discourage* but not actively prevent, or even punish, unlawful arrests. The same authors later conclude, after an examination of the nature of supervision in the force, that:

sergeants do not often supervise police officers outside the police station and when they do observe incidents they are reluctant to exert a direct influence. (p. 284)

In broad measure the same may be said to be true of other supervisory ranks. To a marked extent Smith and Grey (1983) felt that the failure of 'on-the-job supervision' was a consequence of the failure of the force to define its objectives and goals, a practice felt unnecessary in the past since the myth of policing, discussed above, was that of 'the sturdy independence and impartiality of the individual police officer, whose duty is apparently to all of the laws with equal enthusiasm and without fear or favour' (Smith and Grey, 1983, p. 50). As Goldstein (1977, p. 128) puts it:

In fostering [the] image of themselves as ministerial officers, doing precisely what they were mandated to do by law, the police were responding to their understanding of what was expected of them by the legislatures, by the courts and by a substantial segment of the general public.

The knowledge that this stance is simply a managerial fiction; that police officers in practice choose to do or not to do things; that they are directed to enforce particular laws in favour of others or to ignore certain matters in order to concentrate on others; and that all this is a matter of mere whim on the part of those senior managers, leads to the setting of 'unofficial, unacknowledged and implicit' objectives. Some of which may breach the law itself.

It is our already stated thesis that the advent of the Police and Criminal Evidence Act 1984, and the increasing movement towards checks on policing and the administration of justice in Britain is analogous to the 'due process' revolution in the USA in the 1960s. But constraints on police behaviour are as much an internal matter as they are a responsibility of legislators of one kind or another. But from whatever source those controls emanate it is clear that they become more and more necessary.

As we discussed in the last chapter in the context of training, there is substantial evidence that police officers are increasingly using their *existing powers* to harass people from minority group backgrounds, and this says nothing about the occasion when officers step beyond those powers and take the law into their own hands in one way or another. Despite the existence of a sophisticated complaints procedure, the increasing autonomy of the chief officers and the fact that investigation and punishment is a responsibility of the police alone, provides little in the way of confidence to complainants and the public at large that such complaints will be effectively dealt with.

The exercise of discretion and in particular the decision to arrest or not is of fundamental importance. Although there is limited evidence to indicate its occurrence in Britain, certain American studies (e.g. Westley, 1953; Goldman, 1963; Reiss, 1970; Lundman, 1974) have shown that police use their discretionary powers to arrest when 'disrespect' is shown to them. The need to ensure that officers do not lose face and that 'disrespect to the cloth' is a factor in the mind of the British police officer is clearly demonstrated in the Policy Studies Institute report (PSI, 1983, pp. 66–7).

These observations were made in the absence of the wide powers of arrest contained in the Police and Criminal Evidence Act examined in the next chapter, and it is clearly likely that the 'disrespect element' will colour police behaviour, particularly when that lack of respect comes from individuals or groups who have little enthusiasm for police. The American studies tend to show that racial discrimination and prejudice have little bearing on such matters but that people in minority groups, and particularly the young, are more likely to show disrespect: arrest, under the new legislation, for trivial offences now being the most likely form of 'punishment' for such behaviour.

There is little doubt that such 'punishment' does take place and although lengthy detention is now unlikely it is nevertheless true as Smith and Grey (1983, p. 75) point out that:

> In practice ... the process of being arrested, held at a police station, questioned and then charged may often be a much more serious punishment than the penalty (if any) that is subsequently imposed by the court.

POLICE CORRUPTION

Finally it is the case that the police of both nations have been 'found wanting', at one time or another, as a consequence of complaint of extreme behaviour by what is usually a small section of their community. The torpedo of allegations of graft of one kind or another[7] rarely stays submerged for long. (See Reiner, 1985, pp. 65–8 for a full examination of these areas in British policing; and Knapp Commission Report, 1973; Pennsylvania Crime Commission, 1976; Sherman 1976, pp. 6–12; Barker and Roebuck, 1973, regarding the USA.)

COMPLAINTS AGAINST POLICE

Naturally the 'victim' of such behaviour has certain opportunities to seek redress for perceived wrongs.

Prior to the advent of the Police and Criminal Evidence Act, complaints against police were dealt with under legislation contained in the Police Act 1964. The new Act has replaced the old with minimal alteration save in the area of independent supervision of the process.

During its passage through Parliament the legislators debated the whole question of who was to conduct investigations of allegations against police officers. The Police Federation, in what some cynics may see as a political manoeuvre in the face of the new Act, which among other things was seeking to create a new disciplinary offence in respect of 'racist behaviour', insisted that nothing short of a completely independent investigation and adjudication of complaints would satisfy the public who see the current system as biased in the extreme.

The even more cynical might suggest that the move was one calculated to elicit political support for various increases in police powers made in the sound knowledge that investigations undertaken by 'non-police' investigators would be met with non-cooperation, and difficulties only to be guessed at. The belief that such investigations would be less, not more, rigorous might also have been a causal factor in the *volte face*.

Despite that change of mind and some other political pressure the Act does not create a fully independent procedure. The Act provides for the registration of all complaints made against officers and their subsequent investigation by senior police officers (in London of the rank chief inspector and above, and in other forces by officers of or above the rank of superintendent). The investigating officer is required to be outside the immediate chain of command of the officer(s) under investigation.[8]

The Act set up a body known as the Police Complaints Authority (PCA) who are required to be informed by the chief officer of any complaint which alleges that the conduct of an officer resulted in the death or serious injury of another person. Serious injury means a fracture, damage to an internal organ, impairment of bodily function, a deep cut or laceration.

The PCA are also to be informed of particular types of allegation as directed by the Home Secretary, and may have complaints referred to them at the discretion of the chief officer, if they 'consider it is desirable in the public interest'[9] (sec. 89 (2)).

The role of the PCA is purely supervisory. They have no investigatory functions at all, but have certain powers in respect of the conduct of the investigation in that they have control over, may select, veto and must approve, the appointment of an investigator.

Although not contained in the Act, a government White Paper published in 1983[10] gave indications of the nature of their supervision.

The Authority is able, after consulting with the chief officer, to require that an investigation team be augmented by manpower, equipment or other resources. It may give officers conducting investigations 'such reasonable directions as it considers necessary for the proper conduct of the investigation'. It may call upon investigating officers to account for their actions; explain their strategy; and justify lines and depth of questioning and any apparent delay.

The Authority will require a comprehensive report from the investigator and will send a copy of the report to the chief officer and the complainant.

There is a distinction between allegations relating to disciplinary offences and those which relate to 'crime' (in its broadest definition).[11]

On receipt of the report the chief officer is required to submit all allegations of crime in which he considers that the officer ought to be charged with a criminal offence to the Director of Public Prosecutions (DPP) who will decide if there is sufficient evidence to justify a formal prosecution in court. If the report to the chief officer does not indicate a crime or he feels that the officer ought not to be charged he is required to notify the PCA of his decision and the reasons for it, and to indicate if he intends to initiate disciplinary proceedings.

The PCA may direct that particular courses of action are taken, e.g. that the report be directed to the DPP or that particular disciplinary charges are brought.

Allegations of offences which are solely contraventions of the Discipline Code are considered by the chief officer. The Discipline Code deals with a wide range of offences which are shown in full in Appendix IIIa and the legislation provides for a range of punishments that may be awarded after a finding of guilt.

PUNISHMENTS

Under Police Regulations, convictions for disciplinary offences may be dealt with by a range of punishments:

1. Dismissal from the force.
2. Requirement to resign.[12]
3. Reduction in rank.
4. Reduction in the accused's rate of pay for such a period, not exceeding twelve months, as shall be specified in the decision.
5. Fine.
6. Reprimand.
7. Caution.

There are complex regulations regarding the conduct of disciplinary hearings but they do include for the first time, as a consequence of the new Act, the right for officers to be legally represented at such hearings.

For some time, the Police Federation had argued that it was contrary to the laws of natural justice that police officers should be denied access to counsel under such circumstances and eventually achieved the inclusion in the Act of a provision for such representation.[13]

COMPLAINTS AND DISCIPLINE IN THE USA

The Policeman's Bill of Rights

There is a clear similarity between the provisions of the Police and Criminal Evidence Act 1984 dealing with the conduct of hearings following complaints against police officers and the 'Policeman's Bill of Rights' in the USA, which exists in some jurisdictions, including Providence, Rhode Island; New York State Police; San Francisco, California, and lay down a series of specific protections for accused officers including the provision of legal advice.

As Chapman (1982, p. 2) puts it:

> Many police employee organisations throughout the country have made determined efforts to achieve more rights for officers during internal investigations. The feeling of these employee organisations is that policemen should not be treated like second class citizens and should be afforded the same rights as other citizens who are charged with wrong doing under the criminal law.

Once again, there is variation in both the nature and administration of disciplinary functions from jurisdiction to jurisdiction in the USA. For example, the Charleston Police Department in South Carolina has a comprehensive list of available 'punishments', arranged in order of increasing severity, which may be used singly or in combination. (See Appendix IIIb for details of the disciplinary offences in that P.D.)

Punishments range as follows:

1. Retraining.
2. Counselling.
3. Oral reprimand.
4. Written reprimand.
5. Voluntary loss of accumulated time (in lieu of suspension).
6. Voluntary loss of overtime pay (in lieu of suspension).
7. Voluntary uncompensated extra duty (in lieu of suspension).
8. Restitution.
9. Suspension.
10. Demotion.
11. Termination (dismissal).

Mathias et al. (1980) note that 'increasingly the disciplining of officers for "conduct unbecoming an officer" takes the form of due process procedures'. On the other hand, *many police departments, particularly those of a smaller size, will have no procedures or laid down punishments at all.*

THE INDEPENDENT ELEMENT – CIVILIAN INVOLVEMENT

The existence of any civilian or independent element in the investigatory process is similarly far from consistent. Sometimes where civilian involvement has occurred it has foundered on the rocks of police resistance.

In the absence of any office equivalent to the Director of Public Prosecutions in the USA the typically American solution to the introduction of an independent element into the resolution of complaints and allegations against police officers has been the use of Civilian Review Boards of one kind or another. But typically the pressure of police unions and the operation of political manipulation has resulted in these Boards becoming inoperative edifices to the democratic principle, or at best fairly toothless bureaucracies.

For example, the Civil Review Board in Washington DC voluntarily ceased to operate on the perplexing grounds of 'lack of supportive staff', while New York Police's citizen review process was, through a public referendum, voted out of existence following strong resistance from officers in the Department and a campaign presenting the police as the 'thin blue line' between stability in society and communism and anarchy (see Robin, 1980, pp. 83–6, for an examination of the history of this and the Philadelphia CRB). New York City still has a Civilian Complaint Review Board but one consisting of civilian members of the police department (Swan, 1982)!

POLICE REGULATIONS – UK

As has been discussed previously, the centralized resourcing and broad administrative responsibility of the Home Office in Britain has resulted in standardization of many managerial functions. Standardization of discipline in all 43 of the Home Office forces is achieved through two vehicles, the Police Regulations 1965 and the Police (Discipline) Regulations 1985 as amended.

The conduct and conditions of service of individual police officers are controlled by the 1965 regulations. In particular, the first schedule to the regulations, which cannot be added to by any chief officer or police authority without consultation with representative bodies and with the approval of the Home Secretary.

The Regulations set out restrictions on the private life of officers as follows:

1. A member of a police force shall at all times abstain from any activity which is likely to interfere with the impartial discharge of his duties, or which is likely to give rise to the impression among members of the public that it may so interfere; and in particular a member of a police force shall not take any active part in politics.
2. A member of a police force shall not reside at premises which are not for the time being approved by the chief officer.

3. A member of a police force shall not, without the consent of the chief officer, receive a lodger into a house in which he resides, and in respect of which he receives rent allowance, or sub-let any part of the house.
4. A member of a police force shall not wilfully refuse or neglect to discharge any lawful debt.

The aim of these regulations is to ensure that police officers are restricted in such a manner as to ensure the proper exercise of their authority in an impartial manner. Although it is doubtful if any list of rules can ensure impartiality the focus of the regulations is to seek to prevent any officer placing himself under an obligation to a person in the community. The regulations extend, for example, to preventing an officer from having any kind of paid second job (a business interest) – a common occurrence in many, if not all, police departments in the USA.[14]

The British regulations even, in some circumstances, extend to members of the officer's family.

A business interest exists if:

1. The person concerned holds any office or employment for gain or hire, otherwise than as a member of a police force, or carries on any business.
2. A shop is kept or a like business is carried on by the person's spouse (not being separated from him or her) at any premises in the area of the police force in question, or by any relative included in his family at the premises at which he resides.
3. The person concerned, his spouse (not being separated from him) or any relative included in his family living with him has or has had a pecuniary interest in any liquor licence, or any permit or licence for betting or gaming, or for place of public entertainment in the area of the police force in question.

The rules which govern the private lives of officers are very strict and restrictive and have been extended and enhanced in some forces through the development of outlines of 'Guidance for Professional Behaviour' in which many contentious issues in both public and private behaviour, the use of force, discriminatory practices, the rule of law, discretion, membership of 'private clubs or institutions', whose purpose are not generally known or published or whose activities are kept away from the public view' (Newman, 1985).

In general however the main restrictions refer to aspects of 'on duty' behaviour and these are controlled through the vehicle of the Discipline Code contained in the Police (Discipline) Regulations 1985 (See Appendix IIIa).

THE EFFECT OF RULES AND CODES OF CONDUCT

Smith (1985), in a compelling discussion, points out that there are three kinds of rules which dictate and control people's behaviour in an organization. He points out that

'Because a rule exists it does no follow that it rigidly governs day-to-day policing behaviour. At the extreme, a rule may be universally ignored and never invoked to discipline anyone.' He argues that there are three kinds of rule in operation in the police organization. First there are those *working rules* that are internalized by police officers to become guiding principles of their conduct. Second, *inhibitory rules* which are not internalized which are taken into account and tend to discourage them from behaving in certain ways in case they should be caught and the rule invoked against them. Finally there are *presentational rules* that exist only to give an acceptable appearance to the way that police work is carried out.

Although it is only explicitly stated in connection with inhibitory rules, both these rules and working rules share the exercise of sanctions for failure to comply. Sanctions are far less likely in the case of a breach of presentational rules. They may not be explicitly stated and they may not even exist.

Failure to comply with presentational rules could be dealt with under the Police Discipline Regulations only under the headings of 'acting in a manner likely to bring discredit on the reputation of the force',[15] or for 'disobeying a lawful order'; both offences are widely drawn and in any case unlikely to be the subject of major punishment.

But for all that, the existence of a comprehensive code which governs both private and public lives can have consequences beyond the apparently simple questions of efficacy or punishment.

DISCUSSION

The effects of the discipline code – a source of stress?

The existence of such a set of controls over both the public and private lives of British police officers is according to Wegg-Prossor (1979) 'of great importance in protecting the public against the abuse of police power'.

The difficulty is, however, that on occasion the over-enthusiastic pursuit of offenders against the Discipline Code has brought the whole system into, if not disrepute, then certainly the area of police cynicism. Many officers believe that such a comprehensive set of rules is both unnecessary and unprofessional. They argue that the offence at (1) of the code (Appendix III) is sufficient to cover all eventualities and that, as is frequently the case, the diligent search by the investigating officer for *every* discipline offence revealed by the circumstances of the case is both 'bad for duplicity' (a legal phrase meaning that it is an error to charge more than one offence on the same or similar evidence) and causes severe stress.

In 1983 a series of workshops on police stress in England and Wales (Home Office Workshops, 1983) chose to categorize sources of police stress under four major headings: management style, management structure, management systems and traumatic incidents.

It was clear from the studies carried out in the workshops that the behaviour of management in many British police forces, coupled with the often antiquated policies and techniques used in selection, training, promotion, housing and welfare, are major sources of organizational stress for the British police officer.

Above all, the participants identified that poor management styles produce more widespread and long-term stress in police officers than did their operational tasks. They wrote:

> The pressures of police work together with inadequate training and fear of making mistakes foster a negative and fault finding management style. Even the most senior ranks fear criticism and often seek a scape-goat. Excessive attention to minutiae may suffocate innovative ability and make people reluctant to exercise discretion in a rapidly changing society.

Those rather subjective views are increasingly being supported by the objective findings of psychologists. For example, Gudjonsson (1984, p. 235) writes:

> Within the police force certain skills and behaviours are valued and rewarded accordingly. Reward may consist of praise from colleagues and the public, with the resulting increase in self-esteem and self-estimate. . . . Those who are deficient in the valued skills and behaviours may be punished in two different ways. First, they are not allowed to receive the rewards they would otherwise attain. Second, they may be directly punished by losing their job, being demoted in rank or position or being disciplined and sentenced to prison. (sic)

In a comprehensive study of police recruits, constables, sergeants and senior officers Gudjonsson (p. 236) found that 'fear of failure and negative evaluation' significantly increases with experience and seniority.

> Police officers who are very disturbed by failures and negative evaluation may try very hard not to make mistakes. However, mistakes are sometimes difficult to avoid and the perceived fear of the consequences may cause some officers to cover up their mistakes and failures.

A substantial part of the fear of negative evaluation among British police officers springs from the likelihood of falling foul of the discipline code and the range of punishments that can be administered by chief officers.

POLICE DISCIPLINE AND THE 'DOUBLE JEOPARDY' RULE

British officers are, at least, protected from 'double jeopardy' by legislation[16] providing that, where a member of a police force has been convicted or acquitted of a criminal offence, he or she may not be dealt with under the Police Discipline Code on the basis of the same facts.

For the American officer no such protection exists. This is so because cases which fall under both state and federal law are not considered to be subject to the double jeopardy rule.[17]

Table 6.1 The double jeopardy rule for police officers and civilians in the USA in a hypothetical case of assault

	Hearing level	Type of court	
		Civil	Criminal
Police officer	Admin. hearing	*	
	State court	*	*
	Federal court	*	*[a]
Civilian	State court	*	*
	Federal court		

Note: *Signifies a court in which cases may be heard on the basis of the same evidence without breaching the double jeopardy rule.
[a]Civil and criminal hearings in federal courts after hearing in state courts are not considered to be double jeopardy as they deal with breaches of civil rights (18, USC 421–242, Federal Criminal Court Rights and 42, USC 1983, Federal Civil Court Rights). Action under these statutes is not generally applicable to civilians.

For example, an officer alleged to have committed an act amounting to assault and battery may be dealt with under both state and federal, civil and criminal law, *and* be the subject of an administrative hearing with his own PD (see Table 6.1.).

The increasing use of civil litigation in attempts to deal with police misconduct and the award of huge damages may be seen as a response to the failure of the police themselves to deal in any satisfactory manner with such behaviours. Awards of millions of dollars are increasingly commonplace and are taken under Civil Rights legislation. Under the Civil Rights Act 1871, sec. 42, liability does not necessarily have to be based on the intent to violate a person's constitutional rights; liability is based on the doctrine that the officer's conduct had a natural and obvious consequence and that, without intention, the officer's conduct amounted to a denial or deprivation of the person's civil rights.

Not originally intended to do so, the Civil Rights Act was first used to bring action against the police in 1961 and was strengthened by the Supreme Court in 1971 by their creation of a federal cause of action based on Fourth Amendment violations. As Robin (1980, p. 87) accurately puts it:

> The scope of police misconduct covered by Section 1983 of the Civil Rights Act of 1871 under which citizens may bring the police into court is enormous. It encompasses almost everything except the police failing to inform the plaintiff of his or her Miranda rights upon arrest.

But in the USA officers are individually liable for any substantiated claims made against them. Municipalities, police departments, and police officials are not normally liable for the misconduct of their employees or subordinates (Robin, 1980, p. 88), a fact that contrasts markedly with the position in England and Wales.

Although it is the case that under sec. 48 (1) of the Police Act 1964, tort actions in British courts hold the chief officer to be liable for the behaviour of his officers on the basis of a master–servant liability, it is equally the case that sec. 48 (2) of that Act allows that the police fund (i.e. the police authority) shall pay out all monies required by a court award or settlement.

Not only is the American officer unprotected by an interpretation of the double jeopardy rule like that in the UK, he also has to ensure that he has personal liability insurance cover or risk ruin.

In the absence of other satisfactory mechanisms, as Robin (1980, p. 88) puts it: 'the use of civil litigation against the police is the only direct, truly deterrent method for cracking down on police who are racist, brutal, unstable or grossly irresponsible.'

To be sure, in many cases in England and Wales officers are dealt with in two places because the facts are different. And commonly, in serious cases, officers are suspended from duty for months at a time and sometimes for years, but that suspension is on full pay and it is unlikely that threat of civil action in the British courts would produce multi-million pound settlements.

But none the less, some punishments, particularly demotions, can be draconian in their effect,[18] and thus are a major source of stress to many officers.

AN ALTERNATIVE VIEW – CONTROL OF AUTHORITY OR PRESSURE TO PROFESSIONALIZE?

The other side of the coin must also be considered. If police officers in England and Wales are to have the increased powers provided by the Police and Criminal Evidence Act should there not be a mechanism for ensuring that the rules are not broken? The trouble is that no code, however well thought-out, can ever satisfy such a hope. Rules and 'exhortation programmes' can never do more than give guidelines. One can rarely tell when they are formulated, whether rules will be inhibitory, working, or presentational: only their working context will determine that.

A far more fruitful approach might therefore be a combination of stress research and complaints research in the manner of that undertaken in Dallas and Kansas City (Missouri) which seeks to identify patterns of behaviour and the stresses and pressures in police work which affect the performance of individual officers and to correct them (Tamm, 1972; Symonds, 1970) rather than punish them on an *ad hoc* basis. The only other choice, rarely taken in England and Wales, is that of suing the officer in question, or the police force which employs him.

In the USA the absence of any standardized Discipline Code or any comprehensive regulations controlling an officer's private life do not free him or her from similar stressors. The level of financial judgments against individual officers, already at seven-figure levels, are such that fears of multi-million dollar law suits will outweigh, by far, the pressures engendered by the internally imposed discipline of the UK. As Swan (1982, p. 1) puts it: 'the law enforcement community views the trend in police misconduct suits as harassment of the police and a problem only somewhat less alarming than crime itself.' The issue here is, as before, that of the 'professional' nature of policing.

Professionalization

Professionalism is sometimes defined purely in terms of financial remuneration, e.g. professional footballer, professional tennis player or professional plumber. But there is a definition of professionalism which depends upon membership of a profession.

Neiderhoffer (1967) has summed up the attributes of a 'profession' as:

1. High standards of admission.
2. A special body of knowledge and theory.
3. Altruism and dedication to the service ideal.
4. A lengthy period of training.
5. A code of ethics.
6. Licensing of members.
7. Autonomous control.
8. Pride of the members in their profession.
9. Publicly recognized status and prestige.

There is little doubt that in terms of altruism, dedication, pride and a 'special' body of knowledge, the police in the USA and the UK are moving slowly towards the status of a profession.

But in contrast the variable quality of admission criteria, the too often rudimentary training period, the lack of a comprehensive code of ethics, and the inability to demonstrate the capacity for autonomous control, conspire to deprive the American police of their recognition, status and prestige.

Although it is true that the status and prestige of the police in the UK is sometimes in doubt (among certain sections of the population), the high recruitment standards, and the increasing length of training (currently two years, including the probationary period), and the facility for self-regulation (autonomy) move the British police further and faster towards the 'professional' tag than their American colleagues.

Above all, the development of codes of ethics and the existence of a standardized Police Regulations and Discipline Code have this effect. For, although total autonomy, as we have argued elsewhere, is unacceptable (policing in a democratic society, almost by definition, requires civilian involvement), it is the demonstration of a real willingness to 'put one's own house in order' that has a powerful effect in demonstrating to the public that it can perform the self-policing function in a credible way.

SECTION 3

Rights, Realities and Responses: The Practicalities of Policing

CHAPTER 7

Police Powers and Practices: Law Enforcement and Order Maintenance

Wilson (1968) suggested that there are three main styles of policing as follows:

1. The watchman style.
2. The legalistic style.
3. The service style.

He also proposed that these styles are 'matched' to the perception of the function of policing and that there are, naturally, three main functions of policing:

1. Order maintenance.
2. Law enforcement.
3. Public service.

Wilson was engaged in a sociological study of a number of police departments in the USA, but it does appear that his generalized overview of policing styles can be reduced to the individual, psychological level to provide some insight to the philosophy and motivation of ordinary cops.

THE WATCHMAN STYLE

The watchman style of policing is dependent on the perception that the role of the police is one of *order maintenance.* The police officer's role is thus defined more by his perception of his responsibility for maintaining order than by his perception of his responsibility for enforcing the law.

The practice of such police officers would be to ignore certain common violations of the law, especially traffic offences and minor juvenile crime, and to tolerate a certain amount of 'moral' crime, e.g. vice and gambling. The law and the implied *threat of action* are used more to maintain order than to regulate conduct. The officer's definition of 'order' would be drawn in the context of the group (or sub-culture) in which the behaviour occurs.

Judgments about the potential outcome of action against any group or individual in a group are of fundamental importance here. The watchman style does not deny the officer the occasional need for law enforcement but seeks to allow (and encourage) him to make informed decisions about the balance between the need to maintain 'public tranquillity' and the need to enforce the 'rule of law'.[1]

THE LEGALISTIC STYLE

Law enforcement usually means either making an arrest or reporting the offender for subsequent prosecution (a summons). The legalistic style emphasizes that even commonplace situations are matters for enforcing the law rather than maintaining order. Sometimes the model extends to enforcing the law *at all costs* and the officers involved are invited to ignore the possible 'order' consequences of their actions. Typified by large numbers of arrests for fairly trivial matters, high volumes or summonses, the belief of such officers (and police departments) is that there is only one standard of community conduct and that standard is the law.[2]

In the law enforcement style, of course, many 'good arrests' for burglaries, robberies and the like may be made, but in general it is the 'any and all offences require prompt enforcement' attitude which is paramount.

THE SERVICE STYLE

The emphasis here is on service to the community. Although the officer is concerned with order maintainance and although law enforcement prerogatives will be recognized, the general approach is that the role of police is one which is concerned with seeking to improve and enhance the quality of life for all. This officer, whilst not precluding the necessity of arrest, will endeavour to resolve people's problems and to provide both support and, where necessary, protection.[3]

INDIVIDUAL STYLE

Traditionally, the 'service style' has been the claimed style of British policing which, it is said, has had the effect of distinguishing it from the European style which tended to concentrate less on the social role and more on the law enforcement role. However, it is our view, which will be examined later, that 'order maintenance' is the more correct designation for British policing. Although Reiner (1986) in his review of the literature of policing notes that the service role 'was quite deliberately cultivated . . . to secure legitimacy for more coercive functions' (p. 57), there is little doubt that it has a bearing on the manner of the development of the 'image of policing' both in popular culture and in individual psychology. It is significant that, however they end up, the vast bulk of the recruits to the London Metropolitan Police still claim during their initial training period to have joined the force 'to help people'.

THE PERCEPTION OF CRIME

Bound up in all this 'individual psychology' is the need to recognize that above all police officers are human beings. Volumes have been written about the perception of crime in any community which, in summary, tend to show that television and the press generally – and not infrequently the police themselves – generate distorted perceptions of criminality in any given area and that consequently the 'fear of crime' in the population is escalated.

Police officers' images, their 'fear of crime', are affected by exactly the same mechanisms. Not only that, some of them can prove that it's bad – they've been there!

It is just this sort of perception that shifts a 'rookey cop' from his view of the police role as one of a social or service nature to the total law enforcement viewpoint.[4]

The whole effect is then reinforced by notions that 'the public don't care'; 'we are the thin blue line, the last bastion, protecting society from anarchy'; 'the laws we administer are inadequate' or 'court decisions hamper our work'.[5]

Although Wilson's typology was of a sociological nature the definitions are equally applicable to individuals. Both the perceptions of officers and their styles of policing are relevant factors on both sides of the Atlantic and this is so despite the fact that the laws which are administered differ greatly.

But there is another element which has an effect on the psychology of individual officers: the way in which the legislators perceive them and their role and the consequent provision (or denial) of powers provided to them to do their job. An examination of the powers of officers will be conducted in the remainder of this chapter.

THE POLICE AND CRIMINAL EVIDENCE ACT 1984 (PACE)

The progress of this Act through Parliament was not without its difficulties. There was considerable dispute on both sides of the House of Commons regarding almost every clause. The Bill became a battleground between hard-right and hard-left politicians both outside and within Parliament. Spectres of police repression and rampant criminality stalked the corridors of Westminster. The House of Lords saw fit to add a number of amendments. The Bill was shelved for a lengthy period as a consequence of the calling of a General Election and finally, in a much modified form, it received the Royal Assent on 31 October 1984. The Act came fully into force on 1 January 1986.

The Police and Criminal Evidence Act introduces new provisions for the admissibility of documentary (and computer) evidence and rationalizes the law relating to evidence in criminal proceedings, notably that relating to confessions; and rationalizes and consolidates police powers of stop and search, road checks, searching premises and arrest. It provides new measures for dealing with complaints against the police and police discipline, provides statutory arrangements for obtaining the views of the community on policing, and grants a power to the Home Secretary to issue codes of practice on stop and search, searching premises, identification, and the detention, treatment and questioning of persons by police. In the provision of powers to the police and the concerns with civil rights, the legislators attempted to walk a tightrope, balancing justice and humanity in one hand, and crime control in the other.

We have examined some of the problems associated with the issue of controlling police misconduct in Chapter 6, but the necessity for increasing checks and controls over police behaviour is nowhere more clearly demonstrated than by an examination of the content of new Act. For, although the Act consolidates police powers and contains, in the Code of Practice, rules and instructions which aim to exercise controls over a range of matters from fingerprinting to photography, it is control at a cost. That cost is in a dramatic increase in police powers which, by comparison with anything in the USA, are a potential threat to traditional liberties never previously experienced in England and Wales.

POLICE POWERS OF ARREST

For many hundreds of years the existence of a mass of legislation and the absence of a criminal code has caused complication and difficulty in the British legal system. Much academic discussion has been undertaken to consider not only if such a codification was possible but also if it was necessary.

The convolutions and complexities of legislation had undoubtedly led to a good degree of uncertainty for operational police officers in the sense that each Act of Parliament which created an offence or offences had, of necessity, to indicate the circumstances and conditions under which the police could exercise a power of arrest *if such a power was contained in the Act*.

In some circumstances Parliament had seen fit to designate offences, usually of a serious nature, as arrestable offences, a category of offence which replaced, in 1968, the former distinction between felony and misdemeanour. By designating an offence as arrestable Parliament thus provided a powerful and comprehensive power of arrest applicable both to police officers and citizens.

As an alternative to designating an offence as 'arrestable', Parliament occasionally provided in legislation specific powers of arrest, usually of the 'found committing' and 'name and address refused' type, which were for the less serious offences of a 'misdemeanour' type when that category of offence existed in British law.

Prior to PACE, the law had also allowed a third category of offences, those for which there was no power of arrest and which could only be dealt with by way of summons. For most offences in this category, including the bulk of traffic offences from illegal parking to driving without being the holder of a driving licence, the role of the police officer was simply to report the facts to his senior officers who would then decide whether or not to prosecute.[6]

The issuing of tickets for most traffic and similar offences was confined to parking and obstruction type offences but even then, automatic appearance before a magistrate was far from certain, the prosecution decision again resting with police.[7]

The issue however is not in respect of ticketing or otherwise but in the extension of powers of arrest given to police by the Police and Criminal Evidence Act 1984.

Powers of arrest – arrestable offences

The powers themselves are contained in section 24 of the Act, which provides that in respect of arrestable offences:

1. Any person may arrest without warrant –
   (a) anyone who is in the act of committing an arrestable offence;
   (b) anyone whom he has reasonable grounds for suspecting to be committing such an offence.
2. Where an arrestable offence has been committed any person may arrest without warrant –
   (a) anyone who is guilty of the offence;
   (b) anyone whom he has reasonable grounds for suspecting to be guilty of it.

As will be noted these are the powers which were previously applicable through the common law to citizens and form the basis of the 'citizen's arrest' applicable both to the USA and England and Wales. The powers are slightly more confining than those provided for police officers, for in all cases they require that an arrestable offence, as defined, is actually being committed or has been committed. The element of reasonable suspicion attaches to the person suspected of the offence rather than the more general power given to police, where the reasonable suspicion relates both to the nature of the offence and to the suspect. The powers of arrest for constables are:

1. Where a constable has reasonable grounds for suspecting that an arrestable offence has been committed, he may arrest without warrant anyone whom he has reasonable grounds for suspecting to be guilty of the offence.
2. A constable may arrest without warrant –
   (a) anyone who is about to commit an arrestable offence;

(b) anyone whom he has reasonable grounds for suspecting to be about to commit an arrestable offence.

These powers are similar in their nature and effect to those generally applicable to felony arrests in the USA. Again, it is the case that the precise nature of powers will vary from state to state, the broad picture is that spelled out by Robin (1980, p. 30):

When victims or witnesses report crimes, the police may make a warrantless arrest for felonies if there is probable cause – rather than mere suspicion or a hunch – to conclude that a) a felony actually occurred and b) it was committed by the individual to be taken into custody.

Robin continues, however, to define the generally applicable powers of arrest *without* a warrant, for misdemeanours, by contrasting the nature of the reasonableness in the two categories of offence. He notes that:

In arresting suspected felons without a warrant, the officer's decision need only be *reasonable*, not one that is actually 'right' in retrospect ... so long as the 'reasonable person' would have concluded at the time of arrest that a felony had occurred and that the suspect taken into custody was the offender, the warrantless felony arrest was proper. In making a warrantless misdemeanour arrest in many jursdictions, however, the officer must be certain that the suspect committed a misdemeanour. In other words, the officer's decision to make a warrantless misdemeanour arrest must be a 'right' one.

Furthermore, it is generally the case that the law authorizes arrest in such cases only when the offence is committed in the presence of the officer – an insistence on the certainty of guilt – which is theoretically a much higher standard of proof, although in practice easily evaded.

By contrast, the power of arrest in England and Wales for offences other than arrestable offences – which is confined to police officers – still retains the reasonable suspicion in respect of both offence and suspect which, despite the definition of a number of 'arrest conditions' gives a power to police officers to take into custody any person for *any* offence including the most trivial of traffic offences. The power[8] provides that:

1. Where a constable has reasonable grounds for suspecting that any offence which is not an arrestable offence has been committed or attempted, or is being commited or attempted, he may arrest the relevant person if it appears to him that service of a summons is impractical or inappropriate because any of the general arrest conditions is satisfied.
2. In this section 'the relevant person' means any person whom the constable has reasonable grounds to suspect of having committed or having attempted to commit the offence or of being in the course of committing or attempting to commit it.

Nowhere in the Act is there a requirement that the offence should be committed in the presence of the officer and the arrest conditions noted above are as follows:

(a) that the name of the relevant person is unknown to, and cannot be readily ascertained by, the constable;

(b) that the constable has reasonable grounds for doubting whether the name furnished by the relevant person is his real name;

(c) that –

    (i) the relevant person has failed to furnish a satisfactory address for service (of a summons);

    (ii) the constable has reasonable grounds for doubting whether an address furnished by the relevant person is a satisfactory address for service;

(d) that the constable has reasonable grounds for believing that arrest is necessary to prevent the relevant person –

    (i) causing physical injury to himself or any other person;

    (ii) suffering physical injury;

    (iii) causing loss of or damage to property;

    (iv) committing an offence against public decency; or,

    (v) causing an unlawful obstruction of the highway;

(e) that the constable has reasonable grounds for believing that arrest is necessary to protect a child or other vulnerable person from the relevant person.

These powers, we suggest, are an example of the manner in which the legislators view the role of the police. In Britain, there is a good deal left to the discretion of individual officers and the apparent freedom provided by the list of 'arrest conditions' may be contrasted with the entirely more confining power of arrest applicable only in the 'found committing' or 'in his presence' condition. Such differences only served to reinforce the view that the controls exercised over American officers as a consequence of the constraints of the Bill of Rights are far more powerful than those restricting the behaviour of their colleagues in England and Wales.

The extent of the discretion allowed to British officers serves as a starting point to our argument that British police officers are a body that, by and large, conform to Wilson's model of 'watchman' but with an added service element, whilst the American officer matches more readily the legalistic/service paradigm.

We propose to examine this thesis further by comparing and contrasting police practices in a number of practical policing areas.

TREATMENT OF ACCUSED PERSONS – THE JUDGES' RULES AND THE SUPREME COURT

The Judges' Rules

Until the advent of the Police and Criminal Evidence Act 1984, rules of conduct and the admissibility of evidence, matters of real concern to the operational police officer, were contained in the Judges' Rules. These rules had no legal force and were more in the form of guidance for police in the areas of the admissibility of written confessions, and the process of investigation.

It is generally accepted that the origin of the Judges' Rules lies in a letter written by the Lord Chief Justice in 1906, in response to a request from the Chief Constable of Birmingham, for guidance on the 'cautioning' of people who had been arrested. In British legal parlance the word 'cautioning' has broadly the same meaning as the 'reading of rights' in American law. But as we shall discuss, the content and purpose of the process has differed in each country.

The advice given by the Lord Chief Justice confirmed the views expressed some time before that:

> A confession, to be admissible in court, must be made voluntarily and not as a result of any promise or threat, and the accused should be cautioned that 'he is not bound to say anything tending to incriminate himself, but that anything he says may be used against him.' (Wegg-Prossor, 1979)

Later, in 1964, a set of 'rules' drawn up by all the judges to the Queen's Bench Division *on their own* and without reference to the police or to practising or academic lawyers was announced in open court by the Lord Chief Justice and came into force three days later.

A Home Office circular, sent to all chief officers, and entitled, *The Judges' Rules and Administrative Directions on Interrogation and the Taking of Statements,* dealt, in addition, with such issues as the circumstances under which a person was entitled to access to a solicitor or to legal advice. The Rules were later added to by circulars in 1968, 1976 and 1977 which dealt with interviewing, fingerprinting and photographing, children and young persons, the sending of letters by people in custody, the special care needed in interviewing mentally handicapped people, and the need for interpreters when interviewing foreigners and the deaf.

Nevertheless, growing concern developed over the rights of suspects, the conduct of interviews and interrogations in police stations, and the general efficacy of the Judges' Rules. As Irving (1985) puts it: 'What legislation there is can, in a closed twenty-four-hour community, always be avoided.'

The Judges' Rules were not legislation, and Irving's comment was made in the light of the legislation produced as a consequence of The Royal Commission on Criminal Procedure (1981): the Police and Criminal Evidence Act 1984.

The new Act, in effect, brought into legislation the content of the Judges' Rules and has, with the exception of stopping short of producing an 'exclusionary rule', produced regulatory measures over the police (in exchange for a certain clarification of powers) which are similar in force to those Supreme Court decisions in respect of custody and incarceration: *Mallory, Escobedo* and *Miranda.*

THE SUPREME COURT – CONSTITUTIONAL CONSTRAINTS IN THE USA

In order to pursue this examination of police powers, a brief excursion into the constitutional limitations imposed on police in the USA as a consequence of these Supreme Court decisions will be undertaken before and after examination of the contents of the Police and Criminal Evidence Act.

The constitution

The constitutional issues which are applicable at this stage are:

The fifth amendment: which provides, amongst other things, that no person shall be compelled to be a witness against himself, and as such, is similar in nature to the longstanding 'right to silence' in British common law.

The sixth amendment: which provides for a person's right to be represented by counsel; this right exists at every stage during which the accused is in jeopardy[9] and includes interrogation in 'a police-dominated atmosphere'.[10]

The eighth amendment: which allows that people shall be free from cruel and unusual punishment; and

The fourteenth amendment: which makes all these notions binding *as the minimum standard* in all states through its 'due process' provision.

Constitutional cases

Mallory v. US

In *Mallory* v. *US*,[11] the Supreme Court declared that an arrested person should be taken before a magistrate without unnecessary delay. The defendant was a 19-year-old youth of limited intelligence who on his arrest for rape had been interrogated over a ten-hour period. He finally confessed to the crime after the steady interrogation of a police officer using a polygraph (lie detector).

The rationale for the court's decision was essentially that it wished to indicate its opposition to the incarceration of a person for a lengthy period *for the main purpose of securing a confession* to an offence prior to arraignment.

This case in effect declared the start of the so-called 'due process revolution' under Chief Justice Earl Warren, who had been appointed to the post in 1953. Other decisions, which attempted to provide guidelines for the police so that they would abide by the constitution whilst enforcing the substantive criminal law, were not long in coming.

Escobedo v. Illinois

The *Escobedo* v. *Illinois*[12] decision was a severe blow in police circles.

Following the arrest of Danny Escobedo for murder on what has been called 'fragmentary evidence' (Beckman, 1980), a refusal to allow a lawyer to see the accused was almost contemporaneous with Escobedo's making a full confession to the crime. (Evidence was later given that repeated requests for a 'conference' from both the lawyer and the accused were unsuccessful.)

Escobedo's lawyer appealed to the Supreme Court and in their decision the Court indicated that when Escobedo had been refused access to his lawyer his rights under the sixth amendment had been violated. The Court held that *in this case*:

1. The investigation was no longer a general enquiry into an unsolved crime but had begun to focus on a particular suspect.
2. The suspect had been taken into police custody.
3. The police had carried out a process of interrogation that lent itself to the eliciting of incriminating statements.
4. The suspect had requested and been denied the opportunity of consulting with his lawyer.
5. The police had not effectively warned the subject of his absolute right to silence.

Unfortunately, the decision was unclear on many points of practical application and it was not until 1966 that the Supreme Court had the opportunity to lay down some stringent guidelines for the conduct of a 'custodial interrogation occurring in a police-dominated atmosphere'. The question – 'when does a person shift from being "under investigation" to "being accused"?' was thus anticipated and dealt with.

Miranda v. Arizona

The case which finally firmly drew the battle-lines between the police and the judiciary was that of Ernesto Miranda who, in March 1963, was arrested and later charged with kidnap and rape. The charge followed two hours of concentrated questioning by two police officers and the consequently obtained confession was later subject of appeal to the Supreme Court.

The Court resolved to sort out the problems of the *Escobedo* decision and also to try to ensure that in future statements obtained from suspects during 'custodial interrogation' 'were truly the product of free choice'. As Robin (1980) puts it:

The major portion of the *Miranda* opinion is devoted to making and substantiating a single, critical point: regardless of the circumstances under which it occurs, regardless of who the examiners are, regardless of who the suspects are, custodial interrogation is inherently coercive. .... Custodial interrogation makes *any* statements obtained from suspects during this period 'compelled' and thus not 'voluntary beyond a reasonable doubt'.

The clash of police practice with the fifth amendment, 'that no person shall be compelled to be a witness against himself', led to the Court defining a series of safeguards which were spelled out in order to ensure that an individual's right against self-incrimination was upheld.

On any occasion when (a) a person is taken into custody, or (b) otherwise deprived of freedom of action in any significant way, and (c) is about to be subjected to custodial interrogation, the following safeguards are to be observed:

1. Prior to any questioning suspects must be warned, in clear and unmistakable terms, that they have the right to remain silent.
2. Prior to any questioning, suspects must be warned that anything they say can and will be used against them in a court of law.
3. To protect the fifth amendment privilege, prior to questioning, suspects must be clearly informed that they have the right to consult with counsel and to have counsel with them during interrogation.
4. Prior to questioning suspects must be told that if they cannot afford counsel, counsel will be appointed for them if they so desire.

Before attempting to draw some comparisons between the British 'cautioning' requirements and those just discussed a number of additional points must be made.

There are a number of exceptions to the 'safeguard' requirements noted above. *Miranda* warnings are not required when:

1. Statements to be obtained are not intended for use in court or needed to convict.
2. A person makes a completely unsolicited and uninvited statement to the police (a *volunteered* statement).
3. In general 'on the scene questioning' when the concern is with discovering the facts.
4. In street encounters including 'stop and frisk' (see below).
5. In routine 'standard questioning' matters: the completion of accident and incident reports.
6. The evidence sought is 'non-testimonial' in nature, i.e. utterances from the mouth of the accused. The warning is not therefore required when the evidence obtained relates to substances removed from the body, such as blood, even when the substance is obtained without the consent of the accused,[13] provided that the method of obtaining it does not 'shock the human conscience'.[14] This exception also covers fingerprinting, photographing, line-ups, voice prints, voice and handwriting identification, and 'being forced to speak' (Robin, 1980).

More recently (in *Quarles* v. *New York*, 1984), a controversial decision (the Supreme Court in a majority of 5–4), ruled that warnings were not necessary when 'public safety' is at stake. The question 'Where is the gun?' before warnings, which led to the subsequent recovery of a weapon used in evidence, was held to be admissible on grounds of public safety, not only because the accused might potentially make use of the gun but because an accomplice might do so or 'a customer or employee might later come upon it'.

CODE OF PRACTICE – CAUTIONING

The single most important factor for the future development of the law in England and Wales on all or any of the contents of the Act is the provision that 'grants a Power to the Home Secretary to issue *codes of practice*'. Although the codes of practice must be placed before Parliament and must therefore be approved by them, the fact is that changes in the law relating to the matters in the Act can (and will) be altered with a minimum of delay. Once the codes of practice have been approved by Parliament they may be brought into effect by statutory instrument.

The real teeth to this provision regarding codes of conduct, however, lie in section 67(8) of the Act which states that a police officer shall be liable to disciplinary proceedings for failure to comply with any provision of any such code unless proceedings are precluded by section 104 of the Act. The Code of Practice lays down for example that:

> A person whom there are grounds to suspect of an offence (other than a road traffic offence of strict liability) must be cautioned before any questions about it (or further questions if it is his answers to previous questions that provide grounds for suspicion) are put to him for the purpose of obtaining evidence which may be given in court in a prosecution.

The nebulosity of the phrase 'grounds to suspect' raises the problem (dealt with by the Supreme Court) as to the exact circumstances in which a person becomes a suspect. Rather than baldly stating that questions put in a police-dominated atmosphere *per se* requires specific warnings and the application of specific rights, the British Parliament has taken a less restrictive and more 'crime control' oriented position than the 'due process' position of the US Supreme Court.

According to the Codes of Practice, a person need not be cautioned if questions are put solely to establish his identity, his ownership of any vehicle, or the need to search him in the exercise of powers of stop and search.

Alternatively, a person the subject of a 'direct arrest' must be cautioned on arrest unless to do so would be impractical as a consequence of the person's condition or behaviour.

If further questions are to be put to the person after arrest, for the purpose of obtaining evidence, he must be reminded of his previous caution.

The Code lays down the words of the caution as follows:

> You do not have to say anything unless you wish to do so, but what you say may be given in evidence.

Minor verbal deviations are permissible provided that the sense of the caution is preserved.

The contrasts between this form of words and the requirements of 'Miranda' are significant.

First, in the caution there is no mention of the specific 'right to silence', only a form of words that implies its existence.

Secondly, the caution is worded in such a way that some discretion is given to the officer(s) regarding whether the reply will be given in evidence. This must be contrasted with the bold statement of the *Miranda* rules 'that anything they say can and will *"be used against them"* in a court of law'. Traditionally the British legal system has fought shy of the use of a form of words which implies that any words spoken by the accused are *automatically prosecution evidence*. It has been repeatedly argued that the *used against them* form of words may discourage an innocent person from making a statement that will declare and prove his innocence, particularly if that person is uncertain, or has difficulty in expressing him or herself.[15]

Thirdly, there is no mention of the provision of counsel.

However, the Police and Criminal Evidence Act declares that each police station in which prisoners are housed must be provided with a custody officer – a police officer (and thus subject to the Discipline Code provision noted above) whose job it is to look after the prisoners and to keep comprehensive records of their period of detention. The custody officer is obliged (by the Code of Conduct) to inform the accused person immediately on his arrival at the station that:

1. He has a right to legal advice.
2. That he has a right to have someone informed of his detention.
3. That he has a right to examine and consult the Codes of Practice.

He must also provide the person with a written copy of those rights.

1. All such requests must be recorded.
2. Consultation with a solicitor and to have someone informed of his/her arrest must be permitted as soon as practicable and in any case within 36 hours.

Delay in acceding to the request *immediately* may occur in the case of a person arrested for a serious arrestable offence *and* if an officer of at least the rank of superintendent authorizes it. Such delay may only be up to 36 hours.[16]

The delay in providing consultation with a solicitor or communication with a friend may be undertaken for a number of reasons, i.e. if to allow immediate consultation will:

1. Lead to interference with or harm to evidence connected with a serious arrestable offence or interference with or physical injury to other persons, or
2. Will lead to the alerting of other persons suspected of having committed such an offence but not yet arrested for it, or
3. Will hinder the recovery of any property obtained as a result of such an offence.

In the event that the person desires a solicitor but has none of his own he will be provided with a list of duty solicitors from which he may select an individual at random to speak on his behalf.

As in the *Miranda* rules, if such a request is made during questioning the questioning must stop until the request has been dealt with.

THE CUSTODY OFFICER

The role of the custody officer is to ensure that the Code of Conduct and the content of the Act are abided by. As such he is required to make records of any and all events in respect of persons in his care and in particular to ensure that requests for persons to be informed. Another major role is to ensure that the person is not detained in custody for lengthy periods without justification. As a general rule no person may be detained 'without charge' for more than 24 hours.

In any case, in a complex process, the authority of senior police officers is required to detain a person for 'extended periods' (more than six hours and with review periods every nine hours thereafter) up to a maximum of 36 hours. (The normal period of detention without charge being limited to 24 hours.)

After 36 hours the authority of a magistrates court is required for detention for a further 36 hours. A final application may then be made to the magistrates court for a warrant authorizing an additional period of detention up to *the total permissible maximum* period of detention of 96 hours.

Such applications and extensions by police beyond the 24-hour limit may only occur as long as:

1. The detention of that person without charge is necessary to secure or preserve evidence relating to an offence for which he is under arrest or to obtain such evidence by questioning him.
2. An offence for which he is under arrest is a serious arrestable offence.
3. The investigation is being conducted diligently and expeditiously.

CONFESSIONS

Just as the concern in the US Supreme Court in *Mallory* (354 US 499 (1957)) was essentially that it wished to indicate 'an opposition to the incarceration of a person for a lengthy period *for the main purpose of securing a confession* to an offence prior to arraignment', so the British Parliament has seen fit to create legislation that, for perhaps the very first time, seeks to 'police the police'.

Just as the Supreme Court devoted the major portion of the *Miranda* opinion to making and substantiating 'a single, critical point regarding the nature of custodial interrogation', so Parliament has included in the Police and Criminal Evidence Act *laws* which supersede the old Judges' Rules regarding the obtaining of confessions.

Section 76 of the Police and Criminal Evidence Act has sought to clarify the law relating to the admissibility of confessions through a number of measures.

First, the Act defines for the first time what is meant by 'confession'. The word is defined as meaning 'any statement wholly or partly adverse to the person who made it, whether made to a person in authority or not and whether made in words or otherwise.' Secondly, the Act details the circumstances in which such a confession will be inadmissible in evidence.

INADMISSIBILITY

If it is claimed in court (by the defence) that a confession which the prosecution intends to produce was obtained by:

1. The oppression of the person,[17] or
2. The confession was obtained as a consequence of things done or said which was likely to render the confession *unreliable*

then, unless the prosecution is able to prove otherwise, the confession will be excluded.

Alternatively, the court may require, of its own volition, that the prosecution establish that the confession was not so obtained.

However, the provision that even when such a confession has been excluded, evidence obtained as a consequence of it will still be admissible, in marked contrast to the power of the US exclusionary rule discussed in Chapter 3 which makes no distinction between one source of tainted evidence and another.

The most fundamental change in this piece of legislation is the shift from 'voluntariness' to 'reliability' as the test for admissibility.

The *Miranda* rules in the USA, their subsequent erosion,[18] and the case law which surrounds them were nevertheless an attempt to ensure the *voluntary* nature of any confession obtained. But what about the manipulation of the psychological aspects of interrogation?

In its concern to concentrate on the reliability of any confession, Parliament may well have laid the ground for a series of cases which challenge the reliability of statements – apparently made voluntarily – which are none the less produced through some form of psychological manipulation. Is any question put in a police-dominated atmosphere likely always to produce a 'reliable' answer – the US Supreme Court felt that the answer was not likely to be voluntary.

In the quest for 'reliability', the Code of Practice, in an effort to restrict the police from obtaining 'confessions' from suspects by duress or 'oppression' has required that all interviews with those suspected of crime shall be 'contemporaneously recorded'. Although there is the intention to implement the tape-recording of interrogations as a common practice, most, if not all, interrogations are carried on without that facility available. The officers must, in order to comply with the instructions, write down, in long hand, all questions and answers and other conversation *as they occur*.

In 1979 in an English study undertaken in the Brighton police force, Irving (1980) was able to show that most if not all the techniques discussed and considered by Inbau and Reid (1967) were used by officers in eliciting confessions and while conducting interviews.

In 1986, in a replication of the earlier research, McKenzie and Irving (1987) noted that the contemporaneous note-taking requirement had not only all but destroyed the skills of the officers under observation, but that interviews took a significantly longer time even though far less information was gathered.

In the USA, Manuals of Interrogation (e.g. Inbau and Reid, 1967) which concentrate on the psychological manipulation of the interrogation have led Zimbardo (1967) to write:

> It is my professional opinion as a psychologist concerned with the experimental modification of attitudes and behaviour, that current police techniques present a highly sophisticated application of psychological principles which for many are more compelling and coercive than physical torture. Any catalogue of current (psychological) interrogation techniques would show a debasement of human nature and stands as a disgraceful slur on the American system of justice.

There is to date only one manual of the Inbau and Reid type in the UK (Walkley, 1976) although some police forces are developing courses on interrogation techniques. But, in the absence of tape-recorders, any effort to manipulate interpersonal relationships (Danziger, 1976) is potentially doomed to failure. Not only that, where the accused person denies the offence there is little opportunity for any kind of technique to be used in order to seek the truth. That may well have been the intention of the British Parliament, but when the requirements of the code appear to mean, in effect, that allegations by individuals which depend on accounts of events as their main if not sole evidence (e.g. allegations of incest or other sexual offences or child abuse by the victim) can simply be denied by the accused – and that is the end of it, for an admission will rarely be obtained through interrogation, it may be felt that the controls have gone too far.

Parliament may just have restricted, if not prevented, a British psychologist expressing a similar view to that of Zimbardo. But at what cost?

STOP AND SEARCH

Prior to the existence of the Police and Criminal Evidence Act, police powers to stop and search suspects in England and Wales were uncertain as they were based on local legislation which differed from place to place and ranged downward from a strong power in London which allowed an officer to:

> stop, search and detain any vessel boat cart or carriage, in or upon which he had reasonable grounds to suspect anything stolen or unlawfully obtained was being conveyed in any manner or any person reasonably suspected or having or conveying such property in such a manner.

The somewhat archaic language of the provision is not surprising since the source of the power is section 66 of the Metropolitan Police Act 1839. The power applied only to London and although some of the larger cities had similar powers, many areas were left with no substantive power and the necessity for some legal 'distinguishing' to be undertaken to find what amounted to somewhat doubtful powers in some circumstances.

The new Act repealed all former stop and search powers and replaced them with a new power.

Before outlining the provisions of the Police and Criminal Evidence Act a brief excursion into the stop and frisk: street interrogation rules in the USA is called for.

Stop and frisk in the USA

Routine 'field interrogation' may take place on the basis that there is reasonable suspicion that the subject has just committed, is committing, or is about to commit, a felony or a misdemeanour defined in penal law. Typically state codes provide that an officer may demand the person's name and address and an explanation of his behaviour (New York Criminal Procedure, 1979). There is, at this stage, no authority to search.

If during the course of the 'stop' phase the officer has reasonable grounds to suspect that he is in danger of physical injury, he may search that person for any instrument, article or substance readily capable of causing serious physical injury and of a sort not ordinarily carried in public places by law abiding persons. *The 'search' is, however, confined to a pat down of outer clothing.* Continued questioning, etc., might then produce evidence of probable cause and justify an arrest.

Again beset by case law, the legal status of stop and frisk was established by the Supreme Court in *Terry* v. *Ohio*,[19] which laid down the circumstances in which the stop and frisk provisions could take place and defined that the rationale for the frisk is for the protection of the officer and others in the area 'in an attempt to discover weapons with which to assault him'.

After arrest warrantless searches may be conducted of the person's garments and the surface of his body and of vehicles within which the arrested person might readily reach for a weapon or other sizeable item.

THE POLICE AND CRIMINAL EVIDENCE ACT PROVISIONS

In public places and in certain circumstances on private property (i.e. a person unlawfully found in a yard or garden) a constable

1. may search –
   (a) any person or vehicle
   (b) anything which is in or on a vehicle, for stolen or prohibited articles; an 1
2. may detain any person or vehicle for the purpose of such a search.

Prohibited articles include offensive weapons and items such as house-breaking implements, the equipment for stealing motor cars, and items that will assist in 'obtaining property by deception'.

The Code of Practice

The Code of Practice indicates that the stop must be made on reasonable suspicion that *articles* of a particular kind are being carried.

The Code lays down comprehensive guidelines for the conduct of the stop and search; in particular that, although more complete searching may take place out of the view of the public, i.e. in a police van or car – the search in the street is 'a superficial examination of outer clothing'. There is no power to require a person to remove any clothing in public other than an outer coat, jacket or gloves. A more thorough search, e.g. asking someone to take off a tee-shirt or a hat, must be done out of public view. Comprehensive searches must be undertaken by a person of the same sex as the person being searched and may not be made in the presence of any one of the opposite sex.

There are special provisions for intimate body searches, which must take place at police stations under medical supervision; for the recording of such matters; and the information to be provided to the person who has been searched regarding the circumstances, etc.

DISCUSSION

As we have seen, the provisions of the Police and Criminal Evidence Act, at least in the area of the incarceration of prisoners and the obtaining of confessions, have moved British law nearer to the US model although there still remain marked variations.

But it is in the area of 'stop and frisk' and 'stop and search' that the most fundamental *difference* occurs.

In many ways the Police and Criminal Evidence Act has provided in legislation, for the first time, a 'Bill of Rights' that spells out for the individual the expectations he may have about the process, method and practice of his incarceration and questioning, etc. However, Parliament stopped short of providing for the individual the 'cover' provided by the fourth amendment of protection against unreasonable searches *prior to arrest*.

Certain US cases[20] confirm that search after 'custodial arrest' is not a contravention of rights, an area about which there is no dispute in the UK. The major difference in these cases of search pre-arrest and those under British law is the extent to which the officer making the stop is free to conduct the search and the rationale for that action.

The British police officer, like his American colleague, must have 'reasonable suspicion'; but 'reasonable suspicion' of what? For the British officer reasonable suspicion relates to the *possession of articles* rather than the circumstances of their use. The reasonable suspicion for the British officer will be with regard to the possession of stolen or prohibited articles which include offensive weapons, house-breaking implements, the equipment for stealing motor cars, and items that will assist in 'obtaining property by deception'.

For the American officer the search is limited to reasonable suspicion *that a felony or misdemeanour* has been committed, is being committed or is about to be committed, and the 'frisk' is ancillary to that, on the grounds of self-protection, 'for any instrument, article or substance readily capable of causing serious physical injury'.

Allegations have been frequently made that British officers used the previous stop and search law (Metropolitan Police Act, etc.) as a vehicle for harassing individuals, particularly members of minority ethnic groups. The Code of Practice thus draws attention to two factors: (a) the abuse of stop and search powers in the past, and (b) definitions of what *is not* reasonable suspicion.

The Code of Practice reads:

> Statistics on the use of powers to stop and search indicate that in most cases no such article was found, and there is strong evidence that on many occasions these powers have been used where reasonable grounds to suspect the individual concerned of having the article in question on him did not in fact exist. There is also strong evidence that such misuse has played an important part in the mistrust of the police among certain sections of the community. (Stop and Search 1b)

In defining what is not 'reasonable suspicion' the Code states at Annex B:

> a person's colour of itself can never be a reasonable ground for suspicion, and young blacks should not be stopped and searched on the basis that statistics show that they have a higher than average chance of being involved in arrests for certain types of offences. The mere fact that a person is carrying a particular kind of property or is dressed in a certain way or has a certain hairstyle is likewise not of itself sufficient ...
>
> The degree or level of suspicion required to establish the reasonable grounds justifying the exercise of powers of stop and search is no less that the degree or level of suspicion required to effect an arrest without a warrant for any of the suspected offences to which these powers relate.

None the less it is clear that the American officer stops on reasonable suspicion of crime, *a felony or misdemeanour,* the British officer stops on reasonable suspicion that he will find the person in possession of stolen or prohibited *articles:* i.e. the US officer acts after a crime has been committed and for self-protection; while the British officer acts to prevent crime or to recover property and then to prosecute.

It is argued, therefore, that the 'reasonable suspicion' for the US officer relates to 'legalistic issues' of a law enforcement nature, while that for the British officer relates to crime prevention and control issues.

The stop and search/frisk provisions are typical of the differing stances that the legislators of the two nations take. Because the American legislators expect that their police will be 'more free-wheeling and aggressive' (Reiner, 1985) or that they will be 'vigilantes' operating on behalf of the population (Miller, 1977), the legislation and the interpretation of it by the judiciary are reflective of the anticipation that police excesses or over-enthusiasm will need to be curbed.

The British style is more relaxed and, in line with a 'crime control' model, deals with minor infractions as they occur and in accordance with the specific detail of them.[21]

THE STYLE OF POLICING – A NATIONAL ANALYSIS

Traditionally, the relationship between the law enforcement, order maintenance and public service functions of policing has been graphically defined as a continuum along which an operational police officer moves depending on the situation in which he finds himself, selecting eventually the appropriate 'style' – legalistic, watchman or service (see Fig. 7.1) – which fits the circumstances.

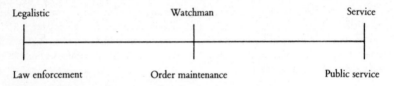

Figure 7.1 The 'Continuum' model of police functions and styles.

This model is often used to define the difference between 'hard' and 'soft' policing and in describing the behaviour of one officer *at any given moment,* or a police department's philosophy in a 'slice of time', such a one-dimensional model is perfectly adequate. But by presenting a complex piece of human behaviour on a continuum of discrete units, it conjures up a simplistic picture of police activity. It is not really a case of either/or, but a balancing act between the components. The balance will shift over time and variations in individual psychology or departmental politics and policies will make it something altogether more dynamic.

Although Wilson (1968) was able to describe the overall effect of policing in a particular city as being in one category or another, by his own admission (Wilson, 1968, p. 13) the cities are not typical of American cities, neither are they atypical: 'they were chosen *because* of their differences' (emphasis added). Furthermore he argues (Wilson, 1968, Ch. 9) that much of the style of the police department is a consequence of the discretionary behaviour of the patrol officer, albeit manipulated by executive decisions and policy. But discretionary behaviour is not an either/or behaviour, it is a complex, multifaceted exercise in which the officer balances his own attitudes and values against his perception of the attitudes and values of the society in which he works. The balance at any one time is as much a matter of the officer's perceptions of the public's *expectations* of his role as it is of departmental philosophies.

It has been consistently argued throughout this book that the dynamics which produce the policing style *of a nation* are related to the psychology, sociology and history of the nation under study. It is argued that in addition to these undoubtedly important aspects, the nature of the process of law-making, the interpretation of the law and the *expectations* (based on past experience) about police behaviour and style on the part of the legislators, the judiciary and the public, also have a marked effect on the overall behaviour of police.

Undoubtedly Wilson (1968) was right in defining certain *police departments* as being typically legalistic, watchman or service-oriented. In the same way we have argued that *individual police officer* style may be identified on similar parameters with the proviso that personal 'shifts' in style can occur, and that, like individual personality, *individual* policing style is dynamic.

The problem of defining the style of a *nation* is no different. The overall paradigm of the process and practice of the police of the two countries under discussion is, it is felt, better described by a two-dimensional model which allows movement in two defined but separate areas and which sees the public service function not as the end of a continuum, but as placed orthogonally to the continuum of law enforcement and order maintenance as in Fig. 7.2.

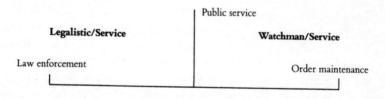

Figure 7.2 The two-dimensional 'balance' model of policing.

Because by definition it must be a generalization, national, 'big picture' policing style is less obviously dynamic than that of an individual officer or even a single city. For this reason we argue that, despite the fact that one may find, as Wilson did, individual and municipal variation, the *overall* practice and expectation in American policing is that typified by a balance between the law enforcement (due process/legalistic) and public service functions, while that of the police in England and Wales is typified by a balance between order maintenance (crime control/watchman) and public service. There are, to be sure, order maintenance policing styles in some American cities but it is entirely possible that Wilson's were 'slice-of-time' observations, the classification of which may have resulted more from contemporary societal factors (which in their turn dictated politically and self-protectively expedient measures), than from any *ongoing* policy imperatives.

Wilson's observations took place in the 1960s at the height of a civil rights/black consciousness movement. In Newberg, one of the 'watchman' cities, Wilson cites an officer as saying that the 'relatively few' arrests of blacks and prostitutes was because, 'the word has come down from the top that we're to lay off the coloured community. With all this Black Power talk, people are afraid of an incident . . . we don't want to make them mad at us' (p. 149). And in any case, as Wilson notes, (p. 149n) that in a stylistic typology *of departments*

> ... no one should assume that these are the only police styles or that every police department in the country displays one or the other of them. I assume if enough departments were studied that one would probably learn of other styles in addition to these and that one would certainly learn that many, if not most, departments display a combination of two or more styles.

We suggest that despite the fact that there may be individual and municipal variation, there is, nevertheless, a 'national character' to policing, which is in large measure determined by the character of the nation itself.

SUMMARY

Put in another way, the *expectations* of the legislators, the courts (who administer the 'due process' model of law), and of the public, are that the style of the American 'cop' is of a legalistic/service nature, and that, as a consequence, his work is to be surrounded by *procedural* rules of law which require him of necessity to think of himself as a *law enforcement* officer. On the other hand, expectations of his British counterpart by Parliament, the courts (who administer the 'crime control' model of law) and the public, are of a watchman/service style. Largely unencumbered by procedural rules (until the Police and Criminal Evidence Act 1984) and merely given advice and guidance (viz. the Judges' Rules), such an expectation leads the British officer to think of himself as a part of the police *service*.

The legalistic/service role in American policing

We have shown that in the history (law enforcement following the pioneers); in the legislatures (laws are concerned with strongly legalistic issues not, by and large, order maintenance/crime prevention issues); in the courts (due process rather than crime control); and in the very nature of the ethnic and cultural mix of the USA and in a huge concern regarding issues of the constitutionality of police behaviour and the role of police in a democracy, the nation's police are expected to enforce the law first and provide help and assistance second.

In a recent case, California police officers who were called to a bar to end a disturbance were held *not* to be liable for failing to provide emergency medical assistance to people found injured. The court stated that such an obligation only arose when the police caused the injuries or caused the parties to rely on their help. 'They have no obligation to offer assistance to injured people who are not arrested.'[22]

It is hard to imagine the upsurge of feeling that would occur in the UK if any officer failed to provide medical assistance to a member of the public in similar circumstances. He or she would most certainly be dealt with under the Police Discipline Code (see Chapter 6) and would probably be dismissed from the force. In the absence of an understanding of the culture in which policing operates the failure of an officer to provide medical assistance to a member of the public is as difficult to comprehend as 'how you can do it without guns?' or 'how you can have guns and not use them?'.

None of this of course denies the empirical evidence that as much as 70–85 per cent of police time on *both* sides of the Atlantic is spent in dealing with non-crime-related matters. There *is* a service role to American policing. But the dynamics are a constant shift of emphasis within the left quadrant of Fig. 7.2, the *balancing* of a legalistic, law enforcement style with a public service/social role style. But, as Johnson et al. (1981) point out, 'the myth of the fight against crime as the sole element of the police responsibility is accepted by the typical citizen and *by the bulk of working police personnel* in the USA' (emphasis added).

The fight against crime becomes a battle against criminal activity, which is not the same thing. The fight against crime is a prevention/crime control philosophy: the battle against criminal activity is a *post hoc,* individual and enforcement philosophy. The latter, it is suggested, produces the 'freewheeling more aggressive style of policing' (Reiner, 1986).

Such a belief, not surprisingly, colours expectations of future performance and perceptions of past performance and the 'law enforcement' element is reinforced and expanded. Placed against a background of public fear of police/governmental power, the development of externally imposed rules (Supreme Court decisions) this is to be expected. Consequently the 'legalistic/service' role develops and flourishes.

The order maintenance versus service role in British policing

In the United Kingdom the history of watchman-type policing, the crime control rather than due process content of judicial decisions, the acceptance of a social role for the police from its inception (for whatever reason), the values and attitudes of a society prepared to tolerate a high level of government involvement in their lives, and a strong insistence still that 'The primary aims and duties of the ... police are to uphold the Rule of Law, to protect and assist the citizen and to work for the prevention of detection of crime and the maintenance of a peaceful society' (Metropolitan Police, 1985), lead British police officers to a different perception of their policing role from their American colleagues.

Thus, the nature of national policing in the UK is typified by a balance within the right quadrant of Fig. 7.2: the maintenance of 'the Queen's Peace' with a strong service role element.

There is, it should be noted, movement in England and Wales towards the legalistic/service role, and many officers would like to see such a movement occur with more haste. The increasing existence of outright hostility to the police from certain communities, allegations of racism and overt criminal activity is stretching the patience of many officers who see such law-breaking take place and are impatient to deal with it at whatever cost to the peace. It is nevertheless the case that concentration on the watchman/service role gives, and has given since the time of Robert Peel, policing its unique flavour throughout the country. It remains to be seen if such a stance can be maintained.

The consequence of a movement towards a more legalistic style in the UK is that the legislators are responding in much the same way as they did in the USA.

The advent of the Police and Criminal Evidence Act 1984 may have an unexpected result. It may be the first concrete step towards the creation of a policing style – this time dictated by society (or at least Parliament acting on its behalf) – which will be more law enforcement than watchman-oriented. As we have seen, police behaviour affects legislators and vice versa, and, by and large, the old police saying still holds good: 'The public get the kind of police they want' (or in some areas, 'the police they deserve').

In this case, of course, it is what the parliamentarians want. Whether what they want is actually effective is, of course, still an open question.

CHAPTER 8

Firearms and Police – The Right to Bear Arms?

In March 1986 newspapers around the world carried a shocking photograph. It was of a British police officer at Heathrow Airport openly resting across his chest a 9 mm fully-automatic Heckler and Koch MP5 machine-gun. The presence of armed officers at Heathrow was nothing new. What was new was the openness with which the armed preparedness of the British police was being demonstrated to the public. Within days response from both inside and outside the police service was forceful. An editorial in *Police*,[1] the official journal of the Police Federation, noted that:

> The deployment of uniformed police officers at Heathrow and Manchester Airports is the latest manifestation of a nation-wide trend towards a more overtly armed police service. The domestic and international image is being altered forever. Far-reaching and irreversible changes are being made at great speed and without consulting the majority of policemen, let alone the public. The process by which these important decisions are being made is not as logical as the decision makers would have us believe.

The appearance of this 'high-profile image' was a response to two terrorist attacks, at Rome and Vienna airports, only days before. But, according to Yardley (1986, p. 20), an ex-soldier and firearms expert, and not a police officer, it was a mistaken and ill-advised response: 'At the most obvious level because walking around in uniform and carrying a sub-machine gun is akin to walking around with a target pinned to you.' And, at a less obvious level, because the weapon itself was 'thoroughly unsuitable even if one does accept the need for overt para-militaries' (Yardley, 1986, p. 20).

These two points typify the dilemma of British policing. On the one hand, there is a growing need for some 'highly visible' response, which at one and the same time satisfies public concern and also ensures that police officers will be armed with something more than the traditional baton or truncheon when faced with the growing terrorist threat, the increased use of firearms in pursuit of crime, and the general deterioration of relationships between the police and certain sectors of the population. On the other hand, though, the selection of such a powerful weapon which, according to Yardley (p. 21), 'demands the highest level of skill on the part of the user' and was described by Mr Colin Greenwood, a former police superintendent and firearms expert, as creating a situation 'where the Metropolitan Police are more dangerous than the terrorists',[2] throws into sharp focus the level of qualification achieved by the officers who respond to those threats by becoming 'authorized shots'.

This kind of ineffectual attempt to maintain tradition, pacify the public, and at the same time appear to provide a 'professional' response was summed up by Mr Leslie Curtis, Chairman of the Police Federation, who told a meeting of police officers:[3]

> It is perfectly absurd to make a high profile public announcement that a police unit, permanently armed, will perform anti-terrorist duties at Heathrow, and, in the same announcement to attempt to reassure the public by pointing out that the automatic weapons carried by these police officers may only be fired by them using the single shot operation, and that they must be fired from the shoulder ... It is incongruous to attempt to deal with the world's worst killers with the world's most pacific police force.

But the world's most pacific police force, and their carrying of firearms, has become a matter of public concern. Not simply because of terrorism or responses to it, not even because of the suitability or otherwise of particular weapons but because of evidence of an increased use of firearms by the police, coupled with a growing number of incidents in which innocent people have been shot by the police.

On the 14 January 1983, Mr Stephen Waldorf, an innocent man, was shot by two police officers and severely injured. He had been mistaken for an armed suspect for whom the officers were searching.[4] A total of fourteen shots was fired by the three officers involved; the third only firing at the tyres of the vehicle. In 1985, armed officers seeking to arrest a man involved in crime and who was reputed to be in possession of firearms entered a house in the Brixton area of south London. During the entry a single shot was fired, seriously injuring Cherry Groce.[5] On 24 August 1985, in Birmingham, an officer who with other armed colleagues was searching a house for a wanted man accidentally discharged his weapon and killed John Shorthouse, aged five.

In what is essentially a 'non-gun culture', the death and injury of innocent people at the hands of the police becomes a matter of acute concern. But the concern is redoubled when researchers began to unearth figures which showed that the level of arms-carrying in a traditionally unarmed police force was at a surprisingly high level. Reiner (1985) notes for example:

> There has been a rapid proliferation of firearms use by the police in Britain although unarmed (apart from the traditional truncheon) on routine patrol, the number of occasions on which firearms are issued to the police has escalated inexorably. In 1970 firearms were issued to the police on 1072 occasions, whereas in 1978 this happened 7462 times.

The 'inexorable escalation' continued beyond 1978. The *Sunday Times* calculated in 1983 that 'guns are issued to police about twenty times a day' (Molyneux, 1985, p. 193).[6]

The estimate was based on figures provided by the Home Office, and related to 'the number of occasions on which one or more firearms were issued in connection with a particular incident involving criminals or other persons known or believed to be armed' (Molyneux, 1985, p. 192) and are (Metropolitan Police figures in brackets):

1980	1981	1982
7275 (5968)	6149 (4983)	7952 (6063)

Following the shooting of Stephen Waldorf, acknowledged as a case in which 'Professionalism, declared policy and training failed',[7] a thorough examination of firearms use and training took place. At the instigation of the Association of Chief Police Officers (ACPO) the Joint Standing Committee on Police Use of Firearms made recommendations in these areas. Since that report was published in November 1983 it is unlikely that the content of it had any effect on the figures for that year. In any case, from that time on, comparison with previous years becomes difficult because the Home Office changed (or appeared to change) the content of their data-base. Figures from 1983 on are on the basis of the number of *operations* in which guns were issued – and show a dramatic fall from previous data.

National figures from 1983 were (Metropolitan figures in brackets): 3180 (2230). By 1984 the national figure had fallen to 2677, fallen again in 1985 to 2488, and by 1986 had fallen slightly to 2453.

The shift from calculation on the basis of 'occasions' to 'operations' makes comparison difficult. Was there really a fall of more than 50 per cent between 1982 and 1983? What is more likely is that the procedures for 'signing out' guns, required for British officers, were tightened. Prior to 1983, and certainly prior to the setting up of a specialist unit to protect royalty and diplomats in 1983, a surprisingly large number of armed static protection posts were covered in London, often by qualified ordinary duty officers from local police stations.[8] Officers filling these posts were drawn from ordinary duty and covered the post of 24 hours in three shifts. Each armed officer would therefore sign for his weapon as an individual entry in the log. At least three such entries would be made in a day; more if officers worked shorter than eight-hour shifts. Each of these entries would be an 'occasion'. The requirement for 'authorization' by a senior officer probably means that each 'authorization', regardless of the number of weapons it involves, is treated as one entry.

There is, to say the least, a problem of interpretation of these data. But, in view of more recent events than those discussed above, the level of public concern remains high. In 1987, the shooting by police officers of four armed robbers (in three different incidents) and of a man armed with a shotgun following a lengthy chase, require a satisfactory indication, to those who are concerned, of the precise level of police armament today. Furthermore, the rampage through the streets of a small Berkshire village by Michael Ryan in August 1987 during which he shot and killed fourteen people, including an unarmed on-duty police officer, but which provoked allegations of a tardy police response,[9] brought into sharp focus the regulations controlling the private ownership of weapons in England and Wales.

Before examining those rules and the conditions under which police are issued with firearms we propose to take a short trip back into history to examine the veracity of the image of the 'traditionally unarmed' police officer in the UK and the 'always armed/trigger-happy' notion about his American counterpart.

AN HISTORICAL DIGRESSION

The somewhat surprising starting point is to note that for the first forty years of organized policing in the USA, like their British counterparts, American officers were *never* armed with revolvers. But the enshrining of the 'right to bear arms' in the second amendment to the American Constitution rapidly changed all that.

The 'right of the people to keep and bear arms' (although originally intended to ensure 'the security of a free State' through a 'well-regulated militia') soon led to criminals carrying firearms, especially hand-guns, and to some policemen, unofficially, carrying concealed small-calibre pistols. Ultimately, as Lee (1971) puts it, 'crime in the streets challenged the very longevity of . . . policemen', and so in the 1880s Boston adopted the revolver for the protection of its officers.

By 1895 the New York City Police Department had chosen the .32 calibre revolver to arm its uniformed officers – not its detectives, who were not armed until some years later. The choice of the .32 rather than the more usual (these days) .38 calibre weapons was, perhaps, a deliberate attempt to keep the level of response to criminal activity at as low a profile as possible and not to encourage escalation to the more powerful weapons on both sides – inevitable though it was to become.

It is the 'low-profile' argument that still largely holds sway in the discussion on arming British police officers. At present only about 10 per cent of the total strength of UK forces are trained to handle firearms. Currently about 12,000 of the 121,550[10] serving officers are authorized 'shots'. No officer is permitted to retain a personal issue of an official weapon; and, despite the fact that he may be legally authorized to possess a weapon in his private capacity (subject to the same legal requirements as any other citizen), he must sign for both the issue and return of any gun, and undertake regular 're-classification'.

Despite the data quoted above, the actual carrying of firearms by on-duty officers in England and Wales is very limited. According to the former Commissioner of the Metropolitan Police, Sir Kenneth Newman, 'less than 1 per cent of the force in London is likely to be armed at any given moment'.[11] More recently, in November 1987, the Chief Constable of Merseyside (Liverpool) declared that 'not one officer in the force is patrolling with a gun at the present time'.[12]

In general it will be seen that the traditionally unarmed British 'bobby' continues to be the rule.[13]

But it nearly was not so.

On 19 October 1867,[14] the *Illustrated London News* reported that officers of the Metropolitan Police were practising cutlass drill in Wellington barracks, an army establishment in central London. This training had been initiated because of the 'increase in murderous attacks' on police officers in the early days of 'Fenian fury'.

The training was for constables but later extended to sergeants and inspectors.

The reporter for the *Illustrated London News* may have missed a major scoop.

On 16 October 1883, in a letter from the Home Office to the Receiver of the Metropolitan Police, comment was made that the Secretary of State had approved the training of 931 constables employed on night-shift, 'in the exterior sub-divisions of exterior divisions' to be authorized to possess firearms whilst on duty. They were to be issued with a lighter model of weapon '*to replace the 1867 issue*'!

On 30 June 1884, a force Police Order gave instructions to the force regarding the issue of firearms to police 'for more effectual protection'. The weapons were to be issued 'only to officers on night duty who can be trusted to use them with discretion'. They would be issued only on application and were for use 'only for self-defence'. A practice that was to continue for many years.[15]

By 1939, in the face of an impending invasion by Germany, 3500 rifles were held in 185 police stations in London, but with the end of World War II the practice of regular issue to officers on nights ceased although the keeping of weapons available at stations has continued.

FIREARMS USE BY POLICE

The Police Federation in the UK has, over the last few years, mounted two separate but linked campaigns. The first determined to improve the training and skills of their members and the second seeking to persuade the legislators that changes in the laws regarding private possession of firearms should be tightened.

England and Wales – the need for training

Although, in the period 1983 to 1986, offences involving violence to the person involving the use of firearms remained relatively static at about 700 per year in London, the figure for robberies involving firearms during the same period rose from 748 in 1980 to 1333 in 1983.[16] A total of nearly 8400 crimes involving firearms was recorded in England and Wales in 1984. In 1986 it was announced that the number of armed robberies in England and Wales had risen from 2104 in 1983 to 2696 in 1985.[17]

These figures provoked the Police Federation into a stance that the availability of arms was of fundamental importance to police but at one and the same time supported the view expressed by Wegg-Prossor (1979) who wrote:

Fears have been expressed that the traditional policy of the Home Office and the police will be altered by reason of the need to provide armed guards for embassies, or because arms are issued to police in special circumstances more often than they were in the past. However, the British police, unlike their colleagues in most countries, will continue to be unarmed. *This is the wish of the public and the police themselves,* although it does mean that from time to time an unarmed policeman will find himself facing an armed and desperate criminal, and policemen may be killed or maimed in the future as there have been in the past. [emphasis added]

But, in the face of increases in criminal activity involving weapons and figures for police possession of weapons which (apparently) show an increase,[18] what is the level of actual use by officers?

POLICE FIREARMS USE

The contrast of data from the USA and England and Wales in this area is so stark that it almost becomes meaningless. Indeed, Wright et al. (1983) are sceptical that such comparisons have any internal validity. They argue that it is virtually impossible to draw valid conclusions without taking into account differences in the collection of crime data and the political, cultural, racial, religious and economic disparities among countries. Such factors, they say, 'are not only tough to compare, they are rarely if ever taken into account'.

The differences between the British culture, which despite increases in the numbers of armed robberies remains an essentially unarmed one, and the 'American fascination with the gun', Parker (1985, p. 198) and its consequent effect on the nature of policing[19], are enormous. But for all that we will continue with the examination.

Police firearms use in England and Wales

In 1980 British police officers fired their guns at ten incidents, in 1981 at four incidents, and in 1982, again at ten incidents. In 1983 guns were used at four incidents. More recently (in 1985) guns were fired by police at seven incidents throughout the year; while in 1986 the figure for gun use was five.

Officers are required by regulations to report any occasion on which their weapon is removed from its holster and this was done on 135 occasions in 1985, and 151 in 1986.

Police firearms use in the United States of America

By contrast, research conducted for this book[20] shows that in New York City during 1983 there were 283 incidents involving the *use* of firearms by police (1.22 incidents per 100 sworn officers), a statistic that supports the finding of researchers for the Police Executive Research Forum (PERF, 1978) that in a survey of 45 police departments policing areas varying in size from populations of 500,000+ to less than 75,000, the number of firearms incidents per 100 sworn officers, ranged from 0.13 to

Table 8.1 Range and median number of incidents in which firearms were discharged per 100 sworn officers.

City size	Number	Low	Median	High
500,000+	8	0.46	3.13	7.99
250,000–499,000	8	0.13	3.34	5.59
150,000–249,000	6	2.37	3.00	8.66
75,000–149,999	9	0.43	0.72	2.84

Note: Adapted from Table 37, p. 53 (PERF, 1978).

8.66 in 1977. The median figure was approximately three incidents per 100 officers, save in the smaller cities where the figure was less than 1 per 100 (0.72). Data are shown in Table 8.1.

Although these data were compiled in the 1970s, it does seem unlikely that they have fallen by any significant amount.

Gun ownership and criminal activity

There are, according to estimates, some 200 million guns of all kinds in the USA and an estimated 55–60 million of those are handguns:[21] over 24,000 handguns per 100,000 population. A new handgun is sold every 12 seconds.[22]

By contrast, the 'non-gun culture' of England and Wales is reflected in the figures for registrations in one city. In London in 1983 there were 8,741 firearms certificates and 29,747 shotgun certificates (Commissioners Annual Report, 1983); in 1986 the figure for firearms certificates stood at 9084 and for shotguns at 41,576. Put another way, there were approximately 113 Part 1 firearms[23] per 100,000 population and 500 shotguns per 100,000 population.

In 1978, in New York City, 23,000 robberies were committed with a handgun, and over 9,000 of these weapons were confiscated by police (Parker, 1984, p. 197). Thousands of guns are stolen every year, and yet in New York City only 26,000 individuals held a handgun licence in 1982 (Parker, 1985, p. 198).

FBI records indicate that in the ten years between 1972 and 1982, 1110 police officers were killed in the line of duty (Sheridan, 1984), although the annual number of killings fell from 134 in 1973 (the peak year of the decade) to 92 in 1982. Some 765 were killed by handguns, 151 by rifles and 127 by shotguns. In the entire history of policing in the UK (with the exception of Northern Ireland) during the period 1830 to 1985, 204 officers died in the line of duty from all causes, including accident. More recently:

> Seventy-nine officers were murdered in the USA (in 1986). ... Seventy were killed by gunfire, 30 in shoot-outs with robbers, 13 while answering emergency calls, 16 while enforcing traffic laws, 9 investigating suspicious circumstances and 7 were ambushed. By comparison 82 officers have been murdered in Great Britain during this century.[24]

As Bayley (1977, p. 221), with what might almost be British understatement, puts it: 'The widespread presence of handguns in the United States makes the environment for police work dangerous.'

Weapons control

It is not our purpose to support either 'gun control' or 'freedom to possess' philosophies, merely to report on the nature of the dialogue between the two sides. The National Rifle Association on the one hand, and Handgun Control Inc. on the other, seem to perform a kind of 'dialogue of the deaf', presenting material which supports their case and ignoring that which denies it or is problematic.

The case of each is dramatically summed up in their own publicity material. 'Guns don't kill people: People kill people' (NRA). 'Guns don't die: People do' (HCI). But the material with which they support their case is, not to put too fine a point on it, partial.

The commonly acrimonious debate frequently revolves around the meaning and interpretation of the Second Amendment to the Constitution: 'A well regulated militia being necessary to the security of a free state, the right of the people to keep and bear arms, shall not be infringed.' NRA claim, for example, that the second amendment is a guarantee of fundamental, *individual* rather than collective right.[25] A similar view is expressed in an academic paper presented to the American Society of Criminology (Blackman and Gardiner, 1986, p. 14), which notes that:

> Constitutional scholars and historians have published extensive research on the Common Law origins of the Second Amendment, on the history of firearms possession in the colonies and in the early days of the republic, and in the intention of the framers of the Fourteenth Amendment to restrict state actions relating to that freedom. What has developed is a body of literature showing clearly that the constitutionally guaranteed to keep and bear arms was plainly understood to exist for each individual and could not be impaired by any government. ... Interestingly there has been little effort by 'gun control' supporters to refute any of this research.

Regrettably, these writers choose to ignore the fact that refutation is hardly necessary. For as HCI literature notes:[26]

> The United States Supreme Court has interpreted the Second Amendment on five separate occasions. In addition, nearly forty lower court decisions have addressed the issue. All have ruled that the Second Amendment guarantees a state's right to maintain a militia.

In 1981, Morton Grove, Illinois, a suburb of Chicago, passed a local law banning handguns. Police officers, jail and prison authorities were exempt. The Illinois Supreme Court and the US Seventh Circuit Court of Appeals ruled that the ordinance was a valid exercise of Morton Grove's police power and that there is no *individual* right to keep and bear arms. The US Supreme Court refused to consider an appeal on that ruling probably because they had said the same thing, albeit about 'technical issues' (Bruce-Briggs, 1977, p. 57), on a number of previous occasions (*US*

v. *Cruickshank* 1876; *Presser* v. *Illinois* 1886; *US* v. *Miller* 1937).[27]

The rejoinder from the NRA[28] is that *Miller* is flawed because the decision was too narrow (it related only to sawn-off shotguns) and that the case for the defence was inadequately presented. (See Caplan, 1976, for a complete exposition of these arguments.)

On the other hand, much of the recent literature from HCI chooses to ignore the empirical research of Wright (1987) and Wright and Rossi (1986) who surveyed a large sample of convicted persons about their 'gun habits'. In summary, the authors conclude that proposals for limited gun control at point of sale would have little effect among hardened criminals (Wright, 1987, calls them 'handgun and shotgun predators') because:

1. Legitimate firearms retailers play only a minor role as direct sources of handguns for adult offenders. Five out of every six 'felons' questioned indicated that they obtained their guns through 'informal transactions'.
2. That gun theft plays a critical role in connecting the adult felony offender to his firearms supply. Many of the informal transactions would be in respect of weapons stolen or unlawfully obtained.

Wright (1987, p. 34) notes that:

The ideal gun control policy would be one that directly affects the illicit user but leaves the legitimate user pretty much alone ... a successful policy for controlling criminal access to firearms must necessarily address the problem of gun theft, perhaps including measures for informing legitimate owners about the extent and seriousness of gun theft and about procedures for adequately securing their firearms.

Something the British believe they have gone a long way towards achieving.

WEAPONS CONTROL IN ENGLAND AND WALES

Legislation for firearms control in England and Wales is powerful and, in summary, requires that possession of every firearm is registered in the area in which the owner resides, is securely stored, and is passed from person to person, whether by way of gift or sale, though a system of official authorization and re-registration. Registration and re-registration are the responsibility of each and every chief constable.

The Firearms Act 1968, sec. 57,[29] defines a firearm as:

Any lethal barrelled weapon of any description from which any shot, bullet or other missile can be discharged[30] and includes:–
(a) any prohibited weapon, whether it is as such a lethal weapon as aforesaid or not;[31] and
(b) any component part of such lethal or prohibited weapon
(c) any accessory to such a weapon designed or adapted to diminish the noise or flash caused by firing the weapon.

With the exception of airguns, air pistols and their ammunition, shotgun cartridges with five or more shot, or antique weapons (i.e. over 100 years old) bought or sold as curios or ornaments, police certificates are required for purchase, acquisition or possession of all permitted weapons. Such certificates are not available for any prohibited weapon (viz. machine-guns, machine pistols, self-loading or semi-automatic weapons, pump action rifles, short barrelled smooth bore guns and 'burst fire' weapons), without special authority of the Home Office.[32]

Certificates are required for what are known as Part 1 Firearms, i.e. all forms of rifled weapons (e.g. rifles, handguns (revolvers and pistols), machine-guns (with the appropriate Home Office approval)) or ammunition for these weapons, and shot-guns.

Certificates will only be granted, on payment of a fee, to a person who can satisfy the chief officer that he has good reason to possess, purchase or acquire the firearm or ammunition. The 'good reason' requirement relates, in general, to membership of an approved club, etc. or in the case of shotguns for legitimate sporting or professional purposes. It is very rarely considered that a 'good reason' for the possession of any weapon is for the 'self-defence/protection' of an applicant. Stringent background checks will be made into all applicants by the police before the issue of a certificate.

Each weapon that a person holds is individually recorded on the certificate, which will also indicate the total volume of ammunition that the person may hold at any one time. The certificate must be produced at the time of purchase of ammunition.

Certain categories of convicted persons are prohibited from holding firearms certificates and some classes of person, e.g. those in the service of the sovereign (including police officers on duty) and other categories of 'professional' users are exempt from the requirements.

All holders of certificates are required to keep their weapons in secure conditions, usually in a locked steel cabinet.

By surprising contrast with the USA, there is no prohibition on mail order sales, although production, to the vendor, of an applicable firearms certificate is required.

WEAPONS CONTROL IN USA

Understandably the legislation over weapons control varies from state to state. Bruce-Briggs (1976, p. 43) describes their position as follows:

> There are some reportedly 20,000 gun-control ordinances in the various jurisdictions of the United States. Most are prohibitions against discharging a weapon in urban areas or against children carrying weapons, and are trivial, reasonable and uncontroversial. Most states and large cities have laws against carrying concealed weapons, the rationale being that no person has a legitimate reason to do so. In a few large cities and states, particularly in the Northeast, a license is required to buy or possess a handgun, and in a very few but growing number of Northeastern cities and states a permit or license is required to possess any sort of firearm.[33]

There is a good deal of opposition to general control of firearms, much of which comes from the National Rifle Association which has 2.5 million members, and is a powerful lobbying force in Congress.

Nevertheless, in 1968, Congress did pass a Federal Gun Control Act which most police officers value as an anti-crime tool. The Act prohibits the import, from one state to another, of handguns, their sale to minors, drug addicts and felons. Many police officers in the USA are members, or strong supporters of the NRA lobby. Many police officers receive their training from the Association and some have appeared in a series of advertisements under the banner 'I am the NRA'.

Recently, however, in a remarkable turnabout, following years of support for them, a group of police chiefs, sheriffs, ordinary patrolmen, bodies representing black police officers and state troopers, turned against the NRA 'gun lobby' and its advocacy of unrestricted gun-ownership.[34] The source of their concern lay in what is described as an NRA attempt to overturn the Gun Control Act (Corrigan, 1986, pp. 8–10) through a controversial Bill known as the McClure-Volkmer Bill.

The Bill, which passed into law on 19 May 1986 under the title Firearms Owners Protection Act, and is known under the label S.49/H.R.945, amended the Federal Gun Control Act 1968. It was roundly condemned during its passage through Congress by the National Association of Police Chiefs, who claimed that it would weaken record-keeping requirements for gun dealers and would 'undermine state and local laws and make our job of protecting the public more difficult' (NACP, Memo to Congress, 1985). Mr Hubert Williams, of the Police Foundation, said: '[The Bill] opens up the door for more weapons to get into the hands of criminals, increases the chances of injury and death, complicates the police officers' job and endangers the citizenry ...' (quoted in Corrigan, 1986, p. 12).

The Bill sought to make a number of changes in federal legislation which included: ending federal licensing of individuals who make 'occasional sales, exchanges or purchases' and thus included pawnbrokers; allowing mail order sale of guns; allowing sale of guns from 'private collections' without any record-keeping requirements; prohibiting 'surprise' inspections of gun dealers, and annulling laws requiring licences to carry weapons in many states. Some sections were carried, some rejected, many amended, often quite substantially.

Not surprisingly both sides claimed success. NRA claimed an 'historic victory', but according to HCI 'the Bill ... did little damage to the 1968 handgun law'.[35]

It is not our purpose to describe the successes and failures, merely to comment that the bottom line is probably that no one won and no one wins; the volume of gun ownership, licit or illicit, remains at its pre-S49 level. The only beneficiaries *may* be the police, but not through any saving of life as a consequence of the Act.

Both sides in the 'shoot-out' described above deployed their most powerful supporters, usually senior police chiefs, who pontificated on the desirability or futility of gun control laws. But the combination into a powerful pressure group of so many of the disparate bodies representing police officers in the USA was a unique occurrence and may herald a more united voice for 'law enforcement'. If only the issues that brought them together were a little more soluble than those connected with gun ownership. For the fact is that illegal or unauthorized gun *possession* is a victimless crime and thus becomes a moral issue. Moral issues are like 'Blue Laws' controlling Sunday behaviour which, as Miller (1977a, p. 128) points out, place the police officer in an untenable position: 'somebody is bound to complain of [either] oppression or neglect of duty.'

Regrettably, one is drawn to the conclusion that the anonymous 'Superintendent of Scotland Yard', quoted by Bruce-Briggs (1976, p. 55) was right when he pointed out that in view of the large number of guns available, prohibition was 'impossible'.

TRAINING AND RELATED ISSUES

As noted earlier, there is an average of about 10 per cent of the national police strength in England and Wales trained to handle firearms, but the actual figure varies markedly from force to force. The Metropolitan Police has about 11 per cent of its strength,[36] some 2700 officers, so trained, many of those officers on specialist duties, royalty and diplomatic protection duty, etc. By contrast the Leicestershire force, largely rural in its operating environment, has only 3 per cent of its strength so qualified.

And, as Mr Douglas Hurd, the Home Secretary, put it in a speech to the Police Federation Conference in 1986:

Last year, the police used firearms in England and Wales exactly seven times – five times in London and twice outside. When I gave this figure recently to a group of US Congressmen, there was a gasp. One of them said that in New York police could reach that figure in one precinct by teatime on a warm afternoon.

Nevertheless, weapons held by British police forces now include: Remington pump action shotguns, Smith and Wesson .223 and 7.56 rifles, .38 Smith and Wesson revolvers, 7.62 Enfield Enforcer rifles with telescopic sights, Heckler and Koch 9 mm sub-machine guns, Parker Hale model 82 7.62 rifles, anti-riot guns, and some CS gas cartridges.

As noted, over the past few years a number of incidents in which innocent people have been shot by armed police have combined to produce increasing public disquiet about the use of firearms by police and a strengthening of the training and selection procedures for firearms officers, adopted by the police.

However, it must be noted that the existence of Home Office Guidelines for the issue and use of weapons, and most importantly the recommendation by the Joint Standing Committee on Police Use of Firearms (set up by the Association of Chief Police Officers), that psychological testing of officers for suitability to handle firearms coupled with an extended training period, now amounting to two weeks (ten working days), seek to prepare more fully the armed British officer for his/her task.

Training in London includes both examination of accuracy in shooting and simulation exercises of the shoot/don't shoot decision-making kind. By contrast

NYPD has a six-day training programme; two days of classroom instruction, three days range practice under the constant supervision of the same instructor plus an additional day of training in combat firing and tactics on the outdoor range. In some states (e.g. South Carolina) although state law mandates training for police officers at the State Academy, the stipulation is that officers should attend that training within the first year after their appointment. In practice this means that often officers remain untrained, including in the handling of firearms, for periods of up to ten months. In some cases, because state laws do not require notification of appointment, officers may have served for a considerable period before the chief notifies the academy that he has an officer on his books who is in need of training.

RULES FOR THE ISSUE OF WEAPONS IN THE UK

In summary the rules for the issue of weapons in England and Wales are that:

1. Arms are issued on the authority of a senior officer.
2. Officers who are to be armed must sign for their arms and ammunition.
3. They must load their pistol under supervision and are given six additional rounds of ammunition.
4. The pistol must not be removed from its holster unless it is necessary to use it.
5. It must never be used unless the officer himself or the person he is protecting are in imminent danger.
6. Any discharge of the weapon must be immediately notified.

USE OF FORCE AND USE OF DEADLY FORCE

Police firearms behaviour in England and Wales is to be viewed within the bounds of the law on the use of force which is dealt with under section 3(1) of the Criminal Law Act 1967 and provides that:

> A person may use such force as is reasonable in the circumstances in the prevention of crime, or in effecting and assisting in the lawful arrest of offenders or suspected offenders or of persons unlawfully at large.

And the question of what is 'reasonable' is a matter for a jury.[37]

By contrast, many American police departments produce quite specific 'continuums of force' culminating in definitions of the circumstances under which 'deadly force' may be applied. Definition of the conditions for the application of deadly force are a requirement for police departments seeking accreditation from the Commission on Accreditation. The rules formulated under these guidelines are comprehensive and often very precise. (See Appendix IV for an example drawn from the Tallahassee Police Department, Florida.)

DISCUSSION

The ability and will to operate as an unarmed police service even in the face of increasing use of firearms in criminal activity is a major element of the unique flavour of British policing. But as we have seen, there are increasing moves (through the provisions of the Police and Criminal Evidence Act 1984) to place at least the legislative side of British police activity on a footing which is nearer, if not totally analogous with, the American model.

We have argued in the earlier chapters of this book that the people-first, law enforcement-second problem of a developing nation, coupled with the legitimized 'vigilantism' (Miller, 1977) which may be seen as an underlying philosophy of American policing, are significant features which dictate the style of that nation's policing. Bayley (1977, p. 222) argues further, that as long as policemen are afraid of being shot,[38] 'they will favour pre-emptive action.... This is not a matter of personality as some have suggested. It is good common sense if there is a risk of being seriously hurt' (p. 222).

Bayley (p. 222), in a slightly more dubious hypothesis, proposes that 'pre-emptive action involving physical domination in encounters with the public will vary directly with the strictness of gun control legislation', and that in part this is a consequence of the fact that many police/citizen encounters are clouded with anxiety: 'policemen will be afraid of being ... shot [and] citizens ... of being shot by mistake.' Police officers, according to this view, are 'take-charge guys' and the presence of guns 'adds a real but incalculable amount of emotion to any police–citizen encounter.'

In a society in which there is acute suspicion of encroachment of governmental power, the police officer, uniformed and armed, is a dramatic exemplar of this power. Although, Bayley argues, police have been called upon to provide a variety of non-enforcement services, such provision is less legitimate and acceptable from an armed rather than an unarmed provider: 'The gun on the hip is a visible reminder that the police have other things to do, that non-enforcement activities are a distraction from main purposes' (Bayley, 1977, p. 222). This contention is supported by noting that at least two cases in the USA declare that the police have no responsibility to protect citizens from attack (*Weiner* v. *Metropolitan Transit Authority*, 55 NY. 2D 175, 1982; *Bowers* v. *Devito*, 686 F.2d616, 1983).[39]

Our model, in Chapter 7, of the law-enforcement/social role behaviour of American policing *vis-à-vis* the order maintenance/social role paradigm of British officers is supported by Bayley's hypothesis (p. 223) that 'disarmed police will be better prepared than armed police to provide mediation not involving enforcement ... the legitimacy of non-enforcement work for the police will be greater in societies with strict gun control'.

There is, and will continue to be, strict gun control in England and Wales. But as James Q. Wilson pointed out,[40] the English situation is slowly eroding. According to Bruce-Briggs (1977, p. 56): 'The key to low rates of violence in England is not in rigorous gun-control laws ... but in the general deferential nature and docile character of the population.' But in 1981 street disorder on a major scale occurred first in Bristol and later in other major urban areas. Sporadic outbursts of disorder occurred throughout the 1980s (Scarman, 1981; Kettle and Hodges, 1982; Benyon, 1984; Reiner, 1985 and 1986; Benyon 1986), and culminated in October 1985 with a major disturbance in the Tottenham area of London in which not only was a constable, PC Keith Blakelock, murdered, but other officers were shot at by an unidentified person while they were attempting to control the disorder.

Critchley (1970) argued that the methodology of the British police for quelling disorder was a 'conquest of violence'; now, as Reiner (1986, p. 259) puts it, 'The carefully constructed traditional image of benign and pacific policing ... seems to have come unstuck.'

There is a deeply-held hostility among inner-city youth towards the police. There were 16,000 assaults on police officers in 1986, an average of 8.2 per 100 serving officers,[41] which resulted in a cumulative total of approximately 22,000 working days lost (Pead, 1987). The armoury of police increases and although the numbers of trained officers have fallen since 1983, there is growing concern that the two-tier response to firearms use by criminals and others is inadequate. (The two-tier response involves the calling of 'local' trained officers,[42] with limited weaponry, as a first resort and only later the calling of 'tactical firearms units', with more sophisticated firepower. This latter course is usually undertaken only with the approval of senior management.)

There are the first signs of a growing interest in weaponry within the British police. Recent issues of *Police* (the journal of the Police Federation) have carried articles on firearms use and, more importantly, even letters on the relative merits of the 'weaver' and 'iosceles' stances.[43]

There is some evidence that the British officer, at least in the inner city, feels in imminent danger of death and certainly that the social role of policing is consigned to a category of 'rubbish' if it does not result in an arrest (PSI, 1983, pp. 62, 64–6). If Bayley's (1977) hypothesis is right, then the level of apprehension in the British officer will inevitably lead to 'pre-emptive action' and may lead to a further rejection of the social role activity. The two models of policing move closer together.

Following a searing attack on the Home Office figures for crime involving the use of firearms in England and Wales, described as 'grossly misleading in a number of ways' (a comment which matches concern over the *actual* number of armed officers on the streets in the country), Greenwood (1986), in what appears to be a veiled call for a permanently armed police force, says in an echo of NRA literature:

Arising from the increase (in armed and violent crime) and from the use of firearms in the Tottenham disturbance, we shall doubtless hear demands for further 'control' on legitimately held firearms. .... It is of course much easier to harass the law-abiding than it is to deal with the criminal.

But, for the time being, we are left with the comforting view of Police Super-intendent A. T. Roberts who wrote a letter of complaint to *Police* (December

1986) following the publication of a picture showing a number of armed police officers. He wrote:

> All you have done is display our organization in such an abhorrent 'macho' image that such weaponry would only be matched by counter-weaponry. . . . I consider you have done the police service a great injustice by bringing these people to the forefront when they have very little part in day-to-day policing.

CHAPTER 9

Policing Public Disorder – Freedom of Speech, Freedom of Assembly, the Redress of Grievances

The term democracy is one which is slippery and notoriously difficult to define. Political philosophers and other great thinkers have struggled hard and long in an effort to come to terms with defining a belief system that apparently provides 'freedom' but at the same time places power into the hands of a few.[1]

It is hard to explain how, on the one hand, the democracy of the German Democratic Republic can be accepted by its people as of a similar quality (possibly better, but certainly no worse) than that of the USA or Britain, and on the other hand, how many people in Britain are bemused by the democratic fervour of Americans to elect everyone from dog-catchers to presidents or to resort to a plebiscite at the drop of a ballot box. The election of a few by many, who place their trust in the elected, is only successful when the voters believe, without reservation, that breaches of that trust will be dealt with rapidly. The elected become the protectors of the freedoms of the people and are at one and the same time both symbolic representations of that trust and practical guardians of it.

There is little doubt that escape from despotism of one kind or another was the spur to both Magna Charta and the Bill of Rights. According to Skinner (1948, p. 269): 'The original victory over tyranny was a constitutional guarantee of personal rights, including the right to protest if conditions were not satisfactory.' But elected politicians cannot defend those rights themselves, thus another *unelected* body, the police, is charged with both protecting and at the same time supervising them.

Goldstein (1977) points out the anomalies of policing in this area of the law. Police officers are, he notes (p. 1), invested with special powers and an authority which is 'awesome in the degree to which it can be disruptive of freedom, invasion of privacy and sudden and direct in its impact upon the individual'.

The authority is delegated to the lowest level of the organization and is exercised without direct supervision or control. Commonly, in dealing with real or potential public disorder, it is exercised in the heat of the moment. Furthermore, in the absence of comprehensive training, such authority is exercised by people who are, above all, human, and will respond to the stresses of crowds and groups in the same psychological set as those forming the crowd themselves.

But as Goldstein (1977, p. 1) continues:

a democracy is heavily dependent upon its police, despite their anomalous position, to maintain the degree of order that makes a free society possible. It looks to its police to prevent people from preying on one another; to provide a sense of security; to facilitate movement; to resolve conflicts; and to protect the very processes and rights – such as free elections, freedom of speech, and freedom of assembly – on which continuation of a free society depends.

It is the aim of this chapter to examine the nature of the police role in supervising that 'right to protest', both peaceful and belligerent; to look at the legal considerations which seek to allow police to 'control' deviant responses; and to discuss the nature of control of the police in these circumstances through both political and non-political means.

THE POLICING OF MAJOR PUBLIC DISORDER

It could be said that the most extreme form of protest is the practical politics of the mob. Immediate, forceful and incapable of being ignored, the riot is the ultimate vehicle for ensuring that the machinery for the 'redress of grievances' is kick-started into life.

The history of both nations is filled with riots of one kind or another. In England, prior to the 'New Police' there was a 'century of upper-class fear of "the mob"' (Reppetto, 1978, p. 16) and, although the causes were varied (intra-religious (1715–16), anti-Irish (1736), political (1770s), and anti-Catholic (Gordon Riots, 1780)) it was the inability of the army to deal with the mob at 'Peterloo' (see p. 13–4 above), rapidly followed by a mutiny of the Guards (1820), which provided the spur of Peel's parliamentary initiative.

On the other side of the Atlantic things were little different. During the eighteenth century disturbances between different groups of immigrants were commonplace but were mild compared to growing anti-British feeling. In 1770, the presence of British troops in Boston afforded 'a recent and melancholy demonstration of the consequences of quartering troops among citizens in a time of peace under the pretence of supporting the law and aiding civil authority'[2] when an ensuing riot resulted in the deaths of five citizens after a party of British soldiers opened fire on the protesting crowd. But even after the establishment of organized policing in New York, and throughout the mid-nineteenth century, feelings between immigrant communities were 'deep and bitter' (Reppetto, 1978, p. 42). The Irish Catholics were at loggerheads with the Anglo-Saxon Protestants. The issue? The nature of Sunday, the so-called 'blue' laws. Disorder in the streets was commonplace. The police even fought each other.

In New York, during the 1850s, arguments about the efficacy of political control of the police had eventually resulted in the creation in New York of an 'alternative' Metropolitan Police Department, in opposition to the already established Municipal Police. The 'Mets' patrolled the same areas as the Municipal force and are reputed to have had such battles over jurisdiction that each would seek to free the prisoners of the other and would interfere with 'police operations' of one kind or another, in an effort to discredit the competition. Eventually they fought a savage battle over a Metropolitan Police attempt to occupy City Hall in order to enable a 'Met' captain to execute a warrant for the arrest of the city's mayor who was protected by Municipal officers (Reppetto, 1978, p. 43).

In 1863, at the height of the Civil War, the Irish population of New York rioted in protest at a conscription law. Elections in 1874 and organized labour disputes in the same year saw similar disorder.

Throughout the late 1870s and through the 1880s and 1890s, strikes, industrial disputes and mob reaction to military presence (see Reppetto, 1978, p. 123) continued with little respite.

Aid to the civil power

The significant difference between the response of organized policing on each side of the Atlantic was the degree of assistance called to the aid of the police.

> [When] the control of civil disorders required assistance beyond the local policing arrangements, forces of special constables or deputies were frequently employed. (Reppetto, 1978, p. 122)

But these were amateurs, 'drunks and drifters who needed the money' or toughs who wanted to 'throw their weight around', which left the state militia as the next on call.

Just as at 'Peterloo', the militia proved to be unsuccessful at quelling riots. But it was the case that 'where a strong police force existed, order was maintained. When regular troops were employed, they too were effective' (Reppetto, 1978, p. 123).

In Buffalo, New York, charges with night sticks dispersed a mob, while in New York City it is alleged that the appearance of the police was sufficient to quell disorder. But in the absence of strong local policing, the militia, often known as the State Guard (i.e. Kentucky Guard), later the National Guard, were commonly the only available assistance to the beleaguered police. The real problem is cogently put by Reppetto (1978):

> The task of dispersing mobs without shooting them is one of the most difficult of operations, requiring a high degree of training, discipline, and confidence between officers and men. It is not something which can be learned by an occasional drill session. In a thousand incidents from Pittsburg in '77 ... through Boston in 1919 to Kent State in 1970, the militia would frequently fail to perform adequately in situations of civil disorder ... instances of indiscriminate shooting, often without orders would be legion. ... In contrast the regular army, whilst sometimes accused of excessive force, would never be charged with a lack of discipline.

But in a society where the multiplicity of local police departments who depend on each other for mutual aid is the norm, such aid can often be insufficient. To this day the procedures of police departments, large and small, will include provision for calling first local and then more widely drawn assistance.

The *Emergency Operations Manual* of Charleston City Police Department defines the role of the chief of police, among other things, as being responsible for 'requesting assistance from other police agencies or from the National Guard': but that call, whenever possible, 'shall be with the specific consent of the Mayor of Charleston'.[3]

Although mainly used for disaster relief the role of the State National Guard remains that of a special state constabulary, called to provide assistance 'in situations calling for skills, organization and capabilities beyond the level of local police, fire and disaster preparedness resources' (Stein, 1984). They may, however, be used in cases of civil disorder at the discretion of the state governor.

The availability of a militia to the police in the USA was, of course, a direct consequence of a desire to avoid a standing army. But by contrast, that standing army was the aid to which the British police were required to turn if necessary.

The British army has a common law obligation to respond to calls for assistance (Carver, 1983). The important point to emphasize, however, is that any application for military assistance is to be made directly by the chief police officer of the area to the appropriate army commander. If the commanding officer did not respond, he would be acting illegally, despite instructions from higher military or political authorities to do otherwise (Carver, 1983). In addition, not only is the local commander bound to assist, by law, but his superiors, including political powers, may not prevent him or his unit from responding.[4]

In contemporary policing in England and Wales, army assistance is rarely called for, save in terrorist incidents when special skills are required.[5] In any case, there is a generally-held view amongst 'service' professionals that currently the use of military assistance would be 'an unattractive hybrid' (Elmes, 1973), or simply too drastic (Carver, 1983), or would escalate rather than placate a hostile crowd through their apparent eagerness to display and deploy special equipment (Thackrah, 1983).

As Reiner (1985) puts it, the secret weapon of the British police 'was not watercannon, tear gas or rubber bullets, but public sympathy'. The control of huge crowds – potential mobs – with unarmed (and largely untrained) police was a direct consequence and extension of Rowan and Mayne's softly-softly policy, and stemmed from the earliest days when fear of a repressive, intrusive police presence on the French model was legion.

The winning-by-appearing-to-lose philosophy of British policing, the generation of public sympathy towards an unarmed, civil police, was nevertheless supported, on occasion, by army assistance.

Although used on a number of occasions in the nineteenth and early twentieth centuries (the last occasion being a police strike in 1919), gradually the non-lethally armed civilian police force became the sole method of riot control (Reiner, 1985).

THE TWENTIETH CENTURY

The USA – from riots to safe streets

There is a saying in Britain that what happens in the USA today will happen in the UK in ten years' time. Usually that assumption is about the nature of fashion, consumer durables and cultural fads but it is applicable to other areas too. Although the time period must be extended from ten to nearly twenty years, both nations have been beset by the severest of public disorder, often aimed at police and the nature of policing, and both have responded in a similar manner, with enquiries seeking to examine the events and their causes and to recommend methods of future prevention that are applicable and feasible, either through legislation or with money, or both.

Violence and protest is one means used against the state to ensure a part in the democratic political process (Vick, 1985, p. 165) and the 'frightening reality of domestic political life' (Robin, 1980, p. 47) came to sharp focus in the USA as a consequence of the riots in the 1960s.

Although the USA had been plagued by riots during the 1940s, issues of civil rights and the treatment of minorities had been reasonably quiet for twenty years. But, when 'discrimination, overcrowded living conditions ... separatism, segregation, lack of police protection, [and] poor police community relations' (Beckman, 1980, p. 288) were instrumental in creating violence as an alternative means of coping, the riots began, 'almost unnoticed and unheeded in 1964 and increased in frequency and severity through 1968' (Robin, 1980, p. 47).

The federal government's response to the riots, the role of police in precipitating them, and the rising fear of crime was 'to establish "crime commissions" to study and analyze the riots, the police, and the fear of crime' (Robin, 1980, p. 47). In particular, the Presidential Commission on Law Enforcement and the Administration of Justice (known as the President's Crime Commission) was later followed by a *National Advisory Commission on Civil Disorders* (the Kerner Commission) which reported in 1968.

The President's Crime Commission reported in 1967 and its main volume, *The Challenge of Crime in a Free Society,* together with six separate taskforce reports, are still considered the most ambitious attempt to examine the relationship between crime, delinquency and the administration of justice. The Kerner Commissioners, on the other hand, were concerned only with the issue of riots and public disorder. And not without some justification.

According to the report itself,[6] during the first nine months of 1967 there were 164 disorders 'officially' recorded and an unofficial estimate of 217. The Kerner Commission (pp. 43–76) also reported that 'typical' rioters were aged between 15 and 24, black, unmarried, highschool dropouts, felt deprived because of discrimination, felt supremacy over whites and were usually anti-white and involved in black rights. They operated in small gangs, and although not participating in the riot in any premeditated way, made plans to take revenge on a store-owner or to loot something that the rioter felt was owed to him (Bernstein, 1967, p. 35).

Within months of the publication of the President's Crime Commission the assassination of Martin Luther King and two months later Senator Robert Kennedy produced 'a time that was "politically right" for the passage of federal legislation ... [and] it was in June 1968 when the Omnibus Crime Control and Safe Streets Act was passed and signed into law' (Robin, 1980, p. 49).

The President's Crime Commission had identified a number of areas of concern and produced objectives to be accomplished in six major areas,[7] in particular for the purpose of this discussion: upgrading the quality and qualifications of criminal justice personnel; and funding improvements in the criminal justice system. Having the advantage of both the President's Crime Commission and the Kerner Report, legislators took the opportunity in the Safe Streets Act to satisfy an increasingly apprehensive public. The action they took was seen by some commentators (cf. Harris, 1971) as provoking the final confusion in the public mind by linking together what were essentially two unconnected issues; rising crime and riots.

The road from 'violence and protest' to federal government response had been strewn with millions of dollars worth of damage and had been polluted by the bodies of the dead, from the unidentified to the brother of a president. There were, in summary, three main responses to the substantial public disorder of the 1960s in the United States. First, an examination of causes and the suggestion of cures, second, legislation, and third, the provision of finance. This latter category was not, it is emphasized, to relieve the underlying political, social and economic problems of the society but to provide for the 'purchase of equipment' and the 'prevention and control of riots'; specific provisions of the Safe Streets Act. How different were things in the England and Wales when, nearly twenty years later, the population were woken from their reverie of 'it can never happen here'? For it did.

England and Wales – from dustbin lids to armoured cars

Castles (1984) has given an integrated account of the mechanisms by which post-World War II Europe, including Great Britain, suffered a labour shortage as a consequence of both the number of wartime dead and the need to rebuild. Although early post-war immigration depended on the 'traditional' source, the Irish labourer, it was not long before the British government started to look elsewhere. First by allowing Polish and other 'fighting refugees' to remain and later by recruiting women from the Baltic countries for hospital work and later by coordinated plans (the North Sea scheme and the Blue Danube plan) covering other parts of Europe (Tannahill, 1958, pp. 19–20). By 1951 there were nearly half a million European workers in Britain (Castles, 1984, p. 41). Because these people were 'aliens' they were restricted within the current legislation and were liable to deportation.

The supervision and record-keeping requirements for 'alien' workers were not a problem for those from British Commonwealth countries. Thus workers from the West Indies, India and Pakistan were actively recruited by London Transport, the British Hotels and Restaurants Association and the National Health Service, but the majority came in response to calls for increased labour for industry. By the mid-1950s about 30,000 non-white New Commonwealth workers were entering Britain each year (Castles, 1984, p. 42). Between 1951 and 1981 the number of UK residents from New Commonwealth countries rose from 218,000 to 1,513,000.[8]

New Commonwealth immigrants settled in large industrial towns in the Midlands and London and could only afford to live in the inner-city areas, the heartland of the working-class Labour voter.

Rapidly, the presence of numbers of non-white workers, appearing greater because of their concentration, became a political issue. Trade unions started to complain of immigrants keeping down wages and taking jobs that should go to 'Englishmen', and although National Trade Union figures (the TUC) advocated equality regardless of status, there was a 'breathtaking gap' between the 'ideals of Congress resolutions and the realities of the shop floor' (Freeman, 1979, p. 22).

Elections were won and lost on racial issues. 'Smethwick rejects a multi-racial society' was the successful platform for a Tory candidate in a local by-election. And the common (if unofficial) political slogan was: 'If you want a nigger for your neighbour – vote Labour.' Parliamentarians, under the guise of trying simply to articulate a 'problem', made what were widely accepted as accurate statements. Their inflammatory and divisive nature was commonly ignored by a huge proportion of the population.

Mr Enoch Powell, the Shadow Minister for Defence and Member of Parliament for Wolverhampton, had been voicing anti-immigrant sentiments for some time when, in April 1968, he declared publicly that the ultimate price to be paid for (black) immigration would be streets running with 'rivers of blood'.[9]

Meanwhile blacks in Britain were developing a political consciousness based directly on their experience of personal and economic discrimination (Hall et al. 1978, p. 331), particularly as a 'race problem' was being identified.

Unemployment was increasing, and had risen to above 4 per cent and concern was rising about the provision of jobs 'for Englishmen'. Then, following an article in the Sunday Times[10] which linked poor housing, poverty, lack of jobs and broken families with the dramatic rise in street crime in Lambeth (Brixton) and pointed to the involvement of black youth in these crimes, the crisis was translated into a problem of 'law and order'.

This linking together of two or more problems, referred to as 'convergence' by Hall et al. (1978), is remarkably similar to the linking between riots and crime referred to by Harris (1971) and discussed above.

But Britain's riots were yet to come. In the meantime the scapegoating continued. National newspaper headlines, mostly relating to alleged abuses of the welfare provisions, tell the story: 'Scandal of £600 per week Immigrants' (Sun); 'We want more money say £600-a-week Asians' (Daily Mail); 'Migrants just here for the welfare handouts' (Daily Telegraph); 'Another 4000 on the way' (Sun).

The riots

One cannot help but be struck by the similarity between the role of the police in England during the 1950s and 1960s and that of the police in New York City nearly a century before.

In Miller's (1977) analysis, the London (and by extension the national) police tradition of impartiality, restraint and the minimum use of force was consequent upon a particular historical period, characterized by political conflict over parliamentary representation and general hostility towards an intrusive police. In America the working classes were divided amongst themselves: 'the native working classes saw a political order they valued threatened by irresponsible foreigners who did not appreciate democracy' (Miller, 1977, p. 11). The police role was thus to 'support a political order ... which seemed threatened by an alien minority' (Vick, 1985, p. 164).

By the 1950s the police in England and Wales found themselves embroiled in the growing politicization of the race issue – the threat by an 'alien minority'. To place Miller's words (p. 20) into this context, the British police, like their American counterparts years before, 'tended to reflect and act out community conflicts instead of trying to establish and maintain standards which transcended the conflicts.' Thus, as growing racism in the community was articulated by both the public and their parliamentary representatives, so the police responded to the covert requirements of the population – to keep order, to take action and to control the 'growing threat' from the 'dangerous classes', the 'volcano under the city'.

In 1958 disturbances, typified as 'race riots' but in reality little more than (usually unarmed) hand-to-hand street fighting, occurred in West London (referred to as the Notting Hill 'race riots', the area is more accurately North Kensington) and Nottingham.[11] The police were caught between white youth on one side and black on the other. The disturbances were quickly over but had a long-lasting effect. In North Kensington two-man 'short patrols' were common. Black clubs were 'raided' with impunity but often without warrants. Probationer constables were encouraged to 'nick-a-nigger-a-night'.[12] The general rule was that 'the dangerous classes' should be kept in their place.

Throughout the period 1959–65, racism, racial abuse and discriminatory discretion were the currency of policing and the teaching materials for the *tabula rasa* of the probationary constable, posted to work in these 'sensitive areas'.

This does not mean that all police officers were rampant racists, merely that, just like the rest of the (white) population, some were affected by the media, the politicians and the demands, made by the 'respectable' middle and working classes, to cap the volcano.

The North Kensington area of London proved to be one of the starting places for other dramatic changes in British policing of disorder.

The Afro-Caribbean population of North Kensington and other parts of London sought, through the early 1970s, to develop a 'carnival' on the model of that tradition in Jamaica and, although small and fairly peaceful in its early days, this became a thorn in the side of policing. In particular, growing allegations of criminal activities in the crowds, robberies, thefts, stabbings and so on, resulting in an increased 'high-profile' police response. High-profile policing was met with high-profile disorder. Youth in the area, particularly black youth, took the opportunity of the anonymity of the crowd to attack groups of police with stones, bottles, bricks and boots or just anything which was handy. The police, totally unarmed and unprepared, were obliged to protect themselves with dustbin lids,[13] an embarrassing and ignominious circumstance. Following that, and a later similar disturbance in Lewisham in South London, police made it very clear that in any future conflict they would not be made to look like amateurs again.

When in 1977 disorder occurred at a march in Lewisham[14] and again at the Notting Hill carnival the same year, riot shields and protective helmets were seen for the first time on the streets of London.

Some limited training was undertaken by the police, although this was mostly confined to developing the dubious skill of 'embussing' and 'de-bussing' as rapidly as possible and to mastering techniques for breaking up comparatively static crowds (trudging and wedging).

But training notwithstanding, in 1980 and during the following six years 'parts of Britain experienced rioting on a scale which had not been seen on the mainland within living memory' (Moore, 1986, p. 88).

In Bristol, at the start of that period, the police failed to contain a riot in a mainly black area of the city, which this time included looting, petrol bombs and considerable damage, and were obliged to withdraw from part of the city (Weigh, 1980). In 1981 police failure in limiting widespread damage and police injuries in Brixton and parts of Liverpool caused such a 'crisis of confidence [among police officers] in the ability of [their] commanders to lead in such circumstances' (Moore, 1986, p. 88) that the Police Federation demanded 'clear strategy [and] firm leadership',[15] the Commissioner of the Metropolitan Police demanded a mini-Riot Act (Reiner, 1985, p. 71) and the parliamentary spokesman for the Police Federation called for 'specially trained squads of men with all the support of helmets, fireproof uniforms, armoured cars – yes, and even guns if necessary' (Daily Express, 6 July 1981). In the end, it was a judicial enquiry which provided the 'more balanced approach' (Reiner, 1985, p. 72).

Just as Kerner had done before him, Lord Scarman pursued an examination of causes and the proposal of cures. Scarman's (1981) report, also like Kerner, was supported (or some might say confused) by other almost contemporaneous publications. First, the triennial report of the Police Complaints Board (1981)[16] was published in 1980 and made recommendations about changing the methods for pursuing complaints against police officers. Second, the Royal Commission on Criminal Procedure (1981) made strong recommendations regarding changes in the nature of police powers and procedures and was the seed for the later published Police and Criminal Evidence Act 1984. Finally in 1983, the report of the Policy Studies Institute (PSI, 1983) produced a blistering insight as to the real nature of police behaviour in London. The concatenation of these separate publications and their translation into legislation which was aimed at ensuring a balance between the rights of citizens and the powers of police was one predictable outcome. The second predictable outcome was, just as the Safe Streets Act had in the USA, to demand improvements in training and standards of police.

Finally came the expenditure of cash. Aimed initially at the inner cities and intended to relieve the underlying political, social and economic problems of the society it shortly became clear that central government was not averse to providing money, as the Safe Streets Act had put it, for the 'purchase of equipment' and the 'prevention and control of riots'. Applications were submitted from chief officers for CS gas, specialist communications equipment, armoured personnel carriers, riot-shields, non-flammable clothing and specialized training.[17] In London, there was a recognition that specially trained police managers are as necessary as trained 'troops'. There are, according to Tendler (1986), 'sixteen teams of specially trained senior officers available across London ... to cope with the strategy and tactics of effective riot policing.'

Most forces now have readily mobilized groups of men specially trained to deal with riots; normally designated Police Support Units (PSUs), Immediate Response Units (IRUs) or some such appellation.[18] PSUs consist of an inspector, two sergeants and twenty constables (called 'a serial') and are conveyed in a 'carrier' (usually a mini-bus).

A distinction must be drawn between PSUs and the availability of Special Operations Teams, including Special Weapons and Tactics (SWAT) teams in the USA. In many large police departments in the USA, activities ranging from hostage negotiation, through undercover surveillance and bomb disposal, to riot control and the policing of disasters are grouped together in a formally organized special operations or tactical component that 'Provides a concentration of resources and specialized expertise at a level that could not easily be achieved by conventional operational elements such as the patrol component or the criminal investigation component' (CAOLEA, 1985). Although there is no expectation that all tasks should be carried out by the same team (indeed, there is positive encouragement to keep hostage negotiation separate from the other functions) there is a clear indication that the application of Special Operations Teams is a full-time commitment. SWAT squads are commonly specialist and *permanent* teams that have responsibility for a number of related law enforcement functions.

By contrast, the men (and some women) on PSUs are not permanent and although they may train, even this function is undertaken with the assumption that officers are unlikely to work beside those they train with at any time in the future. Officers in the large cities may perform short postings to such a duty but cannot ever expect to work with the same colleagues again in a similar way, on any regular basis. Generally outside the major cities, officers are employed on normal police duties but are sufficently mobilizable (on an *ad hoc* basis) to enable them to deal with problems both within their own and other force areas. In addition to riot situations, such bodies, whether rural or urban, may be deployed for manpower intensive activities such as policing static and non-violent demonstrations, labour disputes and in searches for missing children, etc.

There is important distinction to be made between the formation, in the UK, of increasingly specialized units (currently firearms *specialists,* 'who do not participate in day-to-day policing'; PSUs, who do; and the formerly highly contentious Territorial Support Group (criticized by Scarman (1981) when, as a body, they were known as the Special Patrol Group), who are both specially trained and do 'ordinary' duty.

Currently the TSG, consisting of about 900 men, stationed at specific locations in the Metropolitan Police District (MPD) are a permanent mobile reserve, who work together on a full-time basis and are trained in the use of shields and crowd control tactics. Although the units have a role to play in controlling crowds and preventing disorder, the force steadfastly maintains that their major purpose is to provide extra manpower to local divisional commanders, to prevent and detect crime (particularly burglary) and to maintain public tranquillity.

In a move from west to east across the Atlantic, fairly unusual in itself, the Miami Police Department, under the direction of Captain George Green, developed a quasi-TSG philosophy following the disturbances in Miami in 1980. The now consolidated force of Metro Dade PD, policing the Miami area, continue the 'field force' philosophy.

Consisting of a platoon of police officers and sergeants, led by a lieutenant, the 'field force' is formed by six squads – one sergeant and seven officers per squad. The remainder form the Commander's executive squad; provide for specialized 'chemical agent' responses; man a 'prison wagon'; and provide vehicle security.

Unlike the TSG there is no pretence that the activity of the field force is for any other purpose than to respond to 'civil disorder', and to conduct 'high-profile' rescue.

Issued with body armour, jumpsuits (similar suits provided for PSUs and TSG are nicknamed 'babygrows'), shotguns, chemical agent launchers, smoke canisters, and CS gas (boots are recommended as footwear), the 'field force' are specially trained to control crowds, make arrests, use chemical agents and, in other circumstances, provide a professional response to a series of horrifying attacks on private citizens and police officers in their vehicle on public roads at the hands of 'large groups, hostile crowds, and/or riotous mobs' (Hoelscher, 1985).

In the first series of riots in Liberty City major problems of communication, cooperation and control were encountered and the resultant chaos was the spur to 'field force' development. The second series of riots in the same city saw the mobilization of 'field force'; the outcome was remarkably different. 'The keys to the successful use of field force are planning, training, discipline and most of all leadership' (Hughes et al., 1985).

Coordinating the response

In the absence of any National Guard in the UK, and in the face of the reluctance of both the police and the army to use trained soldiers in the control of civil disorder, there is a tendency to rely on principles of 'mutual aid'; the facility which theoretically enables a chief officer to call on neighbouring chief constables for assistance and particularly for manpower resources, etc.

The National Reporting Centre

PSUs are organized and coordinated in an emergency by the National Reporting Centre (NRC) at Scotland Yard, and although not employed to any marked extent in civil disorder of the 'riot' kind, the Centre was activated during the year-long strike of the National Union of Mineworkers, which saw substantial disorder and mass picketing, and drew allegations that the NRC was the precursor to a national police force with much criticism of 'police-state' tactics (Coulter et al., 1984; Reiner, 1984).

Regrettably there is still dispute, at the time of writing, between some of the forces involved in 'mutual aid' over the issue of 'who pays?'. Huge amounts of overtime were incurred as police officers sped from one end of the country to the other. Although the NRC coordinated the operation, no one was certain who paid, from finite, pre-planned budgets – the sending force or the receiving one. Some police authorities have ended up seeking the involvement of the courts to resolve the disputes.

Riot commissions, judicial enquiries and politics

Platt (1971) notes that despite ritualistic statements from 'appointing authorities' about the need for impartiality and the desire to 'represent' the community under examination, the commissioners in US studies of civil disorder have tended to be establishment types which as a consequence limits the likelihood that they will produce any radical recommendations.

In a study of riots from East St Louis in 1917, through Chicago in 1919, Harlem in 1935, Detroit in 1943, Watts in 1965, to the Kerner, Eisenhower and Scranton Commissions, Platt suggests that there are three levels at which such examinations operate.

First, there are the commissioners themselves who are seen as 'symbolic' and 'ceremonial'. Second come the administrators and the lawyers who mediate between the upper and lower levels of the structure and filter out the material not compatible with the establishment views of the commissioners. Finally there are the 'social scientists', who produce research that is characterized by institutional restrictions on the freedom of inquiry, commonly taking the view that riots are a form of deviant behaviour and are dysfunctional from the point of view of social change, assuming that only a minority of the riot-torn community support the disorder and those that do are, in any case, marginal individuals (Platt, 1971, pp. 116–80).

There is little doubt that Platt overstates the bias of the social scientists, for many share the view of Neiberg (quoted in Richert, 1973) that 'violence in all forms, up to and including assassination, is a natural form of political behaviour', and that 'violence may be a binding force ... [or] may have a therapeutic value' (Richert,

1973, p. 129). But there is little doubt that he is accurate in his assessment that the reason for the appointment of commissions is not to seek the causes of violence and suggest possible remedies. Rather, such appointments may be viewed as institutional techniques for dealing with public anxiety. They are designed to contain and deflate public anguish. The simple passage of time, during which evidence is gathered and conclusions are drawn, and the consequent facility which political powers are given to make reference to the 'forthcoming report', thus enables the heat to be taken off.

It is similarly true that the influence of 'hired hands', the social scientists and lawyers, produces in the commissioners an unacceptable level of intellectual and ethical corruption.

The Kerner Commission (1968), for example, was, according to Robin (1980, p. 47), among other things to examine the civil disorder of the 1960s including 'the role of police in *precipitating* them' (emphasis added), and subsequently produced criticism of the police (Kerner, 1968, pp. 3, 5, 8, 18). Used in that way the word 'precipitating' carries with it connotations of blame. But for the social scientist the word has a particular meaning.

The use of the word 'precipitating' in the Kerner analysis is a strong indicator that they were operating on a (then) comparatively new theory of crowd behaviour (Smelser, 1963) which sees the precipitating factor as the *fourth level* of a step-by-step sequence of determining factors leading eventually to riotous disorder.

The precipitating factor is an event 'which is close in time to the riot and looks like a sufficient condition unto itself. But it is not' (Brown, 1965, p. 732). In reality it is the event which brings a crowd, already affected by underlying determinants such as existing political and social strain and generalized beliefs about the source of the strain and the course of action that may relieve it, on to the street (see McKenzie, 1982 for a more complete examination of the 'value added theory'), and requires two more stages to be added before a riot occurs.

A close examination of the in-depth studies of riots contained in the Kerner Report shows that the precipitating factor was in most cases perfectly legitimate, perfectly acceptable and perfectly correct police action – often as mundane as the issue of a ticket for a violation.

Although no one would wish to deny the reality that the police played a part in creating and feeding the *underlying* determinants, to use the (technical) word 'precipitating' without explanation (or citation) is an unacceptable degree of intellectual corruption.

Close examination of the Scarman Report (1981) and analysis of subsequent and previous reports on civil disorder (e.g. Weigh, 1980; Kettle and Hodges, 1982) show that precipitating events (sometimes called 'triggers') are of a similar order in the UK; offers of assistance to an injured man (Brixton, 1981), a legitimate (if insensitive) raid on a drinking club in Bristol (Weigh, 1980), and so on. Indeed, Scarman suggested that such events were 'worldwide', and of a minor nature.

But, to a degree, Scarman, an establishment figure who had already conducted one major enquiry into police action (Red Lion Square, 15 June 1974), was led astray by the evidence of social scientists.

Coleman and Gorman (1982) (the latter a serving police officer) gave evidence that 'the police force attracts conservative and authoritarian personalities, that basic training has a temporary liberalising effect and that continuing police service results in increasingly illiberal/intolerant attitudes towards coloured immigration'. Coupled with the suggestion from other witnesses that the problem in Brixton was with 'young officers', many of the recommendations for training and other improvements in policing were directed at probationary constables and at them alone. Only one paragraph of the report (para. 5.27) deals with in-service training later in a police career and that concentrates on the Police Staff College and the 'courses for senior officers at the Police College [a title which it had foregone years before] at Hendon'. Those that were roundly ignored were the officers who influenced the attitudes of those probationers – the experienced officers who had spent the large part of their service absorbing the 'covert' requirements of the population; to keep order, to take action and to control the 'growing threat' from the 'dangerous classes', the 'volcano under the city', to which we referred earlier.

Attempts to deal with overt or covert, conscious and unconscious racism among these officers have, for various reasons, been roundly rejected (Southgate, 1984; McKenzie, 1986). To date little has been done to resolve that problem.

PSUs SWAT teams and riot squads

In October 1985, PC Keith Blakelock was murdered during rioting on the Broadwater Farm Estate, Tottenham, London. The riots marked the first occasion that the police had been shot at during civil disturbance on mainland Britain and marked also the deployment, but not the use, of specialist officers, with baton rounds (rubber bullets).

Throughout the previous five years many commentators had seen the development of PSUs as 'a de facto third force' (Reiner, 1985, p. 70), but others called for the creation of a professional CRS/National Guard style body, to be deployed only in the event of civil disorder. Some writers, e.g. Morris (1985), argued that the damage to public relations engendered by the use of ordinary duty police officers in such conditions made it necessary to 'make some policemen tougher in order to leave more policemen free to get on with a different kind of work'. He proposed a specialized riot squad under Ministry of Defence jurisdiction, a proposition roundly dismissed by the police and largely ignored by the politicians.

Morris and others draw on what may be called the sociological argument for the creation of such a third force on mainland Britain. There are, however, pressing psychological reasons why this proposition should not be shelved. Recall Reppetto's telling comment:

> The task of dispersing mobs without shooting them is one of the most difficult of operations, requiring a high degree of training, discipline, and confidence between officers and men. It is not something which can be learned by an occasional drill session.

The divisions in society, the existence of racism, real or imagined, the inability of national government to respond to international problems of recession and money supply, to say nothing of national problems relating to the reorganization of society in the age of the microchip, when the work ethic has to be rethought, will inevitably lead to more disorder in the streets.

Riots there will be and it is becoming clear that the police can no longer afford to be in the front line of that battle.

The reluctance of senior management of the police to 'go in hard' at the start of disorder, and the consequent feelings of frustration of the 'troops' were well demonstrated in evidence bearing on the death of Keith Blakelock.

Constable Ian Pyles told the jury at the trial of those charged with killing PC Blakelock, 'We had the manpower and the weapons to stamp it out – but we were not allowed to do so by our superiors.'[19]

But, nowadays, at almost every 'incident', we are presented with evidence that ordinary police officers in PSUs, given inadequate or inappropriate direction by their senior officers, get caught up in the heat of the event, lose control of themselves and, beyond the control of their commanders, do it themselves. When challenged they reply with some justification, 'Well, we're only human.'

Some people see this as 'only a training problem'. 'Get the training right', they say, 'and the men will be able to control themselves and will *only* act on the direction of senior officers.' But however much we would like it to be so, it is impossible to train people to the level at which they can fully control their emotions and respond only to orders given by senior officers and still expect them to carry out their ordinary duties in the traditional way. The use of men and women for such duties, who one day, when on ordinary patrol, are being told 'use your own initiative' and the next are being told 'only do what I say', is a nonsense.

A London police officer recently said:[20]

> At Tottenham I was kitted up with gas mask, baton gun, flame-proof suit and a crash helmet and put in the front line. It was a very aggressive role. It was scaled down. For some days after I was still on a 'high', still very hyped-up, and yet the next day I was knocking on someone's door to see his driving licence. I genuinely found it hard to be civil, because I was still on a high from the previous day. It's a very unfair position, to be in one role one minute and the other the next. There should be a body of men that are trained to deal with riots and that alone. They should not have to go back to basic policing, because the two are not compatible.

Theoretically it *is* possible to train people to control their emotional responses, to act only on command and by the book – a recent film in the BBC Horizon series about NASA astronauts, *Riding the Stack,* showed that – but at what cost? The astronauts become emotion*less;* automata who can, without doubt, deal with potentially life-threatening events at work but who, at home, have difficulty in maintaining relationships, are controlled and distant, and incapable of emotional involvement *in anything*.

One must recognize that, in a society which expects police officers to be alive to community and personal problems, to be involved in, and a part of, the community, such a cost, *in order to train efficient and effective RIOT CONTROLLERS*, would be unacceptable.

The complex job of 'policing' the streets requires sensitive, sensible, efficient and effective *human beings*. But policing riots takes specially trained, controlled and controllable people. As an officer said: 'We can't pat kids on the head one day then shoot them with plastic bullets the next.'[21]

In a very real way this demonstrates yet another element of our thesis that policing in the USA is law enforcement-oriented, while that of England and Wales is more inclined to order maintenance. The presence of specially trained teams in the USA, who are not used for 'ordinary' duties, is a purely 'enforcement' philosophy and rests on the assumption that such bodies exist because, and only because, the requirement to 'enforce' the law becomes inevitable, and the long-term effects become secondary. The circumspection with which the police in the UK move towards the establishment of riot squads is typified by Sir Kenneth Newman who spoke of 'the reluctant stages through which the police have passed from dustbin lids to armoured vehicles.... Each step has been taken cautiously and unwillingly in response to levels of riotous violence' (Commissioners Annual Report, 1987).

Concern in England has always been to ensure that the general acceptance of the role of police in the country was not compromised by what might be seen as heavy-handed action, or might bring police into conflict with a larger sector of the public through adverse reaction than might otherwise be the case.[22] As is regrettably common in police circles, the psychological effects of delay are ignored.

We are well aware that the proposition that riot squads of some kind are necessary for psychological as well as sociological reasons is likely to move at least part of the British model of policing towards that of the American. But the arguments in favour of a third force, specially equipped and trained but not involved in day-to-day policing, might enable the typically British flavour of *day-to-day* policing in England and Wales to be retained.

CHAPTER 10

The Shape of Things to Come: Policing the Future

According to Mathias et al. (1980), comparative studies of the criminal justice process which seek to describe, analyse, compare and reach hypotheses about the international nature of crime, and the societal response to it, are qualitatively different from comparative studies carried out within a nation (i.e. state to state or police department to police department). National studies focus on the 'vertical' aspects of crime: crime within a micro-system of geopolitical boundaries.

Many cross-cultural studies conduct their examination from a national base, seeking to analyse one nation by examining it *against* a particular national perspective. Concentration on *lateral* aspects of criminology within a global macro-system depends on a universal perspective which seeks to examine 'similarities, differences and interrelationships between selected foreign countries' (Mathias et al., 1980, p. 184). These are 'comparative studies in the purest sense': aspects of the systems under study are laid side-by-side not head-to-head.

If one excludes the historical/cultural variable,[1] there remain two major dimensions on which the policing (and to some extent the whole of the criminal justice system) of the UK and the USA may be examined. These are:

1. Aspects of the *organization* of policing, including issues of the role that the police play, their training, their accountability and their organizational response to overt or covert public demand for the provision of service.
2. Issues connected with the *philosophical/legalistic* side of policing; the laws that the police act under and upon, including the way in which issues of personal and individual *rights* are interpreted both by the courts and by the police.

We suggest that there has been slow but identifiable movement of the traditional British model of policing towards that of the American. We have argued that order maintenance with added public service has, for various reasons connected with historical, social, economic and legal factors, been the paradigm for analysis of policing in England and Wales, whilst that of the USA has, for similar reasons, been typified by a more legalistic approach – law enforcement with an added social role – compounded by a multifaceted, complex, non-system (see Chapter 7).

Similarly, the judicial system has been typified as 'due process' oriented in the

USA but based on the 'crie control' model in the UK. And in this context, the changes engendered by the Police and Criminal Evidence Act 1984, particularly in the provision of 'written' rights may, in time, move those to divergent models closer together.

ORGANIZATIONAL CHANGE

Nowhere has the shift of British policing towards the US organizational model been more clearly seen than with the creation of the Crown Prosecution Service, a change removing from the police in England and Wales the centuries-old 'tradition' of being the final arbiters in prosecution decisions.

The prosecution of offences

Before October 1986, the vast bulk of cases heard before courts, at all levels in the judicial system of England and Wales, were initiated, evaluated and prosecuted by the police. That is to say that not only was the evidence provided or collated by the police, but also the decision whether to prosecute or not was taken by a police officer, and often (in the lower courts) the police 'presented' the case to the magistrates for consideration.

The rationale for such a practice lay, of course, in the 'independence' of the chief officer – notions discussed in Chapter 4. In exercising their discretion to prosecute or not in any particular case, the police, it was argued, acted independently of the government and of any local police authority, and were free from the involvement of any judge or magistrate. Although in some special cases the Director of Public Prosecutions could take over cases or the Attorney-General was entitled to direct that prosecutions should cease, these were comparatively rare events.

Generally, in complex or contentious cases, the advice of solicitors (or barristers) was sought, and some police forces maintained their own solicitors' departments for this purpose. Others consulted local firms of solicitors and occasionally had access to the legal department of the local authority. For all that, the final decision regarding prosecution was taken by a police officer.

Through delegated responsibility, such decisions to prosecute were commonly taken by officers down to and including sergeant, although the more complex cases required the decision of a superintendent/chief superintendent and occasionally an assistant chief constable.[2]

Not surprisingly, a process which involved the police in making decisions about the strength of the evidence, gathering details about the background facts of the case, and which was also initiated in many cases by the exercise of 'discretionary' political (Lustgarten, 1986) decisions by a police officer, was the subject of some criticism.

As long ago as 1856 the Select Committee on Public Prosecutors was told by the Attorney-General: 'When the police mix themselves up in a prosecution they acquire a bias infinitely stronger than that which under any circumstance attach itself to their evidence.'

Interestingly,sider them, on the grounds of inadequate or ill-judged evidence, or because of the growing number of cases in which there had been a miscarriage of justice, the prosecutions having been commenced following a police decision to go before a court (Rolph, 1975).

Recently, as a consequence of the Royal Commission on Criminal Procedure – the Commission which initiated the Bill which became the Police and Criminal Evidence Act – Parliament approved the Prosecution of Offences Act 1985, which came into effect in the latter part of 1986. The Act created an entirely new body, the Crown Prosecution Service (CPS), charged with taking over from the police their responsibility to make decisions and to prosecute in all cases.

The role of the Crown Prosecution Service

Although as a consequence of the Act initial charge/no charge decisions *after a direct arrest* continue to be made by an officer of sergeant or inspector rank, review of the case, with the possibility of a decision to withdraw or 'discontinue', is undertaken by the CPS. In addition, the *de novo* consideration of evidence in cases of those reported in order that disposition decisions may be made, or in which evidence is to be considered prior to the application of warrants and so on, previously dealt with by the police, are now taken by the same body. The head of the CPS is the Director of Public Prosecutions; the Attorney-General is the minister responsible to Parliament.

Despite his title, the Director of Public Prosecutions is nothing of the sort. There is no single individual or body of people who are responsible on behalf of the public for initiating prosecutions. (In Scotland there is an official called the procurator-fiscal who serves such a purpose.) Thus, currently, there is no analogy in the criminal justice system of England and Wales to the 'prosecutor' in the American system. But, for a clearer understanding of this fundamental but dramatic change which has altered forever the relationship between the police and the judicial system, we shall examine the system of prosecution in the USA before looking in more depth at the CPS.

The Public Prosecutor in the USA

The role of the Public Prosecutor in the American criminal justice system is complex and comprehensive. Robin (1980) defines the role in accordance with the stage at which proceedings stand, as follows:

1. *Investigation:* The public prosecutor prepares search and arrest warrants.
2. *Arrest:* He screens cases to decide whether to initiate prosecution; and decides that some cases will not be prosecuted. The prosecutor screens and evaluates documents (and, time permitting, may talk to the arresting officer) in order to decide whether to accept or reject the case for prosecution. The prosecutor who decides to accept a case issues a complaint, upon which the suspect is arraigned before a magistrate.

   In some jurisdictions the police, the complainant and the prosecutor will jointly consider the charges. Sometimes the police alone will prepare the charges, usually as a compromise to deal with the heavy workloads of the prosecutor.
3. *First court appearance:* The prosecutor sees that cases accepted for prosecution are arraigned in the magistrates court; he 'cooperates' with the court in summary disposition of minor misdemeanours; requests high bail in felony cases; and may discontinue prosecution in appropriate cases. (For details of the passage of a case through the courts, see Chapter 3.)
4. *Preliminary hearing:* The role of the prosecutor is to establish probable cause before a judge; he may withdraw cases.
5. *Grand Jury:* He establishes probable cause before a Grand Jury in seeking an indictment on a single charge or on multiple counts.
6. *Arraignment:* The prosecutor deals with cases in which defendants enter formal pleas to charges in the indictment: he may allow a defendant to plead guilty to a reduced charge or to a single charge in a multiple-count indictment.
7. *Pre-trial motions:* The role here is to oppose motions commenced by the defence aimed at suppressing illegally obtained evidence or attempts to obtain the dismissal of a case.
8. *Trial:* The prosecutor is responsible for proving guilt beyond a reasonable doubt.
9. *Sentencing:* Recommends harsh or lenient sentencing.
10. *Appeal:* Presents the prosecution case that the conviction was properly obtained and that the finding should not be overturned.
11. *Parole:* The prosecutor may be engaged in opposing early parole particularly in the case of dangerous offenders.

Prosecution in the British courts

With the implementation of the Crown Prosecution Service, the full impact of which is still to be assessed, many changes in procedure were introduced. The following is the current position, contrasted with that which existed pre-1986 where appropriate.

- *Investigation:* The police were entirely responsible for all applications for search and arrest warrants and in general remain so.

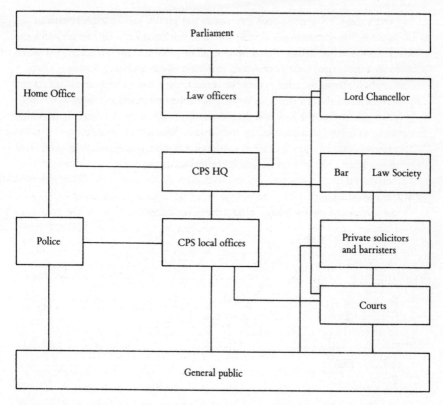

Figure 10.1 The Crown Prosecution Service: place in the criminal justice structure.

- *Arrest:* All cases were and are screened by police, and initial prosecution or 'no further action' decisions are taken by police, but paperwork must be submitted to the CPS for evaluation and decision to continue or discontinue the action.
- *First court appearance:* All cases are now presented by the CPS. Previously most initial appearances were undertaken by the police but in complex or contentious cases a solicitor might have been retained to prosecute (but not to make decisions about prosecution although advice might be sought).
- *Preliminary hearing:* Except in cases where a solicitor was briefed, presentation of a large number of cases in the committal phase was undertaken by police. Now all cases are presented by advocates of the CPS. It will be recalled (see Chapter 3) that the majority of such cases are dealt with on paper rather than through personal appearance.
- *Grand Jury:* The Grand Jury in the UK was abandoned in 1933.
- *Arraignment/pre-trial motions/trial/sentencing:* The entire process of presentation of any case to the Crown Court (see Chapter 3) is undertaken by barristers representing the prosecution. Once indictments have been laid in the magistrates court they can rarely be changed.

Although the CPS system does not match the public prosecution system in the USA in its entirety, the Act provides for the setting-up of the service with the primary function of acting as an independent reviewer of all cases in which defendants are charged or summoned for offences by the police.

The process allows for such review to occur before the court hearing, unless the defendant enters a plea of guilty in writing for specified minor offences.

If it is decided that the case should proceed, it is presented in court by a crown prosecutor, or a lawyer instructed by the Crown Prosecution Service.

The Crown Prosecution Service is national in nature and is centrally controlled through the Office of the Director of Public Prosecutions.

The relationship of the service with other parts of the criminal justice system is shown in Figure 10.1.

The objectives of the CPS have been defined as follows:

1. To be, and to be seen to be, independent of the police.
2. To ensure that the general quality of decision-making and case preparation is of high level and that decisions are not susceptible to improper influence.
3. To provide flexibility to take into account local circumstances.
4. To continue prosecutions while, and only while, they are in the public interest.
5. To conduct cases vigorously and without delay.
6. To undertake prosecution work effectively, efficiently and economically.
7. To seek to improve the criminal justice system as a whole (Arthur Anderson and Co., 1985).

Plea bargaining

There has, in the past, been little opportunity in the English courts for 'plea bargaining' in the American sense of that phrase. Sometimes, when two or more charges have been laid against a defendant, a plea to a lesser offence might have been accepted and no evidence offered on other charges. More commonly, however, where only one charge was laid, and since the prosecution decision had been taken by police, the police decision would be to 'go for it' rather than to accept a plea to a lesser offence. Even in cases in which the police were represented by a solicitor or barrister the acceptance of a plea to a lesser charge would not, in general, be taken without consultation with and approval by the 'officer in the case'. In any case, no *pre-arrangements* for lighter sentences or particular types of sentence (i.e. probation, community service orders, etc.) through prosecution initiatives could or can be made with the judge.

In some cases English law allows for the reduction of an offence if the evidence is insufficient to warrant a conviction for a particular offence but is, nevertheless, sufficient to justify conviction for a lesser one. For example, the serious assault offences may be reduced if the evidence does not establish certain facts, e.g. the *intent* to cause serious injury. In such a case the charge may be dealt with as an offence of causing serious injury in the absence of such intent.

Critics of the plea bargaining practice in the USA have considered it unconstitutional (*Harvard Law Review*, 1970), illegitimate (Dean, 1974)[3] or may lead to innocent persons being convicted;[4] although others (e.g. McCoy, 1980) endorse the practice as a legitimate 'due process' procedure.

The major function of plea bargaining in the US judicial process is to facilitate the 'speedy trial' of a defendant (cf. Bent and Rossum, 1976; Vetri, 1964) and it seems likely that the CPS will develop the 'plea bargaining system' if only to handle the huge caseload which will be placed on the shoulders of a few lawyers taking over a role previously carried out by a large number of policemen. It is said that individual lawyers are required to deal with up to fifty cases a day (Boyle, 1987).

There has been growing criticism of the role of the CPS which is 500 lawyers short of its establishment. Consequently, it uses part-time, and thus uncommitted, junior counsel who are employed on a daily basis. The system is said to have produced 'longer case adjournments' (Boyle, 1987) and to have produced a situation that makes many police officers feel that, if as prosecutors they had done what many CPS employees have done, 'they would be demoted, fined, or even dismissed'.[5] Not surprisingly, the CPS response has been to blame the police for delays and inadequate preparation of paperwork.[6]

The reaction of chief police officers to the introduction of CPS has ranged from enthusiastic acceptance, through apathetic acceptance, to furious antipathy – the latter being the most common.

Many chief officers, and others of lower rank, see this innovation as yet another reduction of their individual, autonomous power and prestige; a further intrusion of 'lawyers' into police decision-making. Above all, police at all levels see it as another example of the swing of the pendulum in favour of the accused and against the prosecution. (CPS, it is said, will be unlikely to 'take a chance' in the face of limited evidence, even when the past convictions had been obtained on the basis of similar facts.)

Finally, of course, it is said to be an example of the manner in which the police are viewed by the legislators and others; that is, as artisans – investigators and enforcers of the law, with no part to play in any of the other realms reserved for the 'professional'. (See Chapter 6 for a brief discussion of the nature of professionalism.) It is thus the case that British officers increasingly see themselves as *ex machina*, with all that that implies in psychological terms.

Other organizational change

The increasing threat of terrorism, the growing use of firearms by criminals in the pursuit of easy gain (see Chapter 9), and the ever-present threat of riot, conspire together to encourage the police in England and Wales to reorganize internally on increasingly specialized lines. Sir Kenneth Newman, during his tenure as

Commissioner of the Metropolitan Police, sought to develop the notion of an 'omni-competent' patrol officer, able to respond to all kinds of demands for service. But despite the rationalization of the organization of Scotland Yard (discussed in Chapter 5), the increasingly sophisticated approach to dealing with potential and real public disorder (including the analysis of 'tension indicators' through District Information Units,[7] the development of comprehensive plans for quelling disorder, dispersal of crowds and the provision of special vehicles for removing barricades, etc.) will lead, inevitably, to the development of more specialism within small groups of officers dedicated to 'law enforcement' rather than 'order maintenance'. Although presented as being for reasons of effective supervision and training, etc., the reduction of the numbers of armed officers is, in reality, the first stage of the development of dedicated bodies of men and women who will not participate in any way in the day-to-day activities of policing.

PHILOSOPHICAL/LEGALISTIC CHANGES

The Police and Criminal Evidence Act 1984, with its intention to strike a balance between the powers of police, on one hand, and the rights of those arrested, on the other, is an historic benchmark, against which all future change and past occurrence must be interpreted.

In particular, the insistence that arrested persons have the right to legal advice which can only be delayed under very specific circumstances has altered entirely the previous position under which the police and the police alone could consistently deny such access *without any legal consequence*. Although it has taken a comparatively long time, we are beginning to see court decisions which are defining the rules in the Code of Practice.[8]

Similarly, the restrictions on stop and search powers and the potential for the creation of an exclusionary rule contained in the Act will, as they are interpreted by the courts, lead to a redefinition of the role of the police in England and Wales away from the crime control model towards the due process model. That shift will occur simply because the police will start to see themselves more and more as victims of the criminal justice system (see Chapter 7).

In his annual report for 1983 Sir Kenneth Newman noted that the crime control model

> ... has a relatively prominent police profile, incorporating assertive patrol activity, high level visibility, extensive use of stop-and-search powers, the likelihood of abrasive street contacts and, on occasions, *a casual attitude towards civil rights*. (*Report of the Commissioner of Police of the Metropolis for 1983*, 1984, p. 7) (emphasis added)

In their concern for 'balance' between control of crime and control of the police (particularly in seeking the elimination of the casual attitude towards civil rights) Parliament may have failed to take into account the potential for a shift in the police role.

As Reiner (1985, p. 198) points out: 'Many changes (in the nature of policing) ... were the *unintended* consequence of reforms aimed at achieving quite different results.' It is entirely possible that the attempt of the legislators to police the police will be roundly ignored by them and simply place them at loggerheads with the rest of the criminal justice system (e.g. see Oxford (1988) *re* 'bluffing' suspects to confess).

Reiner (1985, Chapter 6) has argued that what he calls the 'rational deterrence' model,[9] is not likely to be more effective in policing the police than in policing crime. Indeed, although the police in the USA threw up their hands in horror at the Miranda decision, subsequent studies (e.g. Stephens, 1973) have tended to show that police effectiveness 'may not have been significantly reduced' (Mathias et al., 1980, p. 165). Which begs the question, if the police are still able to perform their function, contrary to their own expectations, what effect do the 'new' rules actually have?

The simple answer is that, just like their colleagues in the USA, British officers will find themselves in a sort of 'no man's land', beyond the pale of the justice system – neither prosecutor nor defender; not professional enough to be trusted but culpable enough to be criticized; an investigator and gatherer of data but having no part to play in the justice process save as cogs in a wheel – a wheel serviced, oiled and turned by lawyers.[10]

It is a significant fact that, for many years, the British police visitor to US police departments would be consistently regaled with 'lawyer' stories, the police equivalent of 'Polak', 'Black' or 'Irish' jokes. This kind of 'lawyerism' was rarely heard in British police culture but now, surrounded by CPS on one side and the increased access to legal advice for suspects on the other, the picture has changed. Lawyerist jokes are on the increase.

The use of the word 'lawyerist' is quite deliberate, for the police are a minority group and respond to prejudice as any human group do. Studies of prejudice by social psychologists have shown that there are a number of consequences for those who are, or perceive themselves to be, on the receiving end. They may (Hashimi, 1973):

1. Become constantly on the defensive, looking for hostile behaviour that may never have been intended which they may then attribute to prejudice.
2. Develop an obsessive concern with, and worry about, doing the 'right thing'.
3. Some may withdraw from all potentially threatening social contact.
4. Become sly and cunning.
5. Strengthen in-group ties and internal organization.
6. Finally, some may deny membership of the group.[11]

The consequence is a growing alienation from the system of which they are supposed to be a part.

Toch (1969) conducted a cogent analysis of the similarity between the aspirations of two minorities in the USA; the police and blacks. He concluded that on the police side:

For his part, the officer feels perpetually persecuted, in that again and again, as he bumbles his way through his awkward personal encounters, the social order (which he represents) appears subjected to unbearable contempt. This leads to cumulative bitterness and increased militancy. When bluff and bluster achieve nothing, it follows that the blame must lie elsewhere. Personal impotence is attributed to national 'criminal coddling'. The officer feels 'handcuffed', not by his own behaviour but by bleeding heart judges and politically motivated civilians. (Toch, 1969, pp. 201–2)

Currently, the railing against CPS, the anticipated effects of PACE and the strengthening of internal organization, are the stage of 'bluff and bluster'. It is entirely likely that effects of the Police and Criminal Evidence Act 1984 will be that, after the dust has settled, crime, detection and clearance rates will be unaffected, but that the nature of policing will be pushed in an unanticipated direction.

Constitutional issues

It is to be hoped that the nature of British policing is such that the 'backlash' effect of the exercise of judicial criticism of police behaviour will be avoided.

But the Police and Criminal Evidence Act 1984 has provided something which begins to look a little like a Bill of Rights. To suggest on the basis of that fact alone that there is any real form of 'constitutional convergence' would, of course, be a nonsense. The constitution of the USA is far more than the Bill of Rights and the unwritten constitution of the UK is of similar complexity. But there is, in the UK, a growing use of the facility afforded by the Supreme Court of Judicature for judicial review. With the facility of that court to deal with matters far more rapidly than their counterparts in the USA, it is entirely likely that issues of breaches of civil rights, at least in the form defined by the Police and Criminal Evidence Act 1984, will be increasingly clearly defined. *Limited* constitutional convergence as a paradigm is less problematic than the 'full-scale' model. If that is the case, it is essential that the police become more readily responsive to changes and re-definitions of the rights of suspects.

In *R* v. *Mason*,[12] a case decided, in early May 1987, it was held that telling a suspect that there was forensic evidence against him when in fact there was none made the subsequent confessions unreliable and thus inadmissable. The conviction was quashed. In December of the same year many operational police officers still had not heard of the decision.[13]

On the other hand, the decision in *R* v. *Samuel*,[14] in December 1987, which held that the right of access to a solicitor could not be denied on the grounds that 'he might advise the person not to answer questions', and that the delay possible under PACE could only be undertaken in the face of *evidence* that the presence of a particular legal adviser would impede the course of justice, was conveyed to street police officers in a letter from the Chairman of the ACPO Crime Committee, dated 12 January 1988. By mid-January most officers were aware of the case.

Rapid assimilation of court decisions about issues of civil rights is of paramount importance to the maintenance of police credibility.

CONCLUSION

We have attempted to show that changes in the criminal justice system of England and Wales have only occurred after many years of openly expressed concern which have subsequently led to sufficient Parliamentary support for the necessary legislation to be initiated.

In Chapter 3 it was suggested that the existence of a written constitution had the effect of slowing legislative change, which is true – but only in the context of changes to the constitution.

The absence of a formal written constitution in the UK has had the effect that, despite huge levels of freedom, the lack of annotated 'rights' for the individual has led to only partly effective, non-legislative, attempts (like the Judges' Rules) to safeguard them. Attempts which were easily evaded and in any case, in the 'big picture', had little effect in moderating, let alone controlling, police excesses.

The movement towards annotated rights for suspects and those involved in the criminal justice process has been as slow, if not slower, than any effort to amend the American Constitution.

There has to be, without doubt, an appropriate climate for change: the time must be right. The values of the society and their expectation of the police role, that attitudes of the courts and the legislators and their understanding of the problems, must coincide in order to initiate such change.

We started this volume with an examination of the complexity of multi-layers of American policing (Chapter 1) and in particular we examined the resistance to 'consolidation' which is manifest at every level of 'police studies', both practical and academic. Undoubtedly eminent figures in the American legal, judicial and police 'systems' have felt the occasional pang of sympathy for the eloquent plea from August Vollmer for policing based on a state structure.

> The ideal sought is a single state police force ... with the control and management in the hands of a single executive ... with the power to hire and fire all subordinates ... protected from political hecklers and unscrupulous politicians ... when all these improvements have been made Americans can expect efficient police administration. (Vollmer, 1935)

But such a structure can only be achieved if the population want it. As long as there is a fear of centralized authority, as long as there is concern over one-man authority for extended tenure, as long as the people do not desire to delegate their public control (accountability) to a faceless bureaucratic body and, above all, for as long as excesses continue to be committed in the name of public security and law and order, such change can never occur.

It is just this centralization of police resources, strong individual authority, absence of satisfactory mechanisms for accountability, and levels of excess that have pushed the legalistic aspects of policing in England and Wales more and more in line with those of the USA. As we have seen, Parliament has taken a similar line to the Supreme Court. Whether that is a wise course to follow, particularly in the face of a need to balance the control of crime and criminality against the need to ensure individual freedom, remains to be seen. For – despite a huge number of differences – the fundamental similarity between our two nations is the 'democratic' heritage we share. Issues of democratic control of the police, professionalization, recruiting, training, organization, police powers and practices and the general efficacy of policing will continue to be sources of concern. But that is only right and proper.

The government – and the police – of a democratic country are meant to be argued about.

APPENDIX I

Amendments to the Constitution of the United States of America: The Bill of Rights

I   Congress shall make no law respecting an establishment of religion, or prohibiting the free exercise thereof; or abridging the freedom of speech, or the press; or the right of the people to peaceably assemble, and to petition the Government for redress of grievances.

II   A well regulated Militia being necessary to the security of a free State, the right of the people to keep and bear Arms shall not be infringed.

III   No Soldier shall, in time of peace, be quartered in any house, without the consent of the Owner, nor in time of war, but in a manner to be prescribed by law.

IV   The right of the people to be secure in their persons, houses, papers, and effects, against unreasonable searches and seizures, shall not be violated, and no Warrants shall issue, but upon probable cause, supported by oath or affirmation, and particularly describing the place to be searched, and the persons or things to be seized.

V   No person shall be held to answer for a capital, or otherwise infamous crime unless on a presentment of indictment of a Grand Jury, except in a case arising in the land or naval forces, or in the Militia, when in actual service in time of War or public danger; nor shall any person be subject for the same offence to be put twice in jeopardy of life or limb; nor shall be compelled in any criminal case to be a witness against himself, nor be deprived of life liberty or property, without due process of law; nor shall private property be taken for public use, without just compensation.

VI   In all criminal prosecutions, the accused shall enjoy the rights to a speedy and public trial, by an impartial jury of the State and district wherein the crime shall have been committed, which district shall have been previously ascertained by law, and to be informed of the nature and cause of the accusation; to be confronted with the witnesses against him; to have compulsory process for obtaining witnesses in his favour, and to have the Assistance of Counsel for his defence.

VII   In suits of common law, where the value in controversy shall exceed twenty dollars, the right of trial by jury shall be preserved, and no fact tried by a jury shall be otherwise re-examined in any court of the United States, than according to the rules of the common law.

VIII   Excessive bail shall not be required, nor excessive fines imposed, nor cruel and unusual punishments inflicted.

IX   The enumeration in the Constitution of certain rights shall not be construed to deny or disparage others retained by the people.

X   The powers not delegated to the United States by the Constitution, or prohibited to it by the States, are reserved to the State respectively, or to the people.

The Fourteenth Amendment, added later, reads, in part:

No State shall deprive any person of life, liberty, or property, without due process of law; nor deny to any person within its jurisdiction the equal protection of the laws.

APPENDIX II

Metropolitan Police (London)

EQUAL OPPORTUNITIES POLICY

The following equal opportunity policy was published in Police Orders on 12 December 1986:

1. The Metropolitan Police is committed to being an equal opportunity employer and is determined to ensure that no job applicant or employee receives less favourable treatment on the grounds of sex or marital status, colour, race, nationality, ethnic or national origins or is disadvantaged by conditions or requirements which cannot be shown to be justified. We also seek to ensure that employees are not victimised or subjected to sexual or racial harassment.

2. Deputy Assistant Commissioner (Personnel) and Deputy Establishment Officer (Personnel) have particular responsibility for implementation and monitoring of this policy and as part of this process working parties and a committee are examining policy and practice within the force. To ensure that line managers and other relevant decision makers understand their position in law and under the force policy, training and guidance will be provided.

3. The law requires that individuals shall not unlawfully discriminate nor help others to do so. Eliminating discrimination and providing equality of opportunity depend upon personal commitment and all members of the force without exception must observe the requirements of the equal opportunities policy and apply its principles.

4. Individuals who feel that they have grounds for complaint in relation to discrimination should pursue their complaints through the grievance procedure.

5. Discrimination is not always intentional or overt. Practices and policies within the force will be consistently monitored to ensure that the equal opportunities policy is being properly implemented and where barriers to equal opportunity are identified any necessary changes will be made.

6. Apart from consideration of equality of opportunity and strict compliance with the law, the efficiency of any organisation will clearly be improved if it seeks to develop skills and abilities of all employees.

APPENDIX IIIa

Police Discipline Code – United Kingdom

EXTRACT FROM POLICE (DISCIPLINE) REGULATIONS 1985

1. DISCREDITABLE CONDUCT which offence is committed where a member of a police force acts in a disorderly manner, or in any manner prejudicial to discipline, or reasonably likely to bring discredit on the reputation of the force or of the police service.

2. MISCONDUCT TOWARDS A MEMBER OF A POLICE FORCE, which offence is committed where–

(a) The conduct of a member of a police force towards another such member is oppressive or abusive, or
(b) a member of a police force assaults another such member.

3. DISOBEDIENCE TO ORDERS, that is to say if a member of a police force disobeys, or without good or sufficient cause–

(a) disobeys or neglects to carry out any lawful order, written or otherwise
(b) fails to comply with any requirement of a code of practice for the time being in force under sec 60 or sec 66 of the Act of 1984
(c) contravenes any provision of the Police Regulations containing restrictions on the private lives of members of police forces, or requiring him to notify the chief officer of police that he, or a relation included in his family, has a business interest within the meaning of those regulations.

4. NEGLECT OF DUTY, which offence is committed where a member of a police force

(a) neglects or omits to carry out with due promptitude anything which is his duty as a member of a police force to attend to or carry out
(b) fails to work his beat in accordance with others, or leaves his beat, point, or other place of duty to which he has been ordered, or, having left his place of duty for an authorised purpose fails to return thereto without undue delay
(c) is absent without leave from, or is late for, any duty
(d) fails to account for, or make a prompt and true return of, any property or money received by him in the course of his duty.

5. FALSEHOOD OR PREVARICATION, which offence is committed where a member of a police force

(a)   knowingly or through neglect, makes or signs any false misleading or inaccurate oral or written statement or entry in any record or document made, kept or required for police purposes, or

(b)   either and without proper authority or through lack of due care destroys or mutilates any record or document made, kept or required for police purposes, or

(c)   has knowingly or through neglect made any false statement in connection with his appointments to the police force.

6. IMPROPER DISCLOSURE OF INFORMATION, which offence is committed where a member of a police force

(a)   without proper authority communicates to any person, any information which he has in his possession as a member of a police force, or

(b)   makes any anonymous communication to any police authority or any member of a police force or

(c)   without proper authority, makes representations to the police authority or the council of any county or district comprised in the police area with regard to any matter concerning the police force, or

(d)   canvasses any member of that authority or of such a council with regard to any such matter.

7. CORRUPT OR IMPROPER PRACTICE, which offence is committed where a member of a police force

(a)   in his capacity as a member of the force and without the authority of the chief officer of police directly or indirectly solicits or accepts any gratuity, present or subscription, or

(b)   places himself under pecuniary obligation to any person in such a manner as might affect his properly carrying out his duties as a member of the force

(c)   improperly uses or attempts to use his position as a member of the force for his private advantage, or

(d)   in his capacity as a member of the force, and without the consent of the chief officer of police, writes, signs or gives a testimonial of character or other recommendation with the object of obtaining employment for any person or of supporting an application for the grant of a licence of any kind.

8. ABUSE OF AUTHORITY, which offence is committed where a member of a police force

(a)   without good and sufficient cause conducts a search, or requires a person to submit to any test or procedure or makes an arrest, or

(b)   uses any unnecessary violence towards any prisoner or other person with whom he may be in contact in the execution of his duty, or improperly threatens such a person with violence, or

(c)   is abusive or uncivil to any member of the public.

9. RACIALLY DISCRIMINATORY BEHAVIOUR, which offence is committed (without prejudice to the commission of any other offence) where a member of a police force

(a) while on duty, on the grounds of another person's colour, race, nationality or ethnic or national origins, acts towards that other person in such a way as is mentioned in paragraph 8 (abuse of authority); or

(b) in any other way, on any of those grounds, treats improperly a person with whom he has been brought into contact while on duty.

10. NEGLECT OF HEALTH, which offence is committed where a member of a police force without good and sufficient cause, neglects to carry out any instructions of a medical officer appointed by the police authority or, while absent from duty on account of sickness commits any act or adopts any conduct calculated to retard his return to duty.

11. IMPROPER DRESS OR UNTIDINESS, which offence is committed where without good and sufficient cause a member of a police force while on duty or off duty but wearing uniform in a public place is improperly dressed or is untidy in his appearance.

12. DAMAGE TO POLICE PROPERTY, which offence is committed where a member of a police force

(a) wilfully or through lack of due care causes any waste, loss or damage to any police property, or

(b) fails to report as soon as is reasonably practicable any loss of or damage to any such property issued to, or used by him, or entrusted to his care.

13. DRUNKENNESS, which offence is committed where a member of a police force renders himself unfit through drink for duties which he is or will be required to perform or which he may reasonably foresee having to perform.

14. DRINKING ON DUTY OR SOLICITING DRINK, which offence is committed where a member of a police force, while on duty

(a) without proper authority, drinks, or receives from any other person, any intoxicating liquor, or

(b) demands, or endeavours to persuade any other person to give him, or to purchase or obtain for him, any intoxicating liquor.

15. ENTERING LICENSED PREMISES, which offence is committed where a member of a police force

(a) while on duty, or

(b) while off duty but wearing uniform, without good and sufficient cause, enters any premises in respect of which a licence or permit has been granted in pursuance of the law relating to liquor licensing or betting and gaming or regulating places of entertainment.

16. CRIMINAL CONDUCT, which offence is committed where a member of a police force has been found guilty by a court of law of a criminal offence.

17. BEING AN ACCESSORY TO A DISCIPLINE OFFENCE, which offence is committed where a member of a police force incites, connives at or is knowingly an accessory to any offence against discipline.

APPENDIX IIIb

Police Discipline – United States

MANUAL OF GENERAL ORDERS, POLICIES AND PROCEDURES

2.18a   Employee discipline shall consist of imposing one of the following steps or any combination of them.

1. Re-training
2. Counselling
3. Oral reprimand
4. Written reprimand
5. Voluntary loss of accumulated time (in lieu of suspension)
6. Voluntary loss of overtime pay (in lieu of suspension)
7. Voluntary uncompensated extra duty (in lieu of suspension)
8. Restitution
9. Suspension
10. Demotion
11. Termination

2.18b   Disciplinary action may be taken against an employee for any one or more of the following reasons:

1. Failure or inability to properly perform the duties and responsibilities required by the position in which employed
2. Insubordination toward a superior or other offensive conduct toward the public, superiors or other employees
3. Violation of attendance requirements or leave privileges; including but not limited to:
    (a)   excessive absenteeism
    (b)   excessive tardiness
    (c)   inexcusable absence without leave or failure to report to work after leave has expired
    (d)   inexcusable abuse of sick leave
    (e)   falsification of a time record or failure to report an absence from duty
4. Conviction of a felony or first degree misdemeanor involving moral turpitude or directly related to the position occupied.

5. Falsification of any application or record of employment.
6. Misappropriation of City funds or abuse or theft of City property
7. Commission of any fraudulent act which prevents the impartial execution of any Charleston Police Department Rule or Regulation
8. Use of or being under the influence of intoxicants or unlawful drugs while on the job
9. Violation of any provision found in these Rules and Regulations.

(Note: Nothing contained in any of these rules shall interfere with the right and duty of the Mayor, Chief of Police or any citizen to file charges on any grounds which they consider justifiable, against any employee.)

2.18c   Any officer who has completed probation who receives notice of a written reprimand, suspension, demotion or termination shall have the following rights:

1. The right to an informal hearing before the Chief of Police at which time the evidence regarding the incident shall be evaluated and discussed, and
2. The right to a formal hearing before the City of Charleston if the individual does not agree to the recommendation made by the Chief of Police at the informal hearing. At the formal hearing the employee has the right to present oral and documentary evidence, and cross examine all adverse parties and witnesses. The individual shall also have the right to be accompanied, represented and advised at the hearing by a representative of his or her own choosing.

Use of Force – Tallahassee Police Department, United States

Tallahassee Police Department General Orders	Date of Issue 7/28/86	Effective Date 7/28/86	Number GO– 60
Subject Use of Force	Reference		Index as Continuum of Force Deadly Force

Amends	Rescinds	Dist. All		Use of Force Use of Force Report

I. GUIDELINES

Although many decisions and actions of police officers have serious consequences, none are so irrevocable as the decision to use force – particularly deadly force. Police Officers are armed and trained in the use of weapons in order to carry out their responsibility to protect themselves or others against assaults from violent suspects and this defensive action is necessary and is supported by the Department.

These guidelines are intended for internal department use only and are not to be applied in any civil or criminal proceeding; nor do they create a higher legal standard of safety or care with respect to third parties. A violation of these rules will be grounds for administrative discipline only, while a violation of the law will be the basis for civil or criminal penalties which may be imposed by a court of law.

II. DEFINITION

Force is defined as that amount of 'active power, strength or energy' which is necessary to overcome a suspect's physical resistance. Officers are trained in the use of a continuum of force (see VII), and are expected to use the least amount of force necessary to effect an arrest or to control a person. If a suspect does not resist, or if the resisting is merely verbal, the use of force by an officer may constitute excessive force.

III.   USE OF FORCE REPORT

If it becomes necessary for an officer to use force to overcome resistance, as delineated in paragraphs IV and V below, a Use of Force Report must be completed by the officer and submitted to his supervisor. Copies of this report will then be forwarded through the Chain of Command to the Chief of Police.

IV.   DEADLY FORCE

The use of deadly force requires medical attention and the following statements apply:

A.   In deciding whether to use deadly force, the value of human life should outweigh all other considerations.

B.   An officer may only use deadly force when he reasonably believes it is necessary in defense of his life or the life of another person. An officer may not become both judge and jury by using force to stop a suspect who poses no threat to him or to the safety of others.

C.   Whenever possible, an officer must give a verbal warning prior to using deadly force.

D.   Warning shots pose a serious danger to other persons who are present in the area and are not to be fired.

E.   Shots at moving vehicles or from moving police vehicles are generally ineffective and are not to be fired unless absolutely necessary in defense of life.

V.   NON-DEADLY FORCE

During incidents involving the use of non-deadly force, a Use of Force Report should be completed when and if:

A.   The Use of Force results in a injury; or

B.   A firearm, nightstick, stungun, chemical agent, or canine is used; or

C.   Any arrest technique having the potential to cause significant injury is used; or

D.   In the officer's supervisor's judgement, the use of even minimal force, under any circumstances, will result in a complaint being filed against the officer.

NOTE: For the purpose of this general order, the pointing of a firearm at an individual constitutes use.

VI.   INVESTIGATIONS

A.   Any time the use of force by an officer results in death, an injury likely to cause death, and/or a shooting, the following units will be notified:

1. Inspectional Services
2. Homicide/Assault Unit

B. All other use of force investigations shall be conducted by the Inspectional Services Section.

VII. CONTINUUM OF FORCE

A. When an individual is arrested, he may

1. Submit
2. Flee
3. Fight
    a. *Passive resistance* – Suspect pulls away from the officer however does not present a threat or actively resist.
    b. *Active resistance* – Suspect actively attacks officer and/or through his/her actions aggressively resists the arrest.
4. Suicide.

B. In response to the above situations the officer should be guided as follows:

LEVEL 1.   OFFICER PRESENCE – Best illustrated when the officer arrives at the scene. This violator sees the officer and does not alter his/her illegal behaviour. The assumption is that the violator knows that the person who has just arrived at the scene is a police officer. They acknowledge the officer's presence because of the marked patrol vehicle, the uniform or the visible badge/identification. Should the violator continue their actions the officer may advance – or escalate – to level 2.

LEVEL 2.   VERBAL COMMANDS – Best illustrated when the officer advises the violator to keep quiet move along, etc. The assumption is that the violator can clearly hear the officer's directions. If the violator continues the illegal actions, the officer may advance – or escalate – to level 3.

LEVEL 3.   CONTROL AND RESTRAINT (empty hand) – Best illustrated when the officer applies a wrist lock, take down or pressure point technique. Most police officer defensive tactics techniques will fall in this area since they are designed for gaining control of the individual and do not have a high potential of injury.

LEVEL 3a.   A slight increase in the level of resistance by the suspect (*punching or increased struggling*) may cause the arresting officer to respond by striking the suspect. These blows should be directed towards areas which are not likely to cause great bodily harm, i.e., motor points, navel area. If these techniques are not effective or if the officer feels that he cannot gain control by using these techniques, he may advance to level 4.

LEVEL 4.   CHEMICAL AGENTS, STUNGUN – Creates a low level of incapacitation with minimal chance of injury. Care should be taken that any time a technique is used (at any level in the continuum) that may cause a violator to fall, his head should not be allowed to strike the ground with a high level of force. If control cannot be achieved at this level, the officer may advance – or escalate – to level 5.

LEVEL 5.   TEMPORARY INCAPACITATION – Best illustrated when the officer is forced to strike the violator with an impact weapon, i.e. a night stick or flashlight when it is the weapon of necessity. These strikes should be directed toward approved striking points. Any blows to the head, neck or shoulder areas are to be avoided. Should the violator pull a knife, draw a firearm or attempt to otherwise kill or seriously injure the officer or the citizen, the officer may advance – or escalate – to level 6.

LEVEL 6.   DEADLY FORCE – Best illustrated when the officer must shoot the violator or strike the suspect with an instrument in a manner that is likely to cause death or great bodily harm.

It is important to note that often because of the suspect's actions, it is necessary to skip levels, i.e. level 1 to level 3. All actions by an officer are predicted by a suspect's actions. Also, the continuum of force works both ways. At all times an officer should be issuing loud verbal commands in an attempt to gain voluntary compliance by the violator. Any time the level of resistance by the violator is increased or decreased, the officer must adjust his/her level of response accordingly.

Notes

CHAPTER 1

1. See for example an interesting discussion of such comparisons of statistical data in Smith, L. J. F. (1983).
2. Which in any case is one of those statistical problems made more complex in the USA by differences between levels of taxation of one kind or another at local, and state level.
3. For example, in California residents of an unincorporated area of a County may petition to form such a district to provide for more intensive coverage than is available from other systems (Commission on Police Officers' Standards and Training, 1976). Such service may be provided by a sheriff, another police agency or a private person or agency. Such a system is currently to be seen in Contra Nostra and San Mateo Counties in California and in Suffolk and Nassau Counties in New York.
4. In November 1987 in a written answer to a parliamentary question, the Home Secretary announced that the Metropolitan Police in London were to come under the scrutiny of Her Majesty's Inspectorate of Constabulary. This is likely to include reviews of efficiency as well as training and force expenditure and appears to be the first step in altering the structure of systems of accountability, particularly in the fiscal area, within that force.
5. That such an issue could have been raised at all contrasts markedly with the lack of enthusiasm shown by those concerned with American policing for anything other than, at the most, a forlornly speculative desire for state policing of one kind or another. For an academic or practitioner to seek national policing in the USA (even if, in so huge a country it were feasible) would probably result in his or her consignment to the outer reaches of academe.
6. Field interviews in consolidation areas in Virginia, California, Minnesota, Kansas and South Dakota and Oregon tended to confirm these views. In particular, 'the two areas of least satisfaction appeared to be traffic control and city ordinance enforcement' (Bureau of Government Research and Service, 1975).

CHAPTER 2

1. In 1752, Horace Walpole the writer and son of Sir Robert Walpole, the Prime Minister, wrote that in London 'one is forced to travel, even at noon, as if one were going into battle'.
2. In the same year a further Parliamentary committee had discussed, and yet again rejected the notion of a full-time police.
3. Writing in 1836, Charles Dickens, then aged 24, wrote with a touch of literary irony:

   The gin-shops in and near Drury Lane, Holborn, St Giles's, Covent Garden and Clare Market, are the handsomest in London. There is more filth and squalid misery near these great thoroughfares than in any part of this mighty city. [Charles Dickens, *Sketches by Boz*]

4. For the US reader it should be explained that the phrase 'knocking people up' refers to giving people a 'wake-up call' and has no sexual connotations whatsoever.
5. Metropolitan Police Orders, 1 November 1830.
6. Inadvertently Peel's strategy also served as the foundation of the stereotype of the policeman as lower-class and ill-educated!
7. Metropolitan Police Act 1839, sec. 54(17).
8. Ibid., sec. 54(16).
9. Ibid., sec. 54(8).
10. See ibid., sec. 60 subsections 1, 2, 3, 7 and 8 which deal with everything from burning materials in the street through beating or shaking a carpet, to leaving open vaults, cellars or sewers, and Metropolitan Police Act 1839, sec. 54 subsections 1–8.
11. See ibid., sec. 54, subsec. 4, 5, 6, 7, 14; and Highway Act 1835, sec. 72.
12. As the US vernacular puts it: 'When you're hot you're hot'; or the more restrained British version, 'Nothing succeeds like success'.
13. However, consideration of the Indians aside, as Becker and Whitehouse (1979, p. 25) put it: 'Justice in those days was swift. It was said that justice was administered with great promptness because there were no lawyers – a happy but short-lived circumstance.'
14. According to Beckman (1980) most early 'full-time' police officers felt that wearing a badge was a sign of degradation and servitude and any effort to enforce 'badge-wearing' was met with stiff resistance.
15. The Pope declared war against Austria.
16. But, as all immigrants have always done, they sought out and stayed with their own kind. New York's Broadway was described by Charles Dickens (1842) in *American Notes* as:

   ... reeking everywhere with dirt and filth. Such lives as are lived here, bear the same fruits as elsewhere. The coarse and bloated faces at the doors have counterparts at home, and the world over. Debauchery has made the very houses prematurely old.

   Here too are lanes and alleys, paved with mud knee-deep; underground chambers where they dance and game: ruined houses, open to the streets, whence, through wide gaps in the walls, other ruins loom upon the eye, as though the world of vice and misery had nothing else to show: hideous tenements which take their name from robbery and murder: all that is loathsome, drooping and decayed is there.

   Clearly Dickens found himself in a New World not dissimilar from the Old.

17. The development in Boston took place because the citizens 'would not or could not protect themselves' (Lane, 1971) and was, according to City Doc. No. 15:

> Intended to initiate, as far as may be, the system of London, were [sic] a similar patrol is established and is found to be of advantage in various ways beside the enforcement of laws.

18. Devery himself later ran for an official post in the Tamanay organization.

19. In Martinsburg, West Virginia, both the local sheriff and his men *and* the local militia 'retired hurt'.

20. The Home Office and the Home Secretary have, in practice, limited jurisdiction over forces outside London. But the whole question of police accountability and control has, as yet, to be fully resolved. The process of reduction of the number of forces to its current 43, even from the 133 which existed in 1949 has tended to increase the level of Office Home involvement. By and large, however, the level of political manipulation, at least in the sense of that discussed in connection with the appointment and tenure of NYPD Commissioners, has been very limited and there is no evidence of corruption or double dealing in the making of such appointments.

21. At the time of the industrial action by the National Union of Mine Workers (NUM) in 1984/85 many commentators were concerned at the apparent political manipulation of the police response to picketing and disorder, and in particular to the activation of the National Reporting Centre (NRC) at Scotland Yard. The NRC operates under the control of the Vice-President of the Association of Chief Police Officers (ACPO) and is responsible for coordinating the response when many forces are involved in 'mutual aid'. For many commentators the existence of NRC was seen as the thin end of the wedge in the creation of a National Police Force (NPF). The equation on many lips was NUM+NRC=NPF (see Chapter 9 for a further discussion of this point).

22. See *R. v. Secretary of State for the Home Department, ex parte* Northumbria Police Authority. Court of Appeal, 18 November 1987. *The Home Secretary has power under sec. 41 of the Police Act to supply CS gas to a Chief Constable without the consent of the Police Authority. It is a power exercised under the Royal Prerogative and is not in conflict with the police authorities' power to equip their force under statute.*

CHAPTER 3

1. Jefferson was not at the 'great debate' for he was in Paris, a witness to the events, including the denial of, and threats to, 'civil rights' which culminated in the French Revolution. He returned to his country convinced that the provision of *written* rights – particularly in safeguarding the right to remain unmolested by government and the authorities, through search, seizure and unlawful arrest and prosecution – was the key to ensuring that abuses did not occur or at least were the subject of judicial review.

2. The Constitution of the United States was described by one of Britain's prime ministers, William Gladstone, as: 'the most wonderful work ever struck off at a given time by the brain and purpose of man.'

3. For example that the monarch will not refuse assent to a Bill which has passed both Houses and Parliament.

4. For example, following the lead of the Temperance Movement in Britain, the US Congress agreed to a Prohibition Amendment to the Constitution which was ratified, by the required three-quarters of the States, on 29 January 1919. It was the eighteenth amendment to the document but within a fairly short space of time it became apparent that the amendment was a mistake. The upsurge of criminal activity as a direct consequence of the amendment is well known. This 'counter-productive legislation' took fifteen years to repeal. When repeal took place, on 5 December 1933, that repeal became the twenty-first amendment to the Constitution.

5. A constitutional issue considered in 1941 by the Supreme Court of the USA (*Cox* v. *New Hampshire*, 312 US. 596, 61 S.Ct 7626,85 L.Ed 1049). The court considered whether the requirement to obtain a permit for a 'parade or procession' on a public street was unconstitutional. They concluded that the state may require such a licence and charge a fee for it.

   See also *Coates* v. *Cincinattii*, 402 US. 91 S.Ct. 1686, 29 L.Ed 214 (1971).

6. Rapid changes in the British Constitution have taken place on at least three occasons, the last being in 1936 at the time of the abdication of King Edward VIII. Parliament has altered its own procedures for making laws – and followed them (Parliament Acts, 1911 and 1949); has declared itself a new body through acts of union (expressly forbidden in the US Constitution) on the incorporation of first Scotland and later Ireland under Parliamentary rule from Westminster; and has even prolonged its own five-year term (although only in the special case of war).

7. In the USA, at preliminary hearings to assess 'probable cause', 'Trustworthy hearsay evidence may be admitted ...' (Watson and McAninch, 1984, pp. 71–2). Such evidence is never admissible in criminal court proceedings in Britain.

8. Since 1967, majority verdicts have been permitted in British courts, with the authority of the judge. A split of 11–1 or 10–2 is the maximum permissible deviation from unanimity.

9. For example, in *Miranda* v. *Arizona* discussed more fully later, the accused was remanded to the trial court for re-trial. Miranda was still found guilty and sentenced to 20–30 years' imprisonment.

10. The modern legal profession has three main branches: judges, barristers and solicitors. At the bottom of the scale are the solicitors whose function is primarily office work and the provision of advice to clients. They are legally trained and are supervised by a professional body, the Law Society.

    The title 'solicitor' is used in South Carolina to distinguish the official known in most states as the District Attorney – a hangover from British Colonial days.

    Solicitors are 'officers of the court' and generally act as advocates only in the magistrates courts. They have however very recently (1985) been granted the right to argue certain categories of case in higher courts. They are liable for action for negligence but can sue for unpaid fees.

11. Beginning their studies in one of the ancient 'Inns of Court', barristers take their Bar Final Examinations after having been registered in an 'Inn' for three years. Success in the examination means that they will be 'called to the bar' (hence bar-rister) and are entitled to practise.

    All barristers are called 'juniors' regardless of age, unless and until they are appointed by the Lord Chancellor as 'Queen's Council'. Called 'taking silk', the Lord Chancellor makes his selection from those who apply on the basis of seniority and eminence.

    Barristers are not liable for actions for negligence but cannot (unlike solicitors) sue for fees owed to them.

12. *US News and World Report,* 1977. There is no overt party political association by judges in the UK.

13. They are know as 'puisne' (pronounced 'puny') judges.

14. In November 1987 in a written answer to a Parliamentary Question, the Under-Secretary of the Home Office indicated that there were about 9000 untried prisoners held in prisons in the UK and that about 900 of them were in police cells.

15. *Police Review,* Vol. 5, No. 4910, 1.5.87.

16. *Kuruma, Son of Kamu* v. *R.* (1941) 28 Cr. Appeal. R.84.

17. Police and Criminal Evidence Act 1984, sec. 78.

18. 22 US 383 (1941).

19. *Wolf* v. *Colorado,* 338 US 25 (1949).

20. In part this was a consequence of federal agents handing to state authorities evidence which would have been excluded in federal courts but which would be admitted in state courts.

21. Not surprisingly, much research has been undertaken to establish the veracity of the allegation that the existence of such a rule in the USA has resulted in a higher level of 'nol pros' decisions, acquittals and other 'rejections'.

   The 'costs' of the rule seems not to have been as large as the concerned might have suggested.

   In the District of Columbia only 1 per cent of a sample of cases was rejected before trial. In a study in four states a 4 per cent rejection rate was found, whilst in a third the major reasons for rejection were found to be insufficiency of evidence, or difficulty with witness evidence or availability. (See Driscol, 1987, for a full discussion of these and other data.)

22. Regrettably the one area that does not seem to have been researched is the practical effect of the rule on 'on the street policing'. Are there any stratagems, tricks of the trade, or manipulations that are undertaken to avoid the effects of the rules? It is entirely possible that the small rejection levels referred to in note 21 are a consequence of some other cause than the overt efficacy of the rule.

23. See McKenzie, I. K., and Irving, B. L., (1987) and Irving, B. L., and McKenzie, I. K., (1987).

CHAPTER 4

1. See Chapter 1, note 4.

2. Some ex-military men continued to be appointed under the 'exceptional qualities' clause, but all chief constables are now full-service regular police officers.

3. Interestingly, a 'police strike' in Boston USA during the same period had the effect of changing what had become an English style of policing to one that was (and is) more typically American.

4. In 1987 the Ministry of Defence police were given the status and powers of regular officers.

5. Hansard, Vol. 213, col. 47.

6. *R.* v. *Metropolitan Police Commissioner, ex parte* Blackburn, 1968.

7. See note 29, Chapter 2.

8. A further example of the manner in which the due process model is used in the USA repeatedly to exercise control of policing and police authority.

9. As are many other posts at lower level, within guidelines issued by the Home Office. Specialist posts, dog-handler sergeants, computer specialists, training staff, are all from time to time to be seen in the pages of *Police Review*.

10. Indiana has a statute that prohibits the consideration of any candidate from outside the state.

11. In one case in Florida closed-circuit TV was installed, as the number of people seeking access to the hall where the interviews were to be held was too large to be accommodated.

12. For all the apparent sophistication of these procedures, in some states (e.g. South Carolina) posts are advertised in the Vacancies column of newspapers. 'Police Chief Wanted' is a fairly common heading in *The State* in South Carolina, although it should be emphasized that these are for posts in one-, two- and three-man departments.

CHAPTER 5

1. Not her – yet. See Lock (1987); Low (1987); Halford (1987). For a more comprehensive view of the role of women in policing, see Southgate (1979), Sullivan (1979) and Jones (1986) regarding the UK; and Martin (1979) and Price and Gavin (1982) regarding the USA.

2. Until the reorganization in 1983 known as A Department.

3. Many of the functions carried out by SO are those of the old C (Crime) Department.

4. Special Branch are a specialized unit dealing with issues of national security, protection of certain high British officials (not royalty), and other matters of a sensitive political nature.

5. Until the reorganization in 1983 known as D Department.

6. Although many officers in the UK will refer to Scotland Yard as 'the Yard' in the manner of detective fiction, most Metropolitan Police habitually use the designation 'CO' (Commissioner's Office).

7. The bulk of these data on NYPD was obtained during research specially conducted in 1983 (and previously unpublished) using an adaptation of the survey instrument used by the Police Executive Research Forum (PERF, 1978) in their study of 45 police departments. The data for the Metropolitan Police were matched on those dimensions.

8. Or a loss of about 18.66 per cent of the 1975 strength.

9. See Becker and Whitehouse (1979, p. 31) for a discussion of these data and their association with a *fall* in the number of grand larcenies, robberies and other serious crimes.

10. The data on pay were updated in 1987 from those obtained by the 1983 survey instrument just prior to a huge surge in the value of the pound against the dollar. The decision to use the standardized unit was thoroughly vindicated. We are indebted to Dr Eli Silverman of John Jay College of Criminal Justice, New York, for the data on rates of pay for senior ranks of the New York Police Department.

11. The rates for detectives as with other uniform ranks is based on a complex multi-tier system with nearly 100 data points for ranks from new patrolman to lieutenant special assignment/commander of detectives. There are 36 data points in the grades between newly appointed captain and long-service deputy chief.

12. Despite the fact that some people believe that these restrictions are a form of both institutionalized racism and sexism, there is no evidence of any potential change.

13. In the late 1960s and early 1970s some forces, in particular the Metropolitan Police in London, were grossly undermanned and accepted applicants with criminal records for minor offences provided that there was no element of dishonesty involved in the circumstances of the case.

14. For example, failing to renew a firearms certificate or vehicle excise licence.

15. Such sessions may include lengthy physical fitness and mental agility components as well as examination of 'leadership' qualities and other more subtle traits.

16. 496F Supp 93. D. NJ. (1980)

17. 52F. F Sup 394 (SD NY. 1981) aff'd 683 F. 2nd 635 (2nd Cir. 1982).

18. The plaintiff had been shot by her husband, a police officer, who then committed suicide.

19. 443 F Sup –D. Haw 1977.

20. 50 N.Y. 2d 85, 405N.E. 2d 679, 1980.

21. *Sunday Times*, 4 May 1987, p. 4.

22. See also Jacobs and Cohen (1978).

23. For many years officers intending to sit the promotion examination were required to obtain a Certificate of Competence signed by a senior officer of commander rank which declared that an officer was 'suited in every way for promotion'. The process of issue of these certificates has become a 'rubber stamp' operation: not because of any ulterior motive but simply because the phrase 'suited in every way' had never been defined. Following a major project within the Metropolitan Police, Certificates of Competence are shortly to be issued against predetermined criteria, measured against operational performance and will therefore lose the 'rubber stamp' ethos.

24. Sufficiently far away from Central London for one senior officer constantly to refer to it as 'The North West Frontier'.

25. *News on Sunday*, 24 May 1987.

26. Police and Criminal Evidence Act 1984, sec. 101(1)B.

27. The Police Training Council (1983), recommendation 8.5 (p. 27).

28. Didactic teaching has been defined as 'a process where the notes of the instructor become the notes of the student without passing through the mind of either'.

29. Some are starting but are in the very early developmental days. See *C. J. International,* Vol. 3 No. 3, p. 29.

30. The huge number of applicants is initially 'weeded' at force level and representatives of the Police Federation are involved in the selection process at this stage.

31. It is entirely possible that the higher rates in New York are reflective of the 'if you pay peanuts you get monkeys' philosophy which is sometimes recommended as a way of avoiding problems of acceptance of graft consequent on low pay.

CHAPTER 6

1. Viz. decisions about the pay and conditions of his officers, decisions about amalgamations, and the requirement to explain his actions (in some circumstances).

2. See Reiner (1985, pp. 75–6) for a view of how non-partisan policing in the UK actually

is. 'The 1979 (general) election seemed to presage a situation comparable to the open politicisation of American Policing ... American police not only wield considerable political clout in determining who is elected, but have many times lobbied to destroy liberal policies...' (Reiner, 1985, p. 75). But it should be borne in mind that Reiner is using a series of political manipulations by the Police Federation and ACPO as the source of his 'allegations': rank-and-file views do not necessarily mirror those attitudes. Many officers remain apolitical save when they see themselves under siege from 'police-bashers' of any political colour.

3. *Fisher* v. *Oldham Corporation* 2KB 264.
4. *R.* v. *Metropolitan Police Commissioner, ex parte* Blackburn 2 QB, 118; *R.* v. *Metropolitan Police Commissioner, ex parte* Blackburn (No. 3) QB 214; *Fisher* v. *Oldham Corporation* 2KB 364.
5. *R.* v. *Chief Constable of Devon and Cornwall, ex parte* Central Electricity Generating Board (1981) 3 All E.R. 835.
6. *R.* v. *Metropolitan Police, ex parte* Blackburn, *The Times* 1 December 1979 (QBD).
7. See Barker and Roebuck (1973) for a full examination of individual police corruption. These authors detail eight types of police corruption: corruption of authority, kickbacks, opportunistic theft, shakedowns, protection of illegal activities, the fix, direct criminal activies and internal payoffs. In Britain, the phrase 'police corruption' is most commonly used to refer to behaviour which accords with the legal definition of bribery. This does not mean to say that the other behaviours in the typology do not occur rather that they are labelled as discipline offences or criminal activity.
8. Although there exist in all forces a body, usually referred to as the Complaints Investigation Branch (CIB) as it is in the Metropolitan Police, the staff do not usually take anything other than a *post hoc* investigative role.
   There is no integrity testing in the UK. The vast bulk of allegations is investigated by officers, not of those specialist branches. CIB deal only with the more serious or contentious cases.
9. The Police and Criminal Evidence Act 1984, sec. 89(2).
10. *Police Complaints and Discipline Procedures,* Cmnd 9072.
11. This definition of crime means that offences like riding a bicycle without lights or depositing litter in the streets fall within the requirement to submit cases to the DPP for decision, subject only to the question of whether the officer ought or ought not to be charged. This decision was taken by Parliament in an effort to restrict chief officers and to ensure that they should not have the 'discretion to prefer a disciplinary charge on a criminal matter rather than take it to the DPP' (Mr Eldon Griffiths, House of Commons *Hansard,* Standing Committee E, 20 March 1984, col. 1838).
12. This differs from dismissal in that in this case pension rights are retained.
13. The Law Society and the National Council for Civil Liberties and the Police Federation made unusual bedmates but their combined forces succeeded in pushing through a section of the Police and Criminal Evidence Act 1984, sec. 102, which means that officers cannot be punished by dismissal, a requirement to resign or a reduction in rank *unless* the officer has had the opportunity to be represented by a legal adviser.
14. In many PDs, e.g. NYPD, officers are permitted to have second jobs only if they have management approval. However, second jobs, including acting as waiters, bodyguards and security men whilst off-duty, are fairly common and seem to raise little complaint. In many jurisdictions there are no restrictions and controls over these matters and some officers may have substantial interests in local companies, etc.
15. The existence of such a widely drawn regulation was one of the main planks in the

arguments of the Police Federation against a specific discipline offence in respect of racist behaviour. But by definition, any offence that talks of 'likely to bring discredit' can either be narrowly interpreted or broadly interpreted. Discredit is in the eye of the beholder. Some minor deviations may be punished but a major infraction ignored.

16. The Police and Criminal Evidence Act 1984, sec. 104.
17. *Abbate* v. *US,* 359 US. 187 (1959).
18. In particular demotion where an officer is not only punished by losing rank, an internal/organizational punishment, but is also punished by reason of a loss of pay which may, over the years, amount to many thousands of pounds or dollars. This latter is an effect of punishment which consequently affects wives, families and the quality of non-working life.

CHAPTER 7

1. The 'Move along' or 'Go home before I have to arrest you' style.
2. The 'Because the law, and that's me, says so' approach.
3. The 'How can I be of assistance?' style.
4. The process is sometimes referred to as 'street nullification' and is typified by the comment of the 'roll call' sergeant in the popular *Hill Street Blues* series on TV. Each week the sergeant tells his men, 'Do it to them before they do it to you'.
5. On the other hand, it is worth pointing out again that, in the USA at least, 'court decisions', in the form of civil suits with seven-figure judgments, have a more powerful professionalizing effect in the promotion of standards and the development of policies and practices than has occurred through years of appeal from academics and others for pure professionalism for its own sake. Furthermore, in March 1986, the Supreme Court declined to put a ceiling on the level of financial judgments against a police officer and further declared that *individual* officers could be held liable for actions even when those actions were the subject of some judicial review, as for instance, when a judge signs a warrant and later it is revealed that probable cause is insufficient!!
6. A process no longer undertaken by police with the advent of the Crown Prosecution Service (CPS).
7. As a consequence of the Road Transport Act 1984, the facility for 'ticketing' has been extended to almost the whole range of traffic offences.
8. Police and Criminal Evidence Act 1984, sec. 25.
9. *Gideon* v. *Wainright* 372, US, 335 (1963).
10. *Miranda* v. *Arizona* 384 US, 436 (1966).
11. 354 US, 449 (1954).
12. 378 US. 478 (1964).
13. *Schmerber* v. *California* 384 US, 752 (1966).
14. *Rochin* v. *California* 342 US (1965).
15. Indeed it is the case that the 'right to silence' itself stems from a concern that the 'ignorant peasant' of English medieval history would simply stammer out an explanation of his presence at the scene of a crime, and would condemn himself, guilty or not.
16. A *serious arrestable offence* includes treason, murder, manslaughter, rape, kidnapping, incest, buggery, certain types of indecent assault, and certain other offences in connection with

explosives, sexual offences, possession of firearms, etc. or any arrestable offence (an *arrestable offence* is any offence for which the penalty is fixed by law. Any offence declared by statute to be an arrestable offence, or any offence for which the penalty on first conviction is five years or more), if it has led, or is likely to lead or is intended to lead to:

  i Serious harm to the security of the state.

  ii Serious interference with the adminstration of justice or the investigation of offences.

  iii The death of any person.

  iv Serious injury to any person.

  v Substantial financial gain or

  vi Substantial financial loss to any person.

(Police and Criminal Evidence Act 1984, sec. 116).

The opacity of the definition under sec. 116(6) (e) and (f) is a source of much legal discussion (see Zander, 1985, pp. 151–2) as no definition of 'substantial' is provided.

17. Oppression includes torture, inhuman or degrading treatment and the use of threat or violence.

18. *Harris* v. *New York* 401 US 222 (1971); *Michigan* v. *Tucker* 417 US. 443, (1974); *Michigan* v. *Mosley* 423 US. 96 (1975).

19. 392 US. 1 (1968).

20. E.g. *US* v. *Robinson* (No. 72–936) and *Gustafson* v. *Florida* (No. 71–1169).

21. 'Circumstances alter cases', as the lawyers say.

22. *Rose* v. *County of Plumas* 119. Cal. Rptr. 842 (App 1984).

CHAPTER 8

1. *Police*, Vol. XXIII, No. 6, February 1986, p. 20.

2. *The Times*, 3 April 1984.

3. Police Federation meeting, January 1987. Stoke. Reported in *Police*, Vol. XXIII, No. 6, February 1986, p. 4.

4. The two officers were later charged with attempted murder and wounding with intent to commit grievous bodily harm and were acquitted. A third police officer fired shots into the back of the car but was not charged with any offence.

5. An incident that was seen as the 'trigger' for subsequent street disorder in the area. An officer was later charged with serious offences but was acquitted.

6. Data are based on calculations published in the *Sunday Times*, 3 April 1983 and 8 April 1984.

7. Report of the Commissioner of Police of the Metropolis for 1983, p. 16.

8. The Diplomatic Protection Group (DPG) and the Royalty Protection Group (RPG) had existed as separate entities since November 1974, although many protection posts tended to be covered by ordinary duty officers. In 1983 following the incident in which a man found his way into the Queen's bedroom in Buckingham Palace, the two units were merged under the supervision of a Deputy Assistant Commissioner, a major upgrading of managerial supervision.

9. See *Police Review*, Vol. 95, No. 4932, p. 1949, 'Thames Valley ACC defends forces' action at Hungerford'.

10. *Report of Her Majesty's Chief Inspector of Constabulary for 1986* (1987).
11. Interview with *Law Enforcement News*, January 1985.
12. Quoted in Kilroy-Silk (1987).
13. The principal author of this volume, in 25 years of police service, was never trained to handle firearms and, like the vast majority of his colleagues, was 'armed' only with the wooden truncheon (also known as a 'stick' or a 'baton'), kept in a special pocket sewn into the inside of the right trouser-leg.

   Furthermore, despite the British police service having been for some years an 'equal opportunity employer', women officers have never been armed *in any way*, not even with a truncheon. Few are authorized shots and only recently has discussion been taking place to identify a suitable 'non-lethal' weapon of protection.
14. Thanks to Mr. L. J. Poole, Director of the Central Planning Unit in Harrogate, Yorks, for drawing attention to this and the following mentioned items.
15. In June 1920, in answer to a question in the House of Commons, Parliament was told that 1006 .32 automatic pistols were regularly issued to officers on night duty 'who can be trusted to use them with discretion' and that this had been the practice for nearly forty years. Similar rules applied to forces outside London.
16. Data should be viewed in the context of a total of 7585 robberies in 1981 which rose to 12,037 in 1983. *Report of the Commissioner of Police of the Metropolis for 1983.*
17. *Report of Her Majesty's Chief Inspector of Constabulary for 1985* (1986).
18. It is regrettable that Reiner (1985) should see fit to comment (p. 72) that the 'seven-fold increase' in the issue of firearms to police between 1970 and 1988 'was matched only by a threefold rise in the reported use of firearms by criminals', as though there was some case to be made that only a one-to-one correlation was acceptable.
19. In an interview with *Playboy* in 1980, James Mitchener said 'Guns, to Americans are aphrodisiacs'.
20. Using a proforma adapted from the design used in the Police Executive Research Forum (PERF, 1978) study, *Survey of Police Operational and Administrative Practices.*
21. The National Rifle Association leaflet, 'NRA Firearms Fact Card 1987', shows between 180–200 million.
22. *Sunday Times,* 27 October 1985.
23. The expression Part 1 firearm is defined below but at this stage the substitution of 'handgun or rifle' will be a sufficient definition.
24. *Police,* Vol. XVIII, No. 12, p. 22.
25. The National Rifle Association leaflet 'NRA Firearms Fact Card 1987'.
26. Handgun Control Inc. (1986) leaflet 'A sampling of Supreme Court interpretations of the Second Amendment'.
27. *US* v. *Cruickshank* 92 US 542 (1876); *Presser* v. *Illinois* 116 US 252 (1886); *US* v. *Miller* 307 US. 174 (1939)
28. NRA (1986) leaflet 'The right to keep and bear arms: analysis of the Second Amendment', p. 12.
29. The Firearms Act 1968 will be amended by the introduction of a new Firearms Act in 1988. The Government White Paper, *Firearms Act 1968: Proposals for reform,* indicates the content of the Bill, which was presented to Parliament on 18 December 1987. It is unlikely at the time of writing that the definition of a firearm will be changed.
30. The definition covers dummy or imitation firearms if the weapon is capable of conversion to discharge a missile, e.g. by drilling a solid barrel or enlarging ammunition chambers.

31. Prohibited weapons include firearms which are constructed or adapted to discharge missiles continuously so long as the trigger is pressed, or until the magazine is empty, or weapons (e.g. aerosol sprays) which can discharge any noxious liquid, gas or other things (e.g. powder).

32. Self-loading or semi-automatic weapons, pump-action rifles, short-barrelled smooth bore guns and 'burst fire' weapons were added to the list of section 5 (prohibited) weapons in the Government White Paper, *Firearms Act 1968: Proposals for reform.* Also included in this category in the White Paper are rocket launchers, bazookas, mortars and stun guns.

33. In 1987 the state of Florida passed legislation which allows anyone to carry a handgun without a licence as long as it is carried openly. Furthermore, provided that an applicant is over 21, has resided in the state for six months, pays $125 for a licence and $21 for a fingerprint check, and has no criminal record or record of alcohol or drug abuse, a person may carry a concealed weapon. Hidden weapons cannot be carried in bars, police stations, schools, colleges, voting places, or in the state legislature, and applicants must show that they have attended a firearms safety course (which is not a shooting qualification). See Gallagher (1987) for an examination of the implications of this statute.

34. As well as a collection of non-law enforcement bodies, the police 'dissenters' included the International Association of Chiefs of Police, the Police Foundation, the National Associations of Police Organizations, the Federal Law Enforcement Officers Association, the National Troopers Coalition, the Police Executive Research Forum, the National Sheriff's Association, the National Association of Black Law Enforcement Executives, the Fraternal Order of Police, the International Brotherhood of Police, and the Police Management Association Officers (HCI leaflet s.49/H.R.945, the McClure–Volkmer Bill).

35. *Washington Report,* Vol. 12, No. 2, Summer 1986. 'NRA's McClure Bill Gutted', p. 7.

36. *Metropolitan Police News Release,* 3 April 1986.

37. 2 All ER 937 (1976) at 947.

38. Skolnick (1966) argued that the dimensions of the US officer's personality are, among other things, predicated on his 'imminent fear of death'.

39. See also note 22, Chapter 7.

40. Quoted in Bruce-Briggs (1976), p. 56.

41. *Police Review,* Vol. 95, No. 4908, pp. 732–3.

42. Although it does vary from force to force, it is comparatively unusual for officers responding to call-out as the first-tier of the response to have their own weapons. Often they are obliged to use the first that comes to hand drawn from the armoury, with the potential for all the problems that result from non-zeroed weapons, etc. (See Yardley, 1986, for a discussion of this area.)

43. *Police,* Vol. XIX, No. 2, p. 34.

CHAPTER 9

1. 'Democracy is the spawn of despotism' as Frazier in B. F. Skinner's (1948) *Walden Two* (p. 268) puts it. He continues: 'Democracy is power and rule. It is not the will of the people, remember; it's the will of the majority.'

2. *Boston Gazette,* 12 March 1770, illustrated in Cook (1973).
3. Stein (1984) argues that as the national guard are increasingly regarded as a vital component of the total national defence network, it is entirely possible that they would be considered a federal body, and would thus be removed from the collection of disaster resources available to local government (see note 4 below). However, since Supreme Court decisions on the Second Amendment seem to indicate that states have the individual right to maintain a militia (see Chapter 8) the consequence would be the creation of state militia charged only with internal security and law enforcement duties.
4. Federal troops are expressly prevented by US federal law (Title 18, US Code sub-section 1385) 'the Posse Commitatus Act' from responding to calls from Federal marshals to assist in law enforcement except where 'expressly authorized by the constitution or by act of congress'. This legislation, confusing and widely misinterpreted (Rice, 1984) was amended and clarified by the Military Cooperation with Civilian Law Enforcement Officers Act (DOD Authorization Act 1982) which allows:
    i. The release of information, equipment, and facilities by the military to include the training of civilian officers in the use of such equipment.
    ii. The provision of assistance through tracking and communication facilities in the enforcement of drug, immigration and customs laws at a border.
    iii. Although still prevented from 'assisting in direct interdiction, search, seizure or arrest of civilians, federal forces may defend themselves or federal property from hostile acts'.
    iv. The military may claim reasonable reimbursement for assistance rendered.
    v. In an emergency, when the size or scope of suspected criminal activity poses a serious threat to the interests of the United States the military may participate in Federal drug, immigration and/or customs enforcement.
Taft (1983) argues that this legislation will produce a more frequent application for military assistance in the detection of sophisticated smuggling operations by land and sea.
5. Viz. the taking of hostages at the Iranian Embassy in London on 30 April 1980, which involved the Special Air Services (SAS) regiment in its resolution.
6. *Report of the National Advisory Commission on Civil Disorders* (1968) p. 68.
7. 1) the prevention of crime; 2) new ways of dealing with offenders; 3) ways of eliminating unfairness and ensuring 'dignified' treatment of all persons in the 'arms of the law'; 4) upgrading the quality and qualifications of criminal justice personnel; 5) expanding research; 6) funding improvements in the criminal justice system (see Robin, 1980, p. 48).
8. OPCS *Demographic Review,* 1977 and 1981 Census.
9. For the full text of this speech, see Smithies and Fiddick (1969).
10. *Sunday Times,* 5 January 1975.
11. These were what are, in today's police-jargon, referred to as 'racially sensitive areas'; at that time they were 'stations to gain experience'. The British author of this book spent the first five years of his police service at such a station (Harrow Road, North Kensington) and thus the comments that follow are based on his personal experience. They may not be representative of the whole picture.
12. The verb 'nick' is British police slang. In this context it means 'arrest' and is similar to the US 'collar'. The word, as a noun, means variously an arrest; a police station; or a prison. The word 'nickname' is said to come from the latter of these definitions.
13. For the US reader, 'trash cans'. Reiner (1985, p. 71) is mistaken in typifying the use of bin lids as 'traditional', such protection had rarely been necessary in living memory.
14. The march in question was of the National Front, a racist, anti-immigrant body. The

police were there to ensure that the marchers were not impeded in their right to 'assemble' and to make their point. A classic example of the anomaly of policing of which Goldstein (1977) wrote, discussed at the beginning of this chapter.

15. James Jardine, Chairman of the Police Federation in his address to the Home Secretary, reported in *Police*, Vol. XIII, No. 10.

16. The body which preceded the Police Complaints Authority, discussed in Chapter 5.

17. In west London a special training area, designed like streets of houses, was set up in order that simulation of riot conditions could be as realistic as possible.

18. In London these are known as District Support Units (DSUs) and are based on the eight police districts, described in Chapter 5. There was a rumour circulating in the mid-1980s that one force had named its emergency team the 'Fast Action Response Team' until the attention of a senior officer was drawn to the acronym.

19. 'PCs' fury over riot blunder', *Today*, 27 February 1987.

20. This and the following quotation are drawn from a transcript of a BBC television programme *The Queen's Peace*, broadcast in October 1986. The transcript was published in *Police*, Vol. XIX, No. 3, pp. 8–9.

21. See note 19.

22. One cannot help but be struck by the realization that these arguments are almost the converse of those employed by the police in the discussions that surrounded the setting-up of bodies of 'traffic wardens' to relieve the police of the 'problem' of conflict between them and the 'motoring public'.

CHAPTER 10

1. 'History is an illusion created by the passage of time' as Douglas Adams put it in *The Hitch-Hiker's Guide to the Galaxy* (Pan, London, 1979).

2. In some cases (e.g. certain serious sexual offences such as incest) prosecution could not be taken without the consent of the Attorney-General.

3. On the grounds that bargaining after arraignment, sometimes with the open connivance of the judge who may serve as 'a catalyst' (Dean, 1974, p. 19), is, in the main, for the purpose of avoiding trial but securing conviction.

4. National Advisory Commission on Criminal Justice Standards and Goals (1973), *Courts*, Washington DC, p. 43.

5. The quote is from Mr Martin Murray (in Boyle, 1987), a former police superintendent, now a defence lawyer. For a period he was employed by CPS as an advocate.

6. 'Crown Prosecution Service rejects "unqualified" claims', *Police Review*, Vol. 95, No. 4932, p. 1951; and Bennett (1987); 'If they kick us do we not bleed?', *Policing*, Vol. XX, No. 1, p. 9; Mayhew (1987), in a speech to magistrates in Sussex, reported in 'Don't let's be beastly to the CPS', *Police*, Vol. XX, No. 4, p. 10.

7. The 'Tension Indicators' of British policing are the 'Indicators of Unrest' of the Miami 'Field Force'. Both depend on the flow of information to a central point. That information is classified in a remarkably similar way to the underlying elements of Smelser's Value Added Theory (Smelser, 1963), usually without acknowledgement.

8. The delay of nearly two years before any substantive 'case law' has started to appear as a consequence of PACE is in marked contrast to that engendered by the Road Safety Act

1968. Within months of its introduction, the Act had generated a huge amount of case law, but then it dealt with the contentious issue of drinking and driving. All those convicted were liable to lose their driving licence. The threatened loss of a driving licence seems to have produced more rapid case law than the issue of civil rights.

9. The 'rational deterrence' model for dealing with crime is 'more police powers = less crime' (Reiner, 1985, p. 174). For the police the equation is 'more court power = greater deterrence = less police deviance + more civil rights'.

10. This is likely to be exacerbated if the practice of suing the police develops to any extent in the UK. This has been a comparatively rare event, for most cases have been settled out of court for what are by US standards derisory sums. The family of John Shorthouse, aged five, shot accidentally by police in 1985, received a total of £13,845 (*Today*, 14 November 1987). Stephen Waldorf, mistakenly shot by police (see Chapter 8) received £120,000. The publication of Clayton and Tomlinson (1987) may mark a watershed in this area. These authors point out that there is an increasing number of civil actions against the police and that 'the only figures available are those for the Metropolitan Police, which show that 126 such cases were dealt with in 1986 compared with only 27 in 1973. The total damages awarded increased from £200 to £377,169 over the same period' (Clayton and Tomlinson, 1988, p. 310).

11. In police circles characterized by telling people you are a 'civil servant' or a 'government employee'.

12. *Times Law Reports,* 23 May 1987.

13. The British author was conducting observational research of police officers throughout the period May to December.

14. *R.* v. *Samuel C.A.* (Crim. Div.); *Independent,* 23 December 1987.

References

American Bar Association (1974) *Standards Relating to the Urban Police Function* (ABA, Chicago, Ill.).

Arthur Andersen and Co. (1985) *The Crown Prosecution Service* (Home Office, London).

Avery, M. and Rudofsky, D. (1985) *Police Misconduct: Law and Litigation* (Clark, Boardman and Co. Ltd., New York).

Baldwin, R. and Kinsey, R. (1982) *Police Powers and Politics* (Quartet, London).

Banton, M. (1964) *The Policeman in the Community* (Basic Books, New York).

Barker, T. and Roebuck, J. (1973) *An Empirical Typology of Police Corruption* (Charles C. Thomas, Springfield, Ill.).

Bayley, D. H. (1976) *Forces of Order: Police Behaviour in Japan and the United States* (University of California Press, Berkeley, California).

Bayley, D. H. (1977) 'The limits of police reform'. In Bayley, D. H. (ed.), *Police and Society* (Sage, London).

Bayley, D. H. (1977) *Police and Society* (Sage, London).

Becker, H. J. and Hjellemo, E. O. (1976) *Justice in Modern Sweden* (Charles Thomas, Springfield, Ill.).

Becker, H. J. and Whitehouse, J. E. (1979) *The Police of America* (Charles Thomas, Springfield, Ill.).

Beckman, E. (1980) *Law Enforcement in a Democratic Society* (Nelson Hall, New York).

Bennett, M. (1987) 'If they kick us do we not bleed?', *Policing*, Vol. XX, No. 1, p. 9.

Bent, A. E. and Rossum, R. A. (1976) *Police, Criminal Justice and the Community* (Harper Row, New York).

Benyon, J. (1984) *Scarman and After* (Pergamon, Oxford).

Benyon, J. (1986) *A Tale of Failure: Race and Policing* (Centre for Research in Ethnic Relations, Warwick University).

Bernstein, S. (1967) *Alternatives to Violence* (Association Press, New York).

Blackman, P. H. and Gardiner, R. E. (1986) 'The NRA and criminal justice policy: The effectiveness of the National Rifle Association as a public interest group'. Paper presented at a meeting of the American Society of Criminology, Atlanta, GA, October 1986.

Boyle, E. (1987) 'The non-prosecution service'. *Police Review*, Vol. 95, No. 4934, p. 2117.

Brogden, M. (1982) *The Police: Autonomy and Consent* (Academic Press, London and New York).

Brown, R. (1965) *Social Psychology* (Collier-Macmillan, London; Free Press, New York).

Bruce-Briggs, B. (1976) 'The great American gun war'. *The Public Interest*, No. 45, pp. 37–62.

Bull, R. and Horncastle, P. (1983) *An Evaluation of the Metropolitan Police Recruit Training in Human Awareness Training* (Police Foundation, London).

Bunyard, R. (1973) *Police: Organisation and Command* (MacDonald and Evans, London).

Bureau of Government Research and Service (1975) *Contracting for Police Services in Oregon* (University of Oregon and the League of Oregon Cities).

Bureau of Government Statistics (1983) *Report to the Nation on Crime and Justice* (Bureau of Justice Statistics, Washington DC).

Butler, A. J. P. (1979) A study of the occupational perceptions of police officers. Unpublished doctorial thesis, Faculty of Law, University of Birmingham.

CAOLEA (1985) *Standards for Law Enforcement Agencies*, Commission on Accreditation for Law Enforcement Agencies (Fairfax, VA).

Caplan, D. I. (1976) 'Restoring the balance: The Second Amendment revisited'. *Fordham Urban Law Journal*, Vol. 5, No. 31.

Carver, Field Marshall (1983) 'The army and the police'. *Police Journal*, Vol. LVI, pp. 30–41.

Castles, S. (1984) *Here for Good* (Pluto, London).

Chapman, G. (1982) 'Personnel management'. In *Local Government Police Management*, ed. Garmire B. L. (International City Management Association, Washington DC).

Clayton, R. and Tomlinson, H. (1987) *Civil Actions Against the Police* (Sweet and Maxwell, London).

Clayton, R. and Tomlinson, H. (1988) 'Police misconduct and the public'. *Policing*, Vol. 3, No. 4, pp. 309–12.

Cochrane, R. and Butler, A. J. (1980) 'The values of police officers, recruits and civilians in England'. *Journal of Police Science and Administration*, 8, pp. 205–18.

Cohen, S. (1979) 'The punitive city'. *Contemporary Crises*, 3, No. 4.

Coleman, A. and Gorman, L. (1982) 'Conservatism, dogmatism and authoritarianism in British police officers'. *Sociology*, February.

Colquhoun, P. (1795) *A Treatise on the Police of the Metropolis*, 7th edn (London, 1806. Reprinted Patterson Smith, Montclair, NJ, 1969).

Commissioner of Police (1983) Report of the Commissioner of Police of the Metropolis for the Year 1983 (HMSO, London).

Commissioner's Annual Report (1987) Report of the Commissioner of Police of the Metropolis for 1986 (HMSO, London).

Commission on Police Officer Standards and Training (1979) *Police Service and Juridictional Consolidation* (Sacramento, California).

Cooke, A. (1973) *America* (BBC, London).

Cook, S. (1984) 'Still a long way to go'. *Police Review*, Vol. 92, pp. 1496–8.

Corrigan, R. (1986) NRA, using members, ads, and money, hits police line in lobbying drive. *National Journal*, 4 January, pp. 8–14.

Coulter, J., Miller, S. and Walker, M. (1984) *State of Siege: Miners Strike 1984* (Canary Press, London).

Critchley, T. A. (1970) *The Conquest of Violence* (Constable, London).

Danziger, K. (1976) *Interpersonal Communication* (Pergamon Press, Oxford).

Dean, J. M. (1974) 'The illegitimacy of plea bargaining'. *Federal Probation*, Vol. 38, September, pp. 19–20.

Donajgrodski, A. P. (ed.) (1977) *Social Control in Nineteenth Century Britain* (Croom Helm, London).

Driscoll, J. (1987) 'Excluding illegally obtained evidence in the United States'. *Criminal Law Review*, August, pp. 553–60.

Eisenberg, T. (1981) *A Systemic Approach to the Selection of Law Enforcement Personnel: Final Report* (Florida Department of Law Enforcement, Tallahassee, Fla).

Elmes, F. (1973) 'Aid to the civil power'. *Police Journal*, Vol. 1, XLVI, pp. 45–8.

Emsley, C. (1983) *Policing and its Context 1750–1820* (Macmillan, London).

Fielding, H. (1751) *An Enquiry Into Cases of the Late Increase of Robbers*. In Price, J. (1983) *The Metoropolitan Police – Why it was established and how it was developed* (unpublished).

Freeman, G. (1979) *Immigrant Labour and Racial Conflict in Industrial Societies* (Harvard University Press, Harvard).

Friedrich, R. (1977) The impact of organisational, individual and situational factors on police behaviour. Unpub. PhD thesis (University of Michigan).

Frinley, R. C. (1971) 'The appelate system'. *Trial* (November/December issue).

Frosdick, R. B. (1920) *American Police Systems* (Patterson Smith, Montclair, NJ).

Gallagher, G. P. (1987) 'Gunslinging in Florida'. *Police Review*, Vol. 95, No. 4934, p. 2113.

Gilbert, K. and Kahn, A. (1975) 'The constitutional independence of a police constable in the exercise of the powers of his office'. *Police Journal*, Vol. 48, p. 55.

Goldman, N. (1963) *The Differential Selection of Juvenile Offenders for Court Appearance* (National Council on Crime and Delinquency, New York).

Goldstein, H. (1977) *Policing a Free Society* (Ballinger, Cambridge, Mass).

Green, J. J. and Young, A. J. (1980) *A History of Police Training in New York City* (New York City Police Department).

Greenwood, C. (1986) Tomorrow's gunmen. *Police*, Vol. XVIII, No. 5, pp. 28–9.

Gudjonsson, G. (1984) 'Fear of 'failure' and 'tissue damage' in police recruits, constables, sergeants and senoir officers.' *Journal of Personality and Individual Differences*, Vol. 5, No. 2, pp. 223–6.

Halford, A. (1987) 'Until the twelfth of never'. *Police Review*, Vol. 95, No. 4933, p. 2019.

Hall, S., Critcher, C., Jefferson, T., Clarke, J. and Roberts, B. (1978) *Policing the Crisis* (Macmillan, London).

Harris, R. (1971) *The Fear of Crime* (Praeger, New York).

Harvard Law Review (1970) 'Unconstitutionality of Plea Bargaining'. Vol. 83, April, pp. 1387–90.

Hashmi, F. (1973) *Psychology of Racial Prejudice* (Community Relations Commission, London).

Hay, D. (1975) *Albion's Fatal Tree* (Penguin Books, Harmondsworth).

Hoelscher, R. W. (1985) 'High profile rescue'. In Hughes, D. W., Hoelscher, R. W. and Coney, J. J., *Field Force Concept* (Metro-Dade Police Dept, Miami).

Holdaway, S. (ed.) (1979) *The British Police* (Edward Arnold, London).

Home Affairs Committee of the House of Commons (1981) Report: Racial Disadvantage (HMSO, London).

Home Office Workshops (1983) *Stress in the Police Service* (Home Office, London).

Hughes, D. W., Hoelscher, R. W. and Coney, J. J. (1985) *Field Force Concept* (Metro-Dade Police Dept, Miami).

Inubau, F. E. and Reid, J. E. (1967) *Criminal Interrogation and Confessions* (Williams and Walkins, Baltimore).

Irving, B. L. (1980) *Police Interrogation: A Case Study of Current Practice*, Research Study No. 2 (Royal Commission on Criminal Procedure, HMSO, London).

Irving, B. L. (1985) The Police and Criminal Evidence Act 1984: In the Police Station. Paper presented to a conference on the Act (University of Leicester).

Irving, B. L. and McKenzie, I. K. (1987) *Evaluation of the Effects of the Police and Criminal Evidence Act 1984 on Police Interrogation* (Police Foundation, London).

Jacobs, J. and Cohen, J. (1978) 'The impact of racial integration on the police'. *Journal of Police*

Science and Administration, 6(2), pp. 168–83.

Jakubs, D. L. (1977) 'Police violence in times of political tension: The case of Brazil, 1968–1971'. In Bayley, D. (ed.), *Police and Society* (Sage, London).

Jefferson, A. and Grimshaw, R. (1981) The organisation and control of policework: A sociological study conducted within an English county force (Unpublished report to the Home Office).

Jefferson, A. and Grimshaw, R. (1984) *Controlling the Constable* (Muller, London).

Johnson, T. A., Misner, G. E. and Brown, L. P. (1981) *The Police and Society: An Environment for Collaboration and Confrontation* (Prentice Hall, Englewood Cliffs, NJ).

Jones, S. (1986) 'Women police: Caught in the act'. *Policing*, Vol. 2, No. 2, pp. 219–40.

Katz, J. (1978) *White awareness – Handbook for anti-racism training* (University of Oklahoma).

Kerner Commission (1968) *Report of the National Advisory Commission on Civil Disorders* (Government Printing Office, Washington, DC).

Kettle, M. and Hodges, L. (1982) *Uprising! The Police, the People and the Riots in Britain's Cities* (Pan, London).

Kilroy-Silk, R. (1987) 'Gaps in the target'. *Police Review*. Vol. 95, No. 4941, p. 2461.

Kinsey, R. and Young, J. (1982) 'Police autonomy and the politics of discretions'. In Crowell, D., Jones, T. and Young, J. (eds) *Policing and Riots* (Junction Books, London).

Knapp Commission (1973) *Report on Police Corruption* (Brazillier, New York).

Koepsell, T. W. and Girard, C. M. (1979) *Small Agency Consolidation: Suggested Approaches* (National Institute of Law Enforcement and Criminal Justice, US Department of Justice, Washington, DC).

Lane, R. (1971) *Policing the City: Boston 1822–1885* (Atheneum, New York).

Lee, E. L. (1971) 'An overview of American police history'. *Police Chief*, October, pp. 51–52 and 257–9.

Lidstone, K. (1984) 'Magistrates in the pre-trial criminal process'. *Research Bulletin*, 18 (Home Office RPU, London).

Lock, J. (1987) 'How long must she wait'. *Police Review*, Vol. 95, No. 4929, pp. 1810–11.

Low, P. (1987) 'Why women should manage'. *Police Review*, Vol. 95, No. 4929, pp. 1812–13.

Lundman, R. J. (1974) 'Routine police arrest practices: A commonwealth perspective'. *Social Problems*, October, pp. 74–5.

Lustgarten, L. (1986) *The Governance of Police* (Sweet and Maxwell, London).

MacNamara, D. E. J. (1950) 'American police administration at mid-century'. *Public Admin. Review*, Vol. 10, No. 3.

Manning, P. K. (1979) 'The social control of police work. In Holdaway, S. (ed.), *The British Police* (Edward Arnold, London).

Martin, S. E. (1979) *Breaking and Entering* (University of California Press, San Diego).

Marwood, W. (1987) 'Why the bail law should not be changed'. *Police Review*, Vol. 95, No. 4906, p. 636.

Mathias, W., Rescorla, R. and Stephens, E. (1980) *Foundations of Criminal Justice* (Prentice Hall, Englewood Cliffs, NJ).

Mayne, Sir R. (1829) quoted in *The Instruction Book of the Metropolitan Police* (Metropolitan Police, London, 1986).

Mayo, K. (1920) *Justice to All: The Story of the Pennyslvania State Police* (Houghton Mifflin, Boston).

McClure, J. (1984) *Cop World* (Macmillan, London and New York).

McCoy, T. R. (1980) 'Plea bargaining as due process in determining guilt'. *Stanford Law Review*, Vol. 32, May.

McDonald, B., Argent, M. J., Elliott, J. E., May, N. H., Miller, P. J., Naylor, J. T. and Norris N. F. (1986) *Final Report of the Stage II Review of Police Probationer Training* (University of East Anglia).

McKenzie, I. K. (1982) 'Unlawful assembly, riot, rout: The mechanics of the mob'. *Police Studies*, Vol. 5, No. 1, pp. 40–6.

McKenzie, I. K. (1986a) 'Racism and the police service – Where to now?' *Police Journal*, Vol. LVIX, No. 1, pp. 56–67.

McKenzie, I. K. (1986b) 'The police of South Carolina'. *Police Review*, Vol. 96, No. 4868, pp. 1354–5.

McKenzie, I. K. and Irving B. L. (1987) 'Police interrogation: The effects of PACE'. *Policing*, Vol. 3, No. 1, pp. 4–22.

Metropolitan Police (1985) *The Principles of Policing and Guidance for Professional Behaviour* (Metropolitan Police, London).

Metropolitan Police (1985a) *Force Re-organisation: Implementation Planning Guidelines* (Internal Metropolitan Police Publication, London).

Miller, W. R. (1977) *Cops and Bobbies* (Chicago, Chicago University Press).

Miller, W. R. (1977a) 'Never on a Sunday: moralistic reformers and the police in London and New York City, 1830–1870'. In Bayley, D. H. (ed.) *Police and Society* (Sage, London).

Molyneux, M. (1985) 'Reasonable force'. In Baxter, J. and Kauffman, L. (eds) *Police: the constitution and the community* (Professional Books, Abingdon).

Moore, T. (1986) 'Public order: the police commander's role'. *Policing*, Vol. 2, No. 2, pp. 88–99.

Morgan, R. and Maggs, C. (1984) *Following Scarman?* (Bath University, Social Policy Papers).

Morgan, R. and Swift, P. (1987) 'The future of police authorities: members' views. *Public Administration*, Vol. 65, No. 3, pp. 259–77.

Morris, T. (1985) 'The case for a riot squad'. *New Society*, 29 November, pp. 363–4.

NACP (1985) 'Memo to Congress: 1985'. In *Sunday Times*, 10 November 1985.

'National Advisory Commission on Criminal Justice Standards' (1973) *Courts* (Government Printing Office, Washington, DC).

Neiderhoffer, A. (1967) *Behind the Shield: The Police in Urban Society* (Doubleday and Co., Garden City, NY).

Newman, Sir K. (1984) 'Policing by consent: The 1984 James Smart lecture'. *Police Review*, 12 October 1984, pp. 1974–75.

Newman, Sir K. (1984a) Letter to all members of the Metropolitan Police, New Scotland Yard, 19 November 1984.

Newman, Sir K. (1985) *The Principles of Policing and Guidance for Professional Behaviour* (Metropolitan Police, London).

Oxford, T. (1988) 'How to bluff in interviews'. *Police Review*, Vol. 96, No. 4943, p. 29.

Panzarella, R. (1984) 'Management v. policing by objectives'. *Police Journal*, Vol. LVI, No. 2.

Parker, L. C. (1985) *The Japanese Police System Today: An American Perspective* (Kodansha International Ltd, New York).

Pead, D. (1987) '16,000 officers assaulted? *Police Review*, Vol. 95, No. 4908, pp. 732–3.

Pennyslvania Crime Commission (1976) *Report on Police Corruption and the Quality of Law Enforcement in Philadelphia* (Commonwealth of Pennyslvania, Philadelphia).

PERF study (1978) *Survey of Police Operational and Administrative Practices – 1977* (Police Executive Research Forum, Washington, DC).

Peters, T. J. and Waterman, R. H. (1982) *In Search of Excellence* (Warner Books, New York).

Platt, A. (1971) *The Politics of Riot Commissions* (Collier Books, New York).

Plumridge, M. D. (1985) 'Dilemmas of police management and organisation'. In Thackrah, J. R. (ed.) *Contemporary Policing* (Sphere Reference, London).

Police Training Council (1983) *Community and Race Relations Training for Police* (Home Office, London).

Police Review (1985) 'Quota problems in New York'. *Police Review*, 13 December 1985, p. 2508.

President's Crime Commission (1967) *The Challenge of Crime in a Free Society* (Government Printing Office, Washington DC).

Price, B. and Gavin, S. (1982) 'A century of women in policing'. In Price, B. R. and Sokoloff, N. J. (eds) *The Criminal Justice System and Women: An Anthology of Women Offenders, Victims and Workers* (Clark Boardman, New York).

Price, J. (1983) *The Metropolitan Police – Why it was Established and how it was Developed* (Unpublished. Part requirement for LLB degree).

PSI (1983) *Police and People in London*, Vol. IV (Policy Studies Institute, London).

PSI (1984) *Black and White in Britain* (Heinemann, London).

Redmond, P. W. D. (1966) *General Principles of English Law* (London, MacDonald and Evans).

Reiner, R. (1978) *The Blue-coated Worker: A Sociological Study of Police Unionism* (Cambridge University Press, Cambridge).

Reiner, R. (1984) 'Is Britain turning into a police state?' *New Society*, 2 August.

Reiner, R. (1985) *The Politics of the Police* (Wheatsheaf, Brighton).

Reiner, R. (1986) 'The modern bobby: development of the British police'. *Policing*, Vol. 2, No. 4, pp. 258–75.

Reiss, A. (1970) 'Police control of juveniles'. *American Sociological Review*, February, pp. 44–5.

Report of Her Majesty's Chief Inspector of Constabulary for 1985 (1986) (HMSO, London).

Report of Her Majesty's Chief Inspector of Constabulary for 1986 (1987) (HMSO, London).

Report of the Commissioner of Police of the Metropolis for 1983 (1984) (HMSO, London).

Report of the National Advisory Commission on Civil Disorders (1968) (Government Printing Office, Washington, DC).

Report of the Royal Commission on Police Powers and Procedures (1929) (HMSO, London).

Reppetto, T. A. (1978) *The Blue Parade* (Free Press, New York).

Rice, P. J. (1984) 'New laws and insights encircle the Posse Comitatus Act'. *Military Law Review*, Vol. 104, pp. 109–38.

Richardson, J. F. (1970) *The New York Police: Colonial Times to 1901* (Oxford University Press, London).

Richert, J. P. (1973) 'The politics of riot commissions'. *Journal of Police Science and Administration*, Vol. 1, No. 1, pp. 127–9.

Robin, G. D. (1980) *Introduction to the Criminal Justice System* (Harper and Row, New York).

Rolph, C. H. (1975) 'The case for a District Attorney'. *The Observer*, 28 September 1975.

Royal Commission on the Police (1962) *Final Report* (HMSO, London).

Royal Commission on Criminal Procedure (1981) *Report* (HMSO, London).

Scarman, LJ. (1981) *The Brixton Disorders: 10–12 April 1981* (HMSO, London).

Sewell, J. (1985) *Police: Urban Policing in Canada* (James Lorrimer, Toronto).

Sheridan, D. (1984) 'Cops who die in the line of duty'. *Centurion*, Vol. VII, No. 2.

Sherman, L. W. (1976) *Police Corruption: A Sociological Perspective* (Doubleday, New York).

Silver, A. (1967) 'The demand for order in a civil society'. In Bordua, D. (ed.) *The Police* (Wiley, New York).

Skinner, B. F. (1948) *Walden Two* (Macmillan, New York).

Skolnick, J. (1966) *Justice Without Trial* (Wiley, New York).

Smelser, N. J. (1963) *Theory of Collective Behaviour* (Free Press, New York).

Smith, B. (1949) *Police Systems in the United States* (Harper and Brothers, New York, 2nd edn).

Smith, B. (1960) *Police Systems in the United States* (Harper and Brothers, New York, 3rd edn).

Smith, D. J. (1986) 'The framework of law and policing practice'. In Benyon, J. and Bourne, C. *The Police: Powers Procedures and Properties* (Pergamon, London).

Smith, D. J. and Grey, J. (1983) *The Police In Action*. In *Police and People in London*, Vol. IV (Policy Studies Institute, London).

Smith, L. F. J. (1983) *Criminal Justice Comparisons*. Home Office Research and Planning Unit, Paper 17 (Home Office, London).

Smithies, B. and Fiddick, P. (1969) *Enoch Powell on Immigration* (Sphere, London).

Southgate, P. K. (1979) 'Women in the police'. In *Police Journal*, No. 54.

Southgate, P. K. (1984) *Racism Awareness Training for the Police*. Home Office Research and Planning Unit. Paper 29 (London).

Spitzer, S. and Scull, A. (1977) 'Social control in historical perspective'. In Greenberg, D. (ed.) *Corrections and Punishment* (Sage, Beverly Hills).

Standen, J. (1983) 'An accountable police'. *Police Review*, December, pp. 2344–6.

Stead, P. J. (1977) 'The new police'. In Bayley, D. H. (ed.) *Police and Society* (Sage, London).

Stein, G. J. (1984) 'State defense forces'. *Military Review*, Vol. 64, pp. 84–8.

Stephens, O. H. (1973) *The Supreme Court and Confessions of Guilt* (University of Tennessee Press, Knoxville).

Storch, R. (1975) 'The plague of Blue Locusts: Police reform and popular resistance in Northern England 1840–57. *International Review of Social History*, p. 20.

Sullivan, P. K. (1979) 'The role of women in the police service – the effects of the Sex Discrimination Act'. *Police Journal*, No. 54.

Symonds, M. (1970) 'Emotional hazards of police work'. *American Journal of Psychoanalysis*, Vol. 30, pp. 115–60.

Swan, J. K. (1982) 'Internal controls'. In Garmire, B. L. (ed.) *Local Government Police Management* (International City Management Association, Washington, DC).

Taft, W. H. (1983) 'Role of the DOD in civilian law enforcement'. *Defense*, March, pp. 2–16.

Tamm, Q. (1972) 'Changes in role concepts of police officers: A research project' *Police Chief*, July, p. 14.

Tannahill, J. (1958) *European Voluntary Workers in Britain* (Manchester University Press, Manchester).

Tendler, S. (1986) 'Police have plans for 16 senior teams to deal with riots by summer'. *The Times*, 21 March 1986.

Thackrah, J. R. (1983) 'Army police collaboration against terrorism'. *Police Journal*, Vol. LVI, pp. 41–53.

Thomas, W. (1976) *Bail Reform in America* (University of California Press, Berkeley, California.

Thurmond-Smith, P. (1985) *Policing Victorian London* (Greenwood Press, Westport, Conn.).

Toberg, M. A. (1981) *Pretrial Release: A National Evaluation of Practices and Outcomes* (National Institute of Justice, Washington, DC).

Toch, H. (1969) 'Cops and blacks: Warring minorities'. *The Nation*, 21 April, pp. 491–3.

US Bureau of Justice Statistics (1980) *Justice Agencies in the United States* (US Government Printing Office, Washington, DC).

US Department of Justice (1980) *Justice Agencies in the United States: Summary Report* (Bureau of Justice Statistics, Washington, DC).

US Department of Justice (1983) *Report to the Nation on Crime and Justice: The Data* (Bureau of Justice Statistics, Washington, DC).

US News and World Report (1977) How to break the logjam in courts. 19 December.

Vetri, D. (1964) 'Guilty plea bargaining: Compromises by prosecutors to serve guilty pleas'. *University of Pennsylvania Law Review*, Vol. 112, April, pp. 168–81.

Vick, C. (1985) 'An introduction to aspects of public order and the police'. In Thackrah, J. R. (ed.) *Contemporary Policing: An Examination of Society in the 1980s* (Sphere Reference, London).

Vollmer, A. (1935). In Stead P. J., *Pioneers in Policing* (Macmillan, London).

Waite, A. P. and Swinden, D. R. (1984) *Police Organisation Development: An Examination of Five Police Departments in the United States of America* (Metropolitan Police, London).

Walkley, J. (1987) *Police Interrogation: A handbook for investigators* (Police Review Publishing Company, London).

Wates, C. J. and Miller, S. T. (1973) *A Visual Approach to British and American Government* (Longman, London).

Watson, P. S. and McAninch, W. S. (1984) *South Carolina Criminal Law and Procedure* (University of South Carolina Press, Columbia).

Wegg-Prossor, C. (1979) *The Police and the Law* (Oyez Publishing, London).

Weigh, B. (1980) Bristol: The Chief Constable's Report. Published in *Police Review*, 9 May 1980.

Westley, W. A. (1953) 'Violence and the police', *American Journal of Sociology*. July, pp. 34–41.

Whitaker, J, (1978) *Almanack* (Joseph Whitaker, London).

Wilson, D., Holdaway, S. and Spencer, C. (1984) 'Black Police in the United Kingdom'. *Policing*, 1(1), Autumn, pp. 20–30.

Wilson, J. Q. (1968) *Varieties of Police Behaviour* (Harvard University Press, Cambridge, Mass.).

Whitham, D. C. (1985) *The American Law Enforcement Chief Executive: A Management Profile* (Police Executive Research Forum, Washington, DC).

Wright, J. D., Rossi, P. H., and Daly, K. (1983) *Under the Gun: Weapons Crime and Violence in America* (Hawthorn, New York).

Wright, J. D. and Rossi, P. H. (1986) *Armed and Considered Dangerous: A Survey of Felons and their Firearms* (Hawthorn, New York).

Wright, J. D. (1987) 'Gun Law USA'. *Police*, Vol. XIX, No. 9, pp. 32–5.

Yardley, M. (1986) 'Wrong!' *Police*, Vol. XXIII, No. 6, February 1986, pp. 20–1.

Zander, M. (1985) *The Police and Criminal Evidence Act* (Sweet and Maxwell, London).

Zimbardo, P. G. (1967) 'The psychology of police confessions'. In *Readings in Psychology Today* (Del Mar (CRM Books), Calif.).

Index